# Flaubert

## The Uses of Uncertainty

In the same series

*Thomas Hardy: The Poetic Structure* Jean R. Brooks

*Aldous Huxley* Keith May

*Henry James and the French Novel* Philip Grover

*The Nouveau Roman: A Study in the Practice of Writing* Stephen Heath

*Stendhal* Michael Wood


In preparation

*Dostoyevsky* M. V. Jones

*George Eliot* Neil Roberts

*E. M. Forster* M. L. Raina

*Mrs Gaskell* Coral Lansbury

*Kafka* Franz Kuna

*Herman Melville: His Craft and Vision* Robert Lee

*Tolstoy* Tom Cain

Novelists and Their World

*General Editor:* Graham Hough
Professor of English at the University of Cambridge

# Flaubert

## The Uses of Uncertainty

Jonathan Culler

 Paul Elek, London

© 1974 Elek Books Ltd.

ISBN 0 236 15467 2

First published in Great Britain by
Elek Books Limited
54–58 Caledonian Road, London N1 9RN

Printed in Great Britain by
John Sherratt and Son Ltd. St Ann's Press
Park Road, Altrincham, Cheshire AA14 5QQ

# Contents

# Acknowledgements

My debt to the work of Jean-Paul Sartre will be apparent to anyone who reads *L'Idiot de la famille* or my notes, but what I owe to the work of Roland Barthes, Veronica Forrest-Thomson, Geoffrey Hartman, Fredric Jameson, and Paul de Man will be less obvious. To them I should like to express my gratitude and to apologize for any violence their ideas may suffer in these pages.

I am also greatly indebted to Professor Graham Hough for his comments on the manuscript and to Professor Alison Fairlie for her suggestions, criticisms, and disagreements. They have helped to make it a much better book than it would otherwise have been.

Jonathan Culler
Selwyn College, Cambridge
May, 1973

# Author's Note

All quotations from Flaubert are identified in the text itself. Upper-case roman numerals (I or II) refer to volumes of the *Oeuvres complètes*, Editions du Seuil, Collection 'l'Intégrale', Paris, 1964, edited by Bernard Masson. Lower-case roman numerals (i–xiii) refer to Flaubert's *Correspondance* in the Conard edition: i–ix to the volumes published between 1926 and 1933 and x–xiii to the *Supplément* of 1954.

All translations are my own.

# Chronology

1821. Birth at Rouen of Gustave Flaubert, son of Achille-Cléophas, Chief Surgeon of l'Hôtel Dieu.

1835. First of his extant juvenilia: 'Voyage en enfer'.

1836. 'Un parfum à sentir', 'Rage et impuissance'.

1937. 'La dernière heure', 'Rêve d'enfer', 'Quidquid volueris'.

1838. 'Agonies', 'La danse des morts', 'Rabelais', 'Mémoires d'un fou'.

1839. 'Smarh'.

1842. Goes to Paris to study law. Completes *Novembre*.

1843. Begins the first *Education sentimentale*. Fails his exams.

1844. Epileptic or apoplectic seizure ('crise de Pont l'Evêque').

1845. Completes the first *Education sentimentale*.

1848. Begins *La Tentation de Saint Antoine*.

1849. Reads *La Tentation de Saint Antoine* to Bouilhet and Du Camp, who advise him to burn it. Leaves with Du Camp for an 18 month trip to the Middle East, Greece, and Italy.

1851. Begins *Madame Bovary*.

1856. *Madame Bovary* published in the *Revue de Paris*. Revises *Saint Antoine* and publishes fragments.

1857. Trial of *Madame Bovary*. Acquitted of offences to religion and morality. Begins *Salammbô*.

1858. Trip to Tunis and Carthage for *Salammbô*.

1862. *Salammbô* published. Public but not critical success. Beginning of life as a society figure.

1864. Begins the second *Education sentimentale*.

1866. Apogee of social success. Named Chevalier de la Légion d'Honneur.

1869. *L'Education sentimentale* published.

1872. Third version of *Saint Antoine* completed.

1874. Failure of his play, *Le Candidat*. *Saint Antoine* published. Begins *Bouvard et Pécuchet*.

1877. *Trois contes* published. Returns to *Bouvard et Pécuchet*.

1880. Sudden death at Croisset. *Bouvard et Pécuchet* unfinished.

# Introduction

> Poor Flaubert has been turned inside out for the lesson, but it
> has been given to him to constitute practically—on the
> demonstrator's table with an attentive circle round—an extra-
> ordinary, a magnificent 'case'.
>
> HENRY JAMES

The reader who encounters Flaubert's works for the first time
is likely to feel rather like Emma Bovary when, a few days after
her marriage, she begins to suspect that she has been deceived
and wonders what exactly in her brief experience is supposed
to correspond to those grand words, 'bliss', 'passion', 'ecstasy',
that she has oft heard repeated. For like love, Flaubert has such
an exalted literary reputation that disillusion almost inevitably
follows hard upon one's first experience. The cynic might even
paraphrase La Rochefoucauld's dictum on love and say that
no one would think of admiring Flaubert if he had not read
about him in books.

Fortunately one does encounter cases of spontaneous admiration, but for most readers Flaubert's reputation is something of
a puzzle. Why should Henry James, who spent time detailing
the flaws of his novels and who was offended by Flaubert's
social manner, have resisted the temptations of condescension
and overcome personal animosity to call him 'the novelist's
novelist' and 'for many of our tribe at large *the* novelist'?[1] Or
why should Ezra Pound, lover of Provençal lyrics and Japanese
haiku, have extended Flaubert's empire to verse as well as
prose: not only does *Un Coeur simple* embody 'all that anyone
knows about writing', but Mauberly, the artist who 'strove to
resuscitate the dead art of poetry', took Flaubert as his ideal:
'His true Penelope was Flaubert.'[2] That may be set down as
metaphor, but even within the realm of the novel it is not
obvious, to anyone comparing Flaubert with his own 'great
novelist', whether he be Balzac, Tolstoy, Dostoyevsky, Proust,
Joyce, why Percy Lubbock, writing of *The Craft of Fiction*,
should call *Madame Bovary*, that tale of provincial adultery, 'the
novel of all novels that the criticism of fiction cannot overlook'.

How are we to explain this prodigious reputation? One clue might be found in the reasons for Pound's praise:

> His true Penelope was Flaubert.
> He fished by obstinate isles.

Flaubert the craftsman, the perfectionist, who found creation such an obstinate process and set such standards for himself that writing became sacramental penance: this is certainly the picture he gives in his letters. Flaubert, like his contemporary Marx, developed a labour theory of value but applied it to literature. Henceforth a text must cost its author a great deal of agony. The *sprezzatura* of the aristocrat who dashed off a sonnet in a spare moment had already been displaced as an ideal; now one could no longer play the inspired Romantic bard swiftly transcribing a moment's illumination. And of course to be as enormously productive as a Balzac, planning to turn out a novel a month, would be to give up any artistic pretensions whatsoever. Even so, one must stress that Flaubert's posture was not that of the classical craftsman who knew how to construct a verse or a period and whose mastery of an art made his task one of finite progress towards definable ends. For Flaubert the artistic process was interminable and the work, by definition, imperfect; but the writer could not, for that, accept his limitations with a philosophic shrug without renouncing his artistic titles. Indeed, Flaubert seems very much at the source of a conception of the artist which is still with us. No doubt part of its attraction and reason for its persistence is the stress which falls on desire rather than accomplishment. The struggling author can interpret the conjunction of a compulsion to write and an inability to compose as proof of his vocation. It is precisely at the moment when one finds it impossible to write anything that one enters the artistic condition.

The Romantic artist was often in agony and may have felt it the necessary accompaniment of his condition, but it belonged to his emotional life and attempt to live in the world rather than to the process of composition. 'Quels délices! quels tourments!' or 'I fall upon the thorns of life, I bleed!' locate agony in an experience of the world and require of the reader an empathetic understanding of possible causes. The ultimate inexpressibility of such states of feeling does not trouble the poem, for that is its implicit subject. An agony which was clearly defined by the poem would not require the reader to explore his own experience for possible analogues and would thus be less effectively profound. The function of inexpressibility is to refer the reader to the world and to make him seek out sources of agony as a condition of understanding the poem.

Flaubert transferred this Romantic agony to the creative act itself and thereby called into question the notion that made literature a communication between author and reader and made the work a set of sentences referring to a shared experience they did not express. The agony becomes a property of the act of writing and does not figure in a communicative process. Inexpressibility, therefore, once a property of feelings, mark of profundity, and possible source of pride, now becomes part of a creative linguistic act and a source only of agony — the agony of the unending search for *le mot juste*.

This agony has been an extremely important feature of modern literature, and to pay homage to Flaubert is one way of expressing solidarity with the writer in his battle with language and obsessive exploration of its possibilities. There have consequently been those who not only held Flaubert in reverence but also, like Gide, would willingly have traded the novels — stories of mediocre quests — for the correspondence, which records this nobler and more poignant struggle. But I think one can say that without the novels the letters would be a grotesquely comic document: Flaubert's desperate reflections on art are impressive only because his novels are, finally, worthy of respect. Otherwise the letters would be the contortions of a sadly exaggerated passion. To explain Flaubert's reputation by the ideal he proposed and the example he set would be to devalue the novels themselves and to nourish a myth of the artist's tragic condition which flourishes quite well enough already.

Another way of explaining his reputation would be to sketch his place in the development of the novel. Part of his eminence is due to the influence he exercised on other novelists. But a study of influence, however scrupulous and methodical, would not explain his importance, for that depends on the view we take of the novel: the historical goals and a-historical purposes that we postulate for it. If we consider only nineteenth-century fiction, Flaubert occupies neither a dominant nor a strategically decisive position; or if we choose to regard the diverse experiments of Joyce, Djuna Barnes, Raymond Roussel, and Robbe-Grillet as aberrations or dead-ends, we can construct a tradition of the novel which accords Flaubert only a minor role. But if we seek to account for the reputation he undoubtedly has, then we cannot view the novel in either of these ways but must consider the possibility of organizing the tradition so that Flaubert represents a significant mutation. When we adopt this perspective Flaubert's role becomes both honourable and insidious: to have established the autonomy of the novel by freeing it from various social functions which had determined its possibilities but, by so doing, to have rendered the novel itself extremely problematic.

At the risk of oversimplifying, we can state this change as follows. Lacking the specific conventions which mark poetry as language subject to an organization different from that of ordinary speech, the novel is, from the outset, placed in the circuit of communication. 'The addresser sends a message to the addressee. To be operative the message requires a context referred to, seizable by the addressee, . . . a code fully, or at least partially, common to the addresser and addressee; and, finally, a contact, a physical channel and psychological connection between the addresser and the addressee . . .'[3] If we locate the novel in this schema, we can see that the text itself functions primarily as contact or channel. Because the author wishes to communicate with men he does not know and cannot address 'directly', he casts his text in written form, relying on shared referential contexts and interpretive codes to insure the transmission of his message. The novel acknowledges the importance of this communicative compact by evoking, through direct authorial address, the circuit of speech and by marking the knowledge and assumptions which speaker and hearer are presumed to share and which place them in a relation of mutual understanding. Indeed, the strength of the assumption that a text is the voice of an author who desires above all to communicate meanings for which he accepts responsibility is shown by the various subterfuges to which Flaubert's predecessors resorted — the conventions of the epistolary novel, the fiction of a manuscript discovered in the secret drawer of an abandoned desk — in order to distance themselves from their works and dislocate the process of direct communication in which readers would attempt to participate.

14

These procedures only conceal the author. Spatio-temporal devices for separating author and manuscript, they do not deny the communicative circuit but only seek to introduce gaps. Flaubert was both more radical and more thorough. He attempted to ensure that the novel was truly *written*. This involved, first of all, a devaluation of content: if he never fulfilled his ambition to write 'un livre sur rien' he at least made it more difficult to define a given novel as a statement 'about' something in particular. Secondly, he attempted through his continual and loudly-trumpeted sacrifices to his implacable demon, Art, to make the novel an aesthetic object rather than a communicative act. It must become what Kant called a purposive whole without purpose, which would be more easily admired than assimilated as message. Hence his desire to write a book in which he would have only to construct sentences, whose polished surfaces might aspire to the condition of sculpture. Finally, he sought to invalidate the communicative contract by purging references to it, by refusing to make assumptions to be shared, by shifting narrative points of view so that no authorial source of messages might be identified. That he recognized the destructive consequences of this form of guerilla activity is amply shown by references in his correspondence to the desire to 'dérouter le lecteur'; the victim must be uncertain what he is supposed to think, unsure whether he is being made fun of, suspicious that the book may after all have been written by an imbecile, even — though this project seems not to have been realized — led astray by false bibliographical references.

The attempt to escape from the circuit of communication, to make the text a written object and not the physical manifestation of a communicative act, gives the novel a new autonomy and artistic status but creates problems of interpretation, especially since it is no longer clear why it was produced. Once it is no longer a means to ends external it becomes increasingly problematic, and the ideal by which Flaubert sustained his activity — 'one must aim at beauty' — was too ill-defined to carry explanatory power. To write in order to convey something to a group of readers is one thing; to write for the sake of writing, at a time when the notion of writing, by virtue of this change in function, is uncomfortably pluralistic, is very much another, and Flaubert realized too clearly — too clearly, that is, for his own peace of mind — its fundamental absurdity.

Filling pages with words, for its own sake, is the very form of stupidity, the most comic and gratuitous of exercises. His life stretches before him, he tells us, as an endless series of pages to be blackened, and it appears that the main compensation may have been the long sessions when he would summon his friends and read his drafts, 'jusqu'à la crevaison des auditeurs'.

In approaching Flaubert's work, then, an important question to bear in mind is why write a novel at all. Whatever we may think of novelists like Balzac and Lawrence who seem to have espoused and pursued with determination a particular communicative project, their activity is not difficult to understand. Whether we think they failed or succeeded, their efforts can be placed in a general economy of human action and the works themselves interpreted in terms of this thematic project. Any doubts about the novel as a form can be bracketed or saved for an ironic peroration in which the difficulties of purveying truth through fiction are noted. But in other cases it is crucial not to forget that the novel, once it becomes an end in itself, is fundamentally gratuitous; that the writing of novels is not a natural and spontaneous activity; that therefore we must attempt to make the text answer for its own existence. 'Why write a novel?' is not primarily a biographical question, or at least I do not mean to treat it as such. Nor does it ask simply what effect a novel might have for its readers. It is designed, rather, to reveal a gap between these two questions and focus on the problem of teleological explanation.

To explain a work by reference to a final cause is perhaps the basic mode of literary criticism. When an ultimate purpose can be named, the critic's task is to show how everything in the work contributes to this end and to demonstrate the teleological determination of its unity. But in the case of problematic novels which seem to have arisen outside the communicative circuit, the question, 'Why write a novel?' or 'Why write this novel?' points towards an absent answer, a kind of empty meaning which must serve as teleological determinant of our reading. That is to say, if critical discourse is designed to demonstrate the presence of a controlling purpose in all the parts and their interrelations, then the fact that the most sophisticated and 'aesthetic' novels show a purposiveness without purpose cannot but affect our reading of them.

The easiest solution, designed to permit critical discourse to continue in the absence of a purpose to explicate, is that of a formalism which attempts to make the problem into a solution by taking the existence of the work, which at first seemed to require justification, as the ultimate purpose to which all its elements contribute. Everything, from technical devices to thematic patterns, exists in order to bring into being the literary work whose function is simply to exist.[4] The most wily and distinguished practitioner of this mode of criticism is Henry James, whose Prefaces surprise the reader by how little they explain in the expected sense. Thematic properties of the novels, which we expect to see explained as purposes, are treated as solutions to the technical problem of bringing the work into existence. Thus, it is not a matter of writing a novel to convey *What Maisie Knew*; the child's knowledge is the solution to the problem posed by the technical ambition 'of giving it *all*, the whole situation surrounding her, but of giving it only through the occasions and connections of her proximity and her attention.'[5] And the thematic silences of *The Golden Bowl* are determined by the desire to make the book 'subject to the register, ever so closely kept, of the consciousness of but two of the characters.'[6] One might say, analogously, of Flaubert, that the novels are determined by the desire to write a certain kind of sentence, and this would bear a measure of psychological truth as well as establishing the formal teleology that criticism requires.

But to proceed in this way, to use even so formal and empty a final cause, is to make what may be an unwarranted presupposition of coherence. The notion that works of art must be unified and that the task of criticism is to demonstrate this unity derives, at least in part, from the communicative model and the metaphysics of presence on which it rests. The work tries to express an essence which presides over it as its source and its purpose. To capture the truth of the work is to recover that essence and make it present to consciousness. Criticism, in short, is an unfortunate necessity forced on us by our fallen condition; it tries to recover a moment outside of time where forms and meanings are one; it attempts to make present the truth which forms would communicate directly in a prelapsarian world where there was no gap between appearance and reality, no need for mediation, no possibility of error.

If we reject this nostalgic desire to recover essences as a

metaphysical option which determines our experience but is not determined by it, then we can say that while much art does strive towards versions of 'natural' or organic harmony and constructs models of unity to replace a lost natural unity, the most self-conscious works are aware of the ultimate impossibility of the task and manifest this awareness by the styles of their failure. If novels themselves reveal the problematic nature of attempts to extract truth from appearance, to relate action to meaning, and to produce unity from chaos, we may at least try to suspend the requirement of teleological unity which critical discourse tends to impose.

How then should one read Flaubert? The question is crucial for a number of reasons. First of all, it is not simply a matter of critical strategy but has an important bearing on the thematic properties of the novel. For if the genre is, as we say, an interpretation of experience, an attempt to make sense of the world, then we are confronted from the outset with the problem of relating the procedures which we use in interpreting the novel to those which narrators and protagonists attempt to use in ordering their experience. Both are instances of imagination trying to invest its objects with significance, and whether the processes are made to accord or whether they resist close identification, the relationship between them will be of considerable thematic importance. The novel is itself already a study of the process of reading, and if criticism is not to be more blind than the discourse it studies it must consider its own procedures of reading.

Secondly, the problem of reading is crucial because our notions of what to do when confronted with a text are the major constituents of the institution of literature. The meaning of a work is clearly not the sum of the meanings of its sentences; to 'understand' a work requires more than knowledge of a language. The institution of literature is a repository of conventions and assumptions, expectations and interpretive operations, which enable readers to take up a text, order it, and produce meaning from that ordering. An author writes within and at times against the set of conventions of reading which he takes to be operative in his culture, and to understand the form within which he is writing one must attempt to make explicit the expectations and procedures of readers which it presupposes.[7] And when the novel has become self-conscious and problematic, then the expectations and interpretive operations of readers become doubly important, for they constitute, in one sense, its subject: to read the novel is to observe the ways in which it frustrates one's attempts to make sense of it.

In studying Flaubert, then, close attention should be paid to the process of reading without allowing this scrutiny to lead to paralysis. One must attempt to show that among the procedures of reading which our culture makes available — which constitute the institution of literature — some are more appropriate and effective than others. There are three ways in which this argument can be developed. First, one can take as one's model the psychoanalytic cure and maintain that the validity of one's proposals will be shown by the reader's recognition that they do make sense of his own reactions and problems. Criticism, like the discourse of the psychiatrist, makes explicit the subconscious interpretive operations, and one can reject the proposals of other critics on the grounds that they conceal or avoid rather than confront responses and difficulties which one takes as given. In some cases this line of argument seems highly appropriate. For example, the concept of boredom is as frequent in the experience of reading major works as it is infrequent in critical discussions of them. Or, at least, when critics do use it, it becomes an empty gesture of rejection. But boredom is a literary category of the first importance; it is the background against which the activity of reading takes place and which continually threatens to engulf it. The strategies of reading and interpretation must be understood as attempts to avoid boredom, and, on the other hand, boredom itself is a literary device whose usefulness modern literature has increasingly forced us to appreciate. To recognize the potential sources of boredom in a work and the different rhythms of reading which can be used to neutralize them is to discover important facts about its structure.

Nevertheless, I should not like to ground critical argument entirely on this appeal to the spontaneous reactions of readers. For the notion of a natural and unmediated response to literature is clearly a myth: someone who had no acquaintance with literature and the discussion of it, far from providing a 'pure' response against which critics might test their corrupt and elaborated versions, would simply not know what to make of a poem or novel, because to read it *as* a poem or a novel (as we say with emphasis to those who use literature for other purposes) is to read it in accordance with the procedures that have been developed by a cultural tradition and are gradually assimilated during one's literary training. One cannot assume, therefore, that we have full and complete reactions to a text which criticism must simply make explicit. Reactions are likely to be awkward when we lack the formal machinery for considering them. What we cannot say we are less likely to feel. And therefore critical discourse must be recognized as a process of producing meanings and allowed to produce new meanings. Operating within the general cultural system of reading, it must be allowed to show that certain well-attested procedures work against other assumptions and desires and to suspend the former in order to see what results. This does not, of course, deprive the reader of his rights, nor does it introduce critical relativism of any sort, for the critic himself must convince the reader that he knows what he is talking about by describing the effects he identifies in terms which make them plausible and by making the operations he performs sufficiently explicit that the reader can see how they lead to the proposed effects. If the meanings and the means of producing them cannot be made plausible in terms of the general cultural conditions for making sense, then the critic's discourse will seem incoherent. One cannot, as Roland Barthes says, 'make sense in just any way whatsoever (if you doubt it, go ahead and try)'.[8]

One can, then, advocate some styles of reading and reject others not only by appeal to spontaneous reactions which the latter obscure but also by reference to more fundamental cultural assumptions about coherence and efficacy. By exposing the conventions or operations on which a critical reading is based one can either reveal the tenuousness of that connection or else attempt to show how these conventions hamper the functioning of more fundamental critical assumptions and desires. In these cases the testing ground is the reader's reaction not to a literary text but to the coherence of the proposing critical discourse.

But argument must still be carried out at a third and final level, which is that of the teleology of criticism itself. I have already suggested that some types of interpretation are to be avoided because they spring from critical systems which are guilty of what has been called premature teleology. They have, that is to say, arrested the play of criticism too soon, defined its purpose too readily, erected as its determining force too precise a final cause. To the question, 'What is criticism for?' or 'What does criticism do?' the answers that it 'reveals meaning' or that it 'reveals unity' seem premature determinants. The first is a relatively modern, certainly post-Symbolist, reply and makes criticism an attempt to produce as much meaning as possible. The second has Aristotelian roots but reaches full growth only with theories of organic form; it makes criticism an attempt to display harmonious wholes in which nothing is superfluous and all contributes to a single end. To challenge these particular teleologies one need only say that literature can be valued for qualities other than the unity or meaning it leads one to produce; one can also value the resistance to meaning and the resistance to unity. If one wishes at least to preserve those possibilities one requires a more formal teleology which avoids foreclosure.

One might say simply that criticism exists to make things interesting. If one thus avoids foreclosure at the cost of vacuity, that is, I believe, a necessary operating expense. To be more precise is difficult and dangerous, but one can at least say that one of the preoccupations of such criticism will be to differentiate a work or the work of an author both from other works and from oneself. Difference will be a source of value and variety the predicate of literature as a whole.

To defend this particular teleology is not difficult, for it accords more closely than others with the traditional demands we make of literature. It is valuable, we say, because of the ways in which it leads us to rethink our experience, 'renews our perception', and increases our 'awareness of the possibilities of life'.[9] We recognize, in short, that value is connected with the stimulus to new thoughts but stop short, in a typical premature foreclosure, of the more radical consequences because of a communicational and representational theory of art. We value new perceptions of what the work talks about or shows: the world. To extend this criterion so that it applies to criticism as well, we have only to say that the text itself is an object and part of the world (and a more important object than many which novels present) and that the process of interpretation forms a greater part of our experience than the making of fine moral judgments. If literature is valued for making more interesting, by the theories it embodies and the discriminations it encourages, various aspects of experience, then criticism should be valued insofar as it awakens interest in that aspect of our experience which it analyses and exercises.

The reason for taking this particular imperative as criticism's final cause is not that it offers particular guidelines or even the rudiments of a program but that it may help to loosen the hold that 'meaning' and 'unity' have obtained on criticism. It was not always thus. Discourse about literature formerly allowed margins of irrelevance: elements of a work could be treated as material already given, or 'explained' by citing literary and biographical sources, or treated as an independent stratum under the heading 'style'. There was no anguished sense, such as many now feel, that the critic had failed if he could not see how some element or aspect of the work contributed to the effect of the whole or bore meaning. Perhaps it was simply that with God's creation for a model — whose apparent inconsistencies and absurdities were sufficiently obvious — one scarcely could expect perfection in the creations of men, but that once man became sole creator, harmony and significance were fervently demanded since there were no other sacred objects. The reasons do not matter, since in any case there can be no question of returning, but one might at least suggest, without attempting to disparage the achievements of modern criticism, that the long tolerance of some disorder and irrelevance may tell us something important about literature: that interest and admiration need not depend on unity and meaning.

If one wishes to remain open to this possibility one must try to observe with some scepticism the basic activity of 'recuperation' which one's critical discourse performs. Recuperation may be defined as the desire to leave no chaff, to make everything wheat, to let nothing escape but integrate it in a larger scheme by giving it a meaning. This operation is inseparable from critical discourse (to talk about a work is to organize and name) and perhaps from culture itself. We admit to and tolerate an absence of meaning in nature but we are ill-prepared to do so in culture: a haphazard arrangement of leaves on the ground has no meaning,[10] but the description in a poem or novel of a haphazard arrangement of leaves is immediately taken up and given a meaning, and even the most aleatory series of words and phrases will be made to signify and read, if nothing else comes to mind, as signifying absurdity. We cannot arrest or escape the process of recuperation; it always overtakes us in the end and puts a name, albeit abstract, to what we have done. All we can do is observe the process for what it is, attend to whatever blocks one sort of recuperation and sends the whole operation, with great grinding of gears, one stage higher into a more abstract mode, and try to see that the final recuperation to which we are subject is not a premature foreclosure but allows us room for play and includes an awareness of its own process under an abstract and formal heading like 'the difficulty of making sense'.[11]

For some time Flaubert's works proved resistent to recuperation, except of an abstract sort, because he was labelled a 'realist' and anything the text described was justified by that representational project. But of late a more active critical recuperation has won the field, inspired by his reputation as the meticulous craftsman whose every detail served a purpose. The two main strategies are the impressionistic and the symbolic: the first justifying all that it can as a description of what the characters observe, think, or feel, and hence as a device of characterization which contributes to meaning; the second justifying details by extracting from them semantic features, opposing these features to produce contrasts, and organizing the contrasts in symbolic patterns.

Both procedures are most reputable ways of dealing with literature, and I seek neither to impugn them as such nor to play the Luddite and reject particular interpretations as 'overly ingenious'. My claim would be, first, that if we attempt in our reading of Flaubert to make everything contribute to thematic effects, and if we take this unity in meaning as our standard of artistry, then we should be compelled to admit that Balzac is the greater artist, for the simple reason that there, as we are so imperiously shown by the narrators themselves, nothing escapes the recuperative process and facts are immediately transformed into knowledge which takes its place in a developing system. So that modern critics' decided preference for Flaubert, while they adhere to this standard of values, seems very much a case of self-serving: to write about Balzac is more superfluous, for the production of meaning is done by the novels themselves, whereas Flaubert requires interpretation and offers the critic himself more scope to develop thematic and symbolic patterns.

The critic is therefore effectively valuing, as the source of interest in Flaubert, precisely the absence of what he himself produces. He is interested in Flaubert because of the empty spaces his own discourse can fill.

Secondly, and here we move to another level, the recuperative procedures that such discourse uses are undercut by the novels themselves, which contain by example a theory of interpretation. In approaching Flaubert we place ourselves in a paradoxical situation whose interest we cannot enjoy if we seek easy exits. The novels concern the difficulties of bringing interpretive models to bear on an experience, but in order to reach the point where we can derive this theme as an interpretation, we must employ exactly those interpretive processes whose failures the novels display. And further, if we try at a second remove to unify the novels in these terms and see them as an attack on meaning and organization, we fail abysmally, for they are so insistently novels, that is to say, not novel, that they slip away, in ironical evasion, when we try to graft elaborate and revolutionary theories to them. 'What is all this fuss?' they might say. 'We are just novels: stories of Emma Bovary and Frédéric Moreau, of Salammbô, Bouvard and Pécuchet, and Saint Antoine. What has all this to do with us? Why are you trying to conclude?'

That is the problem. The novel is an ironic form, born of the discrepancy between meaning and experience, whose source of value lies in the interest of exploring that gap and filling it, while knowing that any claim to have filled it derives from blindness. Rather than display by my own example the impossibility of achieving completion when analysing each novel as a unified artifact, I have chosen to disperse and fragment them: to create from their fragments a context in which reading can take place. The first chapter, however, departs from this scheme, and, reading the juvenilia against the problems posed by Flaubert's literary situation, seeks to extract a series of projects which lead an uneasy life in the later novels. The second chapter explores the ways in which the mature novels resist recuperation while at the same time inviting it and sketches what might be called a pathology of the novel. The third chapter investigates what might qualify as two unifying concepts: Stupidity, a major category of Flaubert's discourse, which brings about in formal terms the fragile co-existence of notions which have little common substance; and Irony, a central category in critical discussions, whose affirming and negating qualities offer the possibility of representing through it the complexities of Flaubert's technique. Finally, the problem of reading towards a positive meaning is posed and explored through *Salammbô* and *Trois Contes*. An Afterword offers some retrospective justifications and tries to indicate how Flaubert is interesting.

# I
# The Rites of Youth

Je m'ennuie, je voudrais être crevé, être ivre, ou être Dieu, pour faire des farces.

*Agonies*[1]

## A. *Precocious Boredom*

Flaubert's boredom, as he hastens to point out, was not 'that common and banal boredom which comes from idleness or illness, but that modern boredom which gnaws the very entrails of a man' (i, 151). The condition was well known at the time and had been diagnosed by Chateaubriand in his *Génie du christianisme* as the prerogative of an advanced state of civilization. The ancients were too stoical, too active, too resistant to the debilitating influence of women, to have succumbed to this disease; nor were they helplessly exposed to so many books. Reading and writing made disillusionment no longer the fruit of experience and possession of old age but something any child could acquire in idle hours in his father's library. The concept of life as *desengaño*, a process of running down towards boredom and despair, decreased in aptness with the success of the writings which propounded it. 'In our early youth,' wrote Schopenhauer, 'we sit before the life that lies ahead of us like children sitting before the curtain in a theatre, in happy and tense anticipation of whatever is going to appear. Luckily we do not know what really will appear.'[2] But soon everyone knew. If they did not read Schopenhauer — no one, it seems, did — they read the poets and novelists. It is not a little ironic that the fervour with which they announced that happiness lay in innocence, lack of self-consciousness, and ignorance of the world awaiting one, prevented anyone with the least squib of intellectual curiosity from passing an innocent youth. Books, as Chateaubriand said, 'make one clever without experience. One is disillusioned without ever knowing the joys . . . and without having tried anything one is cynical about everything.'[3]

Flaubert himself claims 'a complete presentiment of life' in early youth: 'it was like the smell of nauseous cooking that pours through a kitchen ventilator. You don't need to have eaten any of the food to know that it will make you vomit' (i, 201). This is from the mature vantage point of twenty-five years. But seven years earlier he had devoted a long letter to the subject, bewailing his own and his fellows' tendency to suffer from imagined or anticipated evils, to sow their own paths with brambles: 'Today's generation of schoolboys are incredibly stupid. They used to have more flair and spend their time on women, duels, orgies; now they're all wrapped up in Byron, dream of despair, wantonly close their hearts, and vie with one another who can look the palest and best bring off the line: "I'm blasé." Blasé! What a joke! Blasé at 18.' He prefers to strike the alternative pose: 'I'm for the popping cork, the stuffed pipe, the naked whore!' (i, 46–7).

The poses, of course, go together: that he should try to treat the one ironically by taking refuge in the other shows how firmly entrapped he is. Indeed, his letters of the period and the juvenilia suggest, by frequent juxtaposition, that Romantic Satanism is the other side of Romantic despair, and that both are essentially conditions or roles. That is to say, there had been a time when *Weltschmerz* came with a shock of discovery and offered at least the pleasure of investigating and deepening it ('it is sweet to believe oneself wretched when one is only empty and bored'[4]), and when Satanic activity could be a spontaneous response to a world bereft of values and a negative attempt to restructure the world between the poles of God and Satan. But now, though these roles might be deeply felt as the given alternatives of existence, to *act* in either is to imitate. If one does anything, one apes some Romantic character. They had already wept, killed themselves, been blasé, fought duels, self-consciously called for whores. As Sartre has argued at some length, the varieties of action open to the second generation of Romantics — the generation of Flaubert, Leconte de Lisle, Baudelaire — were exceedingly sparse, for the dramatic actions whose models were available seemed to demand an aristocratic condition, and the young doctor's son would have felt exceedingly odd challenging anyone to a duel.[5] Self-consciousness and the wrong condition made action impossible.

This is less important, however, than the new temporal structure of *ennui*, due to the fact that the Romantics had been there already. Previously one had earned the right to disillusionment;

27

wisdom was the result of living a *Bildungsroman,* which gave it both a temporal thickness and a coefficient of optimism. Despair implied nostalgia for a state that had actually been experienced and could be seen as the repository of values. Once identified, as that which time had destroyed, these values could be lifted out of any temporal moment of experience and made into the moral imperatives of a transcendental world whose manifestations must be recalled or imagined in a nostalgic or prophetic mode. Thus a major figure of Romantic literature is that of the aged solitary: Cain, Ahasuerus, Faust, the Ancient Mariner, the narrator of *The Prelude,* and later, Tithonus, all of whom have in their ways passed beyond life and can speak of its lessons. The poetic posture is one of looking back, whether from the distance of eternity or only of 'five long winters', as in *Tintern Abbey.* Hence the structure of the statement relates the disillusionment that knowledge brings to a temporal process which is the source of knowledge. The poem assumes history as the condition of wisdom and disillusionment. The source of hope, then, is that the history might be prevented from taking place, that the innocence whose loss defines the passage of time might be preserved in others. Or else there is the more elaborate Nietzschean strategy, which is not of the period but confirms the form of the problem, of attempting to preserve the values of spontaneity within the flux of time itself by denying time the character of historical development *toward* something. One may reconquer innocence by going beyond the knowledge that transforms time into history.

For the second generation of Romantics this crucial temporal structure of boredom and despair is altered. Despair requires no temporal distance, needs no history, and so to escape from history is no escape at all. They begin to write at a time when they have as yet no experience to write about but know the conclusions they would reach should they trouble to reduplicate experiences. And the conclusions being known, it is difficult to feel enough innocence for disillusionment to be lived as empirical history. There is no need for the writer or his works to assume history as the condition of knowledge, and the temptation was to substitute spatial for temporal distance and rise above the world to condemn it, not through a story of losses and gains but *sub specie aeternitatis.* Thus, the major form of continuity employed by Romantic discourse was no longer a structural necessity. Works as different as Coleridge's *Ancient Mariner* and Constant's *Adolphe* had been unified by the fact that the narrator spoke from a perspective of experience and produced a story commanded by the meaning he was able to extract from it. The meanings had such novelty and urgency that the tale itself must function as demonstration and participate simultaneously in the empirical and symbolic mode.

For the generation of Flaubert and Baudelaire there was no reason to produce such demonstrations, no need for a history to function as proof. If they chose not to imitate their predecessors directly their situation offered two possible strategies. The first, adopted by Baudelaire, is marked by the striking feebleness of temporal structures. Those that do appear are denatured, shifted from the place of power they occupied in Romantic verse. References to the future are but metaphors for desires and fears. Quests take place in space rather than time, which obviates the need for inventing a history to represent the process of disillusionment in one who remains in the same place. *Chant d'Automne*, *Voyage à Cythère*, and especially *Le Voyage*, dispense with the passage of time by reference to spatial displacement and thereby move immediately into a symbolic mode without passing through the empirical:

> Nous avons vu des astres
> Et des flots; nous avons vu des sables aussi;

the plurals lead towards conclusions without the trouble of establishing a series of particulars.

> Amer savoir, celui qu'on tire du voyage!
> Le monde, monotone et petit, aujourd'hui,
> Hier, demain, toujours, nous fait voir notre image:
> Une oasis d'horreur dans un désert d'ennui![6]

There is no need to explain and motivate disillusionment but only to explore its forms and consequences. And when the Romantic history is used as a temporal passage, it is, as in *Bénédiction*, lifted away from an experience and made allegory. Even nostalgia, the theme whose temporal structure one would expect to find most indestructible, is treated, as in *L'Ennemi*, as an experience given rather than acquired, expressible without depiction of the paradise lost.

What seems to have happened is that all the Romantic

themes are taken for granted as the modes of experience itself
rather than as conclusions to be extracted from an experience.
Baudelaire can begin a poem,

> Quand le ciel bas et lourd pèse comme un couvercle
> Sur l'esprit gémissant en proie aux longs ennuis,[7]

secure in the assumption that this is the common experience of
a generation and that despair need not be provided with a
history. Memory does not so much create a thematic order
from past history as open a space for the sport of imagination.[8]
Hence the unparalleled rhetorical quality of Baudelaire's verse
which has puzzled commentators and made them impugn his
seriousness. The despair of Hugo's *Tristesse d'Olympio*, for
example, is properly serious since it is extracted from an
empirical history and naturalized by the text as an explicable
reaction. But the despair of Baudelaire's *L'Irrémédiable*, with its
reflection on its own production of images, or of the 'Spleen'
poem beginning, 'J'ai plus de souvenirs que si j'avais mille ans',
is just a point of departure, a condition in which the imagination can work out its metaphors. And the paralysing ennui that
is the ostensible theme is undercut by the rhetorical energy
which proliferates images in a spectacle of self-dramatization:
'Je suis un cimetière abhorré de la lune . . .'[9]

Henry James maintained, with purest intent to blame, that
Baudelaire's 'care was for how things looked, and whether some
kind of imaginative amusement was not to be got out of them,
much more than for what they meant and whither they led
and what was their use in human life at large', and that one is
'constantly tempted to suppose that he cares more for his
process — for making grotesquely-pictorial verse — than for
the things themselves.'[10] This is perfectly true, but scarcely
cause for reproach. To have valued the writing of poems above
the objects they treat was, in his case, extremely healthy; and
as for his attempts at imaginative amusement, this reflects a
more fundamental and pitiable despair than that of a noble
Romantic posturing, for it is the despair of knowing already
what things mean and that they are of no use in themselves,
which lacks even the consolation of pride in one's discovery.
To have come after was to have inherited *ennui* as the atemporal
condition of the poet, to be unable to make this theme the
burden of a continuous discourse based on temporal forms, and

to be left only with the possibility of exploring this theme in discontinuous ways through a frenzied but self-conscious rhetorical activity, to which *La Béatrice* bears best witness.

To dispense with time and attempt to extract 'la beauté du mal' in a rhetoric which reveals a despair of ever escaping a condition felt as given was not a strategy effectively open to Flaubert. He was too critical of rhetoric and too self-protective to adopt these modes of poetic elaboration. But the problem was very much the same: what to do with these Romantic themes which define the artist's condition but which no longer seem to demand development through the temporal forms which organize Romantic literature and produce unity and continuity even when the theme is one of alienation and discontinuity? Flaubert's strategy was almost an exact inversion of Baudelaire's: whereas the latter, chosen by poetry, neutralized temporal structures and sought poetic power in a rhetoric of imaginative display and self-dramatization, the former, working in prose, not only eschewed self-display and the flaunting of imaginative conclusions but attempted to find ways of using temporal structures while undermining their unifying power and the continuity they implied. He would write novels, tell stories that unfolded in time, but he would avoid the nostalgic retrospective structure which transforms time into intelligible history as viewed by one who has lived through it and would deflect the possible transitions from action to knowledge.

But to state Flaubert's approach in this way is not to imply that he was presented with a strategy which he deliberately chose. The juvenilia record long hesitations, experimentation in various derivative Romantic modes, and he did not even begin to discover his strategy until he had succeeded in determining the status of his own experience. That is to say, until he had derived from the set of Romantic models presented him and from his own social and economic situation a sense of what the condition of artist would entail in his case, he could not formulate a strategy, for the simple reason that he did not know from where he spoke and consequently had no sense of how his texts would relate to readers. The function a writer's language is given depends on the position he conceives himself as taking in the world. What does the writer do? What, therefore, must one do to become a writer? How is the experience of the doctor's son from Rouen to be related to the models of the artistic condition which the cultural tradition provides?

It was clear, first of all, that he could not be Chateaubriand, Vigny, Hugo. He could not aspire to play the aristocrat, looking down on the world from the posture of dispossessed monarch, feeling it still to be his kingdom, though dominated at present by inimical forces. A more plausible model was Chatterton, the dying swan — friend of young lords, to be sure, but living in a bourgeois milieu which kills him. Or Vigny's other poet, Stello, who attempts practical life but finds it impossible and is persuaded that his duty lies in withdrawal. The artist, by this model, was a cursed creature, who accepted death and failure as proof of his singular sensibility. Sartre argues that the *poète maudit* was the only model available to the 'knights of nothingness' of Flaubert's generation, for whom poetry is defined by the impossibility of the poet's condition and who, consequently, must seek failure in order to become poets.[11] To enter the confraternity, they must find existence intolerable, and with the youth of France continually meditating their suicides, one understands Pétrus Borel's suggestion that the government provide a self-service guillotine at 100 francs per head.

But this does not seem to have been the only role open to Flaubert. True, he does prate in this vein: 'If I didn't have in my head and at the tip of my pen a Queen of France of the fifteenth century, I would be completely disgusted with existence and a bullet would long ago have delivered me from this poor joke called life' (i, 14). But that was at age twelve. Later his precocious boredom and conviction that experience will always fall short of expectations lead to a desire to disengage from the world and take arms against it. 'Really I have profound admiration for only two men,' he writes at age seventeen, 'Rabelais and Byron, the only two who wrote with the intent to harm the human race and to laugh in its face. How splendid to be a man so placed before the world!' (i, 29). But even when he is not dreaming of revenge the role he projects differs from that of the *poète maudit*, for while the latter may be excluded from human society, he is scarcely blasé:

Il meurt dans ce qu'il pleure et dans ce qu'il espère;[12]

and aware, with Baudelaire's poet, that 'la douleur est la

noblesse unique', he grooms himself for immolation. Flaubert did not balk at sacrifice, but self-sacrifice was scarcely his forte. He did not want to undergo a painful experience in order to bear witness; he tries, rather, to convince himself that he has already lived, grown old in thought and feeling, and can now separate himself from the world which need no longer function as theatre of experience. He is not going to live a history because he can make of his first twenty years a cycle which includes all the pale possibilities human existence offers. 'You thought me young, but I am old' (i, 230), he writes to Louise Colet. 'I have lived a great deal, Louise, a great deal. Those who know me well are surprised to find me so ripe, but I am even more ripe than they suspect' (i, 382); 'beneath my envelope of youth there lies an extraordinary old age' (i, 429). Between 1846 and 1849, says Sartre, every letter Flaubert writes at least alludes to his precocious old-age.[13] He will not be the *poète maudit*, writing in a frenzy of active desire and disappointment. He will be an old man who has passed beyond experience and can survey the world with disdain: 'I have now reached the point where I can look on the world as a spectacle and laugh at it. What is the world to me?' (i, 30).

This is what he regards as God's view of the universe: a divine amusement imposed, as if by *fiat*, on an acerbic *ennui*. Omniscience, such as we can conceive it, would make everything boring indeed; there would be no surprise or anticipation, no opacity and no achievements for understanding. Nothing could be of any interest, for interest is a structure of incompletion. Yet at the same time, considering oneself and one's situation with supernatural lucidity, one would be keenly aware of the absurdity of eternal boredom and might find that omnipotence made it possible to escape with a divine guffaw.

The desire to play God is coupled with a congenital distaste for practical action. Sartre locates its source in the family situation which gave Flaubert from the outset a negative self-definition. Unwanted child, deprived of the success both inside and outside the family that went, as if by right of primogeniture, to his brother Achille, he was from the first defined as the non-Achille, the idiot of the family. Like any younger child, he could not in early years match his brother in physical and intellectual activity, but unlike most, if we are to believe Sartre, he was defined by that alone. Nothing is expected of him; he is not defined by others as a subject who will have his own history; he is only an object of adults' discourse, which he believes implicitly. His future can be prophesied but it cannot be created. He is, Sartre says, deprived from the outset of the basic categories of *praxis*: 'it is not simply that he detests practical life; he does not *understand* it. It forms no part of his limited universe . . . Everything has happened, even the future; man's directed efforts will never be more than a futile quivering on the surface of a dead world.'[14]

Sartre's account is certainly just as a dramatization of the result, whatever its status as causal analysis. The rejection of a world of *praxis* is the common denominator of Flaubert's life at Croisset, his attitude towards language as an object to be worked and polished, and his life-long obsession with stupidity. When he writes in a letter, 'I can never shave without laughing, the process seems so ridiculous' (i, 262), he reveals the basic mechanism. Shaving is ridiculous in itself, but not as the response of an individual to annoying stubble on his chin. In that context it is a practical activity directed towards a certain goal; but destroy the human intentionality that gives it a meaning, consider it solely as object, and it becomes as ridiculous as a word repeated over and over until it becomes meaningless. This is what he calls 'the ridiculousness intrinsic to human life itself, which emerges in the simplest action or most ordinary gesture' (i, 262). The perception of intrinsic ridiculousness is based on a refusal to understand, a willingness to suspend the human project which gives the object unity and purpose. But since this brings about a renewal of perception, the role of 'l'idiot de la famille' promises well as artistic posture. He will write what he sees, from the vantage point of stupidity and alienation: magnifying, reducing, and generally arresting the world of *praxis* in a mode which will come to be called realistic but which is *de-realizing* in the sense that it does not show men actively making their destiny but allows that world of action and effective choice to collapse at the reader's touch.

These three strains in Flaubert's character are projected onto his literary practice as three possible artistic postures: the tragic figure of the *poète maudit* speaking his griefs, the bored old man who has died to life and now rails against the world, and the passive artist who records a world which he eschews and does not comprehend. They intermingle in the juvenilia and appear now and again in the letters of maturity. But they meet for one crucial moment: the epileptic or apoplectic seizure known as the 'Crise de Pont l'Evêque'. Whatever the facts of the incident, it is clear that for Flaubert himself it is the effective manifestation of a number of projects and the decisive event of his life.[15] For the *poète maudit* the crisis proves his singularity and cursedness, his inability to live as other men, and like an attempted suicide establishes his credentials. For the youth prematurely old, whose experience already suffices, it is the death long predicted from which he can be reborn on the other side of life, freed from the need to live a personal history and free to look back with disdain on what he has left behind. For the idiot of the family it consecrates his passive role; he need not attempt to be a subject of experience; he can abandon his attempts to pass his law exam and remain in his family as the younger son incapable of activity. He can even be defined as an aristocratic *rentier* rather than a bourgeois who earns his living.

That the crisis had these functions is evident from the letters in which he looks back on it. 'Je suis vraiment assez bien depuis que j'ai consenti à être toujours mal' (i, 172), he writes. To be defined as *always* ill is a strategic solution, permitting an 'irrevocable good-bye to practical life'. There is now, he says, 'so great a gap between me and the rest of the world that the most natural and simple things I hear astonish me.' Separation from the world will be the source of a literary technique: 'for a thing to be interesting one need only look at it long enough.' (i, 192). And he has now attained a condition where this will be his main activity. Further events are excluded: 'I am now in an inalterable condition . . . When I think of everything that could happen I can't see what could change me, that is to say, me, my life, my daily routine' (i, 201). The crisis was 'the conclusion, the close, the logical consequence' of his youth (i, 230). He can now stand back from that life and regard it as closed, without having entered a new life which could count as empirical history. He will not engage in activity but will observe the world as a spectacle:

> Celui qui vit maintenant et qui est moi ne fait que contempler l'autre qui est mort. J'ai eu deux existences bien distinctes. Des événements extérieurs ont été le symbole de la fin de la première et de la naissance de la seconde. Tout cela est mathématique. Ma vie active, passionnée, émue, pleine de soubresauts opposés et de

sensations multiples, a fini à vingt-deux ans. A cet époque, j'ai
fait de grands progrès tout d'un coup, et autre chose est venu.
Alors j'ai fait nettement pour mon usage deux parts dans le monde
et dans moi: d'un côté l'élément externe, que je désire varié,
multicolore, harmonique, immense, et dont je n'accepte rien que
le spectacle, d'en jouir; de l'autre l'élément interne que je con-
centre afin de le rendre plus dense . . . (i, 278).[16]

This letter is dated 1846. He has completed the works now
classed as juvenilia and will soon begin the first version of *La
Tentation de Saint Antoine*. He has achieved that neutralization
of his own experience which seems a necessary correlate of his
mature artistic posture; but that in itself does not offer much
guidance as to how he should write or what the activity of
writing entails. To discover the functions his language can bear
was the work of some years and required considerable experiment with derivative Romantic forms. In order to understand
how it became possible for him to write the mature novels and
what repressions form the bases of their techniques, we must go
back and observe the hesitations with which he tries out narrative postures in the juvenilia.

## B. *Narrative Strategies*

*Voyage en enfer, Rage et impuissance, La Dernière Heure, Rêve d'enfer,
Passion et vertu, La Danse des morts, Ivre et mort* — the titles of
Flaubert's early works suffice to indicate the thematic preoccupations of the adolescent beginning to write in the years
1835–1840. Whatever his admiration for Voltaire, the Romantic agony was his stock in trade. And though the *cause célèbre* of
the decade, Hugo's *Hernani*, had introduced him to the attractions of historical melodrama (represented by *Mort du duc de
Guise, Un Secret de Philippe le prudent, Deux Mains sur une couronne,
La Peste à Florence, Loys XI*), these exotic excursions are less
interesting than the series of works which bear the direct
expression of the moment's *Weltschmerz*. For there he must
devise ways of bringing home to imagined audiences inherited
truths about the human situation: that life is impossible in this
world ruled by Satan or an absent God, where passion is fruit-
less, all endeavour hopeless, and the only solace a directed
railing or a contemplation of temptations to which one might,
if one is lucky, be asked to succumb. 'Tout est dit, et l'on vient

trop tard'; but it must be said again, with feeling. Experiment is relegated to the realm of form, though that may lead to the discovery of a new project.

There are three narrative strategies used in this early period, which one might call the authorial stance, the confessional stance, and the prophetic stance. In each case the narrator adopts a different contractual relationship with his reader, which affects the treatment of time and the production of meaning. In each case he must discover appropriate sources of authority which can give assurance to his role and make his works acts supported by the institution of literature.

The authorial stance predominates in the earliest works, as is perhaps to be expected, since the young author is primarily excited by the fact that he is writing. 'Perhaps you don't know what a pleasure it is to write', he exclaims at the end of *Un Parfum à sentir*:

> Ecrire! oh! écrire, c'est s'emparer du monde, de ses préjugés, de ses vertus et le résumer dans un livre; c'est sentir sa pensée naître, grandir, vivre, se dresser debout sur son piédestal, et y rester toujours . . . Je suis maintenant fatigué, harassé, et je tombe de lassitude sur mon fauteuil, sans avoir la force de vous remercier si vous m'avez lu . . . (I, 67).[17]

The essence of the posture is there. Thrusting himself forward as author, asking us to admire his creative activity more than the story itself, he engages the reader not to involve himself in the tale but to take it as an artifact which reveals the daring and cleverness of the creative project: 'I have sought to rail against prejudice and will perhaps arouse indignation against an author as impudent as myself' (I, 66). We are called to admire not the profundity of the story but the profundity of the author who has been clever enough to conceal deep thoughts in it: 'I shall offer you no explanation of its philosophy. It has one — painful, bitter, sombre and sceptical; find it for yourselves' (I, 67).

Set in this framework is the story of Marguerite, ugly wife of a poor saltimbanque, who, unable to bear the misery of her condition and her husband's alternation between brutality and indifference, kills herself, hounded as a madwoman by the Parisian crowd. The potential temporal structure of the story is negated by the authorial posture, for Marguerite's condition is given in advance, as that of which the author wishes to speak, so that there is no process of development or of discovery but only the gradual movement towards a pre-ordained result. I am going to show you, the author says on his opening page, 'all those hidden pains and wounds masked by false laughter and circus costumes . . . in order to make the reader ask: whose fault?' (I, 55). And the answer follows hard apace: it is the fault of social prejudice and institutions but also the fault of fate, 'which crushes men in its iron fist like a giant juggling with dried skulls' (I, 55). That double and ambiguous vituperation, with its possibilities of contradiction, indicates one of the problems of this narrative stance. The pre-eminent value accorded to the moment of writing and the process of creation makes the theme of misery simply a given whose causes and conditions need not be explored in a temporal process. We must attend to the author and not to Marguerite's problems.

The authorial stance, is, of course, potentially viable, but those works which employ it usually invoke the activity of writing as a tragic or problematic process and thus offer a greater source of interest than shouts of jejeune satisfaction. In such cases the difficulty of writing is a theme which can be read against or integrated with others adumbrated in the text, so that, for example, *Les Faux-monnayeurs* poses the problem of the relationship between ways of composing a novel and ways of composing a life, and *Tristram Shandy* relates a never-ending and disordered discourse to the 'frankness' that a confessional ordering of one's life implies, thereby posing the problem of composition at both levels. Even texts constructed around triumphant references to the process of writing — like the sonnets which proclaim that 'this verse will make you immortal' — succeed by making these references metaphors for the praise that is the subject of the poem. Finally, of course, there is the self-reflexive *Künstlerroman* which refers to its own process of composition but presents it as the outcome of a history, prepared by a series of experiences and adopted as a solution to problems of living.

The success of the authorial stance, then, would seem to depend on giving the process of writing a history or making it a metaphor for other themes in the work. Either one of these solutions will establish the rights of authorial discourse, whereas in Flaubert's version there is no such support: authority is vested solely in the person of the writer, since his stories are explicitly adduced as created *exempla* designed as much to show that he can write as to demonstrate a particular thematic truth. The discourse of the author is not supported by analogies with the story which enable it to be integrated; it takes up the story too quickly and, allowing it no independent existence, cites it as an example of authorial daring.

*Rage et impuissance,* for example, is subtitled 'Conte malsain pour les nerfs sensibles et les âmes dévotes', and uses the brief tale of a man buried alive in error to demonstrate the absence of God. Trying to break out of his coffin, the doctor turns from raging despair to prayer and believes he is about to be delivered, but no answer comes and he dies cursing God. 'Eh bien', asks our author,

> aimable et courageux lecteur, et vous, bénévolente et peu dormeuse lectrice, que pensez-vous qu'eût répondu notre homme du cercueil, si quelque maladroit lui eût demandé son avis sur la bonté de Dieu? Eût-il répondu: peut-être? existe-t-elle? que sais-je? Pour moi, je pense qu'il eût dit: J'en doute ou je la nie. (I, 87).[18]

There we have our proof. And here, he continues, 'is the whole moral of this foolish work': I engage you all to cast your existence in God's face when it is bitter. The story, needless to say, scarcely survives the manner of its telling.

*Quidquid volueris* does survive, largely because of its singularity: Djalioh, the hero, offspring of a forced experimental union between an ape and a Negro slave, is introduced to society by the amateur scientist, Monsieur Paul, as an orphan, and not surprisingly finds life an intolerable burden. He is the man with a soul, dreaming, in best Bovaresque fashion, of taking Paul's wife in his arms and fleeing through woods, fields and prairies to the shade of a palm tree where he might sit and gaze into her eyes. Aware of his desires but not of his difference, he is the *poète maudit* who cannot live, nor even read and write. But nature will take its revenge on an oppressing society, and Djalioh, not willingly but almost experimentally, dashes her child against the ground and amorously rapes the weeping mother, who dies of the shock; after which, lacking more sophisticated means, he kills himself by running head on against the mantelpiece. The moral is not far to seek in Flaubert's pathology: the son as true artist, a monster capable only of dreams but forced into a human condition for which he is unequipped. Indeed, this is the problem our posturing author explores; but the tale he recounts is so singular and so much richer than his interpretations of it, that it is not immediately taken up by an authorial discourse and seems, in fact, to escape his control, though he tries to label it a clever folly, a dream of his poetical brain: 'Come, mad dreams of my sleepless nights, . . . children of my brain, give me one of your mad tales and strange laughs . . .' (I, 102). The author hovers over his story, explaining the failings of the 'reasonable man', praising the poetical cast of Djalioh's soul, commenting self-consciously on the romantic elements in his tale, and underlining its thematic constants. At the end he asserts most blatantly his authorial control: 'You want an ending at all costs, don't you? And you find I'm awfully slow in producing one; very well, here it is!' (I, 113). But this procedure, which in other cases reduces the story to a pale example, does not seem to function in that way here, for the simple reason that the tale exceeds the thematic demands made on it by the narrator. Had Flaubert made his hero a constitutionally mute and inglorious Milton, condemned to a life of frustrated passion, then the failure to ground the tale in an empirical history would have made it nothing more than the weak vehicle for the *Chatterton* theme: the young poet crushed by an unsympathetic society. But Djalioh as chosen vehicle both blocks the narrator's ready assimilation of the tale (the poet who is *literally* a monster must be rather a special case) and stands apart for the reader as surplus of the *signifiant* which has escaped the author's deadening grasp. The Flaubertian text, one might say, has discovered excess as a source of power, but the young Flaubert misinterprets this lesson and cannot apply it with success until much later and in a different narrative mode.

The authorial mode fails because the author tries simultaneously to cite his tales as examples illustrating a thematic truth and to emphasize that they are his own creations. He cannot, consequently, speak with any real authority. On the one hand, any claim that his discourse is based on a profound and detailed knowledge of the world is undercut by the briskness with which he moves from rudimentary story to moral and by the insistence that the texts are children of his brain. On the other hand, the experience of the narrator is not presented in such detail as would enable us to take it as the source of authority. Not only the mode of presentation but the choice of details recounted prevent us from finding in the voice that speaks the authoritative statement of truths distilled from the world or the compelling plaint of an anguished personal experience. It is not a question, need I say, of the actual knowledge or sincerity of the individual, Gustave Flaubert, but only of the failure of the text to project an experience which might serve as its basis. And the reason for this seems to be that the narrator's interest in his own role as author precludes him from naturalizing his story as an effective history compassing change and development and from offering the predicament of the author himself as a sufficiently complex experience worked out in time. To take either of these courses would seem a possible solution; to take them simultaneously, by making the author both hero and narrator and recounting his history, is to adopt the confessional stance.

The form is a familiar one and its literary success may be due to the elegance with which it resolves the problem of authority. A narrator recounting his own life is, inevitably, a most knowledgeable person, and we grant without question people's right to speak of themselves, though we may often prefer not to listen. But that is only the first level of authority. The confessional mode is based on a temporal structure which separates the subject who speaks in the present from himself as an object who lived through the past, and it marks this separation by the judgments which the former passes on the latter. Since the reader is also a subject passing judgment on the object whose history is recounted, he will test the authority of the narrator by seeing how well the judgments offered concur with his own and will gain a sense of just how far and in what respects he may accredit the narrator's discourse. Either the narrator becomes a representative man or, if he deviates widely, a pathological case enunciating a personal view which we can understand because we know his history. Either way the narrator's discourse is grounded.

Flaubert, however, has difficulties with this form because of his problems in coming to terms with the writing of history. Alternating between a desire to deal with experience in an empirical mode and offer particular causes for disillusionment and a desire to achieve swift generalizations by displaying a pervasive fatalism, he leads his readers to expect an intelligible history and then fails at crucial moments to provide it. *La Dernière Heure*, the first of this series, starts in a most promising way: the nineteen-year-old narrator has sealed his room and lit a coal fire, whose fumes will kill him in an hour: 'There is still enough paper on my desk to set down hastily all my memories of life and the circumstances which affected this ridiculous but logical series of days and nights, of tears and laughter, which people call a man's life' (I, 88). The function of his confession will be to show suicide as the logical outcome of his experience and to reveal, through the logic at work here, the futility of existence. But in fact this project is most inadequately realized. The first event in the narrator's downward course is the death of his sister, which upsets him for essentially selfish reasons: he prays for his playmate to be restored to him but his prayers are not granted, which produces both local rage ('her soul! her soul is nothing to me!') and general alienation. In other respects, as he hastens to tell us, he possesses all the ordinary prerequisites of happiness: healthy, wealthy, well-travelled and loved, he is a fortunate soul who creates his own misery by asking, why do I exist? why does anything exist?

> Souvent, en regardant tous ces hommes qui marchent, qui courent les uns après un nom, d'autres après un trône, d'autres après un type idéal de vertu, toutes choses plus ou moins creuses et vides de sens, en voyant ce tourbillon, cette fournaise ardente, cet immonde chaos de joie, de vices, de faits, de sentiments, de matière et de passions [je me suis dit]: 'Où tend tout cela? sur qui va tomber toute cette fétide poussière? et puisqu'un vent l'emporte toujours, dans le sein de quel néant va-t-il l'enfermer?' (I, 89).[19]

The summary is so brief, so obviously the result of a particular optic rather than the distillation of an experience lived at normal rhythm, that the plane of empirical history is abandoned and the reader is left uncertain whether he is supposed to read the confession as the document of an unmotivated pathology or whether he must himself supply causes. The desire to create a narrator who can speak directly and in the most general terms of his disgust for life leads Flaubert to lift the tale away from a particular history which might have served as demonstration and thereby to weaken the narrator's authority.

*Mémoires d'un fou* displays in more explicit fashion the same problems. The confessional form seems to call for the presentation, from the perspectives of maturity, of a series of incidents through which innocence is tarnished and youthful optimism destroyed, and if the life portrayed is to prove representative it must appear to the reader as a process of natural development, with at least local uncertainties, in which the particular configuration of experience which happens to be encountered is a plausible cause of disillusionment. But Flaubert, whether because he himself has not lived or because others have been here before him, is little-inclined to adopt this necessary temporal structure. He is still writing tracts and, despite the use of a confessional mode, is still strongly tempted to take up an authorial stance. 'Why write these pages?' he begins, they are but the ravings of a madman. 'I'm going to set down everything that comes into my head . . . I will use up a packet of pens and a bottle of ink and bore both the reader and myself' (I, 230). The time of writing is more important than the time of experience, for the document is primarily charged with presenting the scepticism, despair, and madness of a particular view of the world.

'I'm going, then, to write the story of my life,' says the narrator, but in fact I have scarcely lived. I am young and have not experienced the world or entered society. My life consists not of events but of thoughts: 'How many long and monotonous hours have been spent in thinking, in doubting!' (I, 230). Thought is not a response to events which might offer an empirical justification of it; it is something independent, the pure creation of the authorial mind. By this separation of thought as a life in itself, we are already at one remove from the project of advancing a view of the world by showing how it emerged from events, but it would still be possible to display a life of thought as a progressive development, through which the reader might be led step by step. In fact, however, the narrator's thoughts do not appear to grow; they are given as a Romantic *désespoir sans cause* and adduced as instances of a general critique of existence. This book, he tells us, speaks of the world, 'ce grand idiot, qui tourne depuis tant de siècles dans l'espace sans faire un pas, et qui hurle, et qui bave, et qui se déchire lui-même' (I, 230).[20] Read this story, he says, of an empty life so full of thoughts and tell me afterwards si tout n'est pas une dérision et une moquerie, si tout ce qu'on chante dans les écoles, tout ce qu'on délaye dans les livres, tout ce qui se voit, se sent, se parle, si tout ce qui existe . . . Je n'achève pas tant j'ai d'amertume à le dire. Eh bien! si tout cela, enfin, n'est pas de la pitié, de la fumée, du néant! (I,232).[21]

His life is to be all lives and serve as a demonstration of these propositions, but uncertainties in the narrative posture render this project extremely problematic. The tale of an individual who had become a raving madman through his attempt to come to terms with an ordinary experience might fill the requirements; the narrator, in this case, would stress his essential similarity to other men and diverge from them only in the rigour with which he lived out conclusions which others glimpse but shy away from. But the narrator of *Mémoires d'un fou*, pleased with the profundity and originality of his thoughts, prefers to stress his singularity and set himself against his readers: 'A madman, that horrifies you' (I, 230). Since his view of the world is not justified by a portrayal of events, he must ground it in his own cast of mind. And so he tells us of his admiration for Romantic poets, his youthful nightmares, his general lassitude, his ill-fated love for a married woman, mixing this indiscriminately with a general railing against the age and a wish that civilization might die. And then, in Chapter XX, a few pages from the end, as if realizing that his narrator is not fulfilling the function assigned him, Flaubert abruptly introduces a second narrator with whom the reader may identify more closely and who can, therefore, with greater authority announce the message. Each of us, he begins, sees the world through his own prism. Some see only practical affairs, others a sublime plan, still others an obscene farce. Those who see the world as a pile of mud are unusual people and difficult to take. 'Vous venez de parler avec un de ces gens infâmes . . . ceux-là sont des gens sans principes qui regardent la vertu comme un mot et le monde comme une bouffonnerie. De là ils partent pour tout considérer sous un point de vue ignoble' (I, 244).[22] Passing judgment on the first narrator, identifying his view as a deviant one, the second narrator makes himself a normative figure; and then, in order to accomplish the task which defeated the first narrator, he challenges the reader to open his eyes to this vision of the world: think on your condition, 'homme faible et plein d'orgueil, pauvre fourmi qui rampe avec peine sur ton grain de poussière' (I, 244).[23] You think you are free, superb, majestic, but you know nothing, control nothing, and die like the miserable animal you are. This narrator, who has tried to characterize himself as a reasonable man, attempts to remedy the failure of the confessional mode by taking up the same themes in a prophetic mode. The implication is clear: Flaubert has not yet learned how to make use of a temporal history and can accomplish his purposes only by moving outside of time altogether.

The last of the confessional series is *Novembre*, Flaubert's most ambitious work before the first *Education sentimentale* and one which he did not disdain to show to friends even much later in life. Indeed, it is rather more successful than *Mémoires d'un fou*, though the problems posed and solutions adumbrated are rather similar. The narrator is a young man who feels that his life has already reached its term and who meditates on his past with rather more curiosity and uncertainty than Flaubert's other confessional narrators. 'Il me semble quelquefois que j'ai duré pendant des siècles, que mon être renferme les débris de mille existences passées. Pourquoi cela? Ai-je aimé? ai-je haï? ai-je cherché quelque chose? j'en doute encore' (I, 248).[24] He does not begin with a thematic account of the world, formulated from a perspective outside time but, in an attempt to account for his own despair, leads the reader through the stages of his development. And he is perceptive enough to recognize that the process of writing his own history cannot be wholly divorced from his own life but must be considered as an action which he has chosen and which is as pointless as another. He is, moreover, sufficiently self-critical to measure himself against the Romantic models that inspired him and perceive that his failure to be a dramatic figure — René, Werther, Don Juan — is a major source of *ennui*.

J'étais donc ce que vous êtes tous, un certain homme qui vit, qui dort, qui mange, qui boit, qui pleure, qui rit, bien renfermé en lui-même, et retrouvant en lui, partout où il se transporte, les mêmes ruines d'espérances sitôt abattues qu'élevées, la même poussière de choses broyées, les mêmes sentiers mille fois parcourus, les mêmes profondeurs inexplorées, épouvantables et ennuyeuses. N'êtes-vous pas las comme moi de vous réveiller tous les matins et de revoir le soleil? las de vivre de la même vie, de souffrir de la même douleur? las de désirer et las d'être dégoûté? las d'attendre et las d'avoir? (I, 252–3).[25]

He discovers happiness only in fragile moments of natural communion. When he tries to give love a practical manifestation the result is an acute sense of the disparity between desire and its empirical fulfilments. Later it seems that he has found a kindred soul, but failure is a structural necessity, and with a terse 'I never saw her again' the manuscript tails off into a nostalgia tinged with bitterness at the foolishness of nostalgia.

At this point, however, a second narrator enters and provides, as in *Mémoires d'un fou*, a commentary on the tale of the first. But the differences in the relationships between the two narrators in these works are a splendid indication of Flaubert's new and surer grasp of narrative strategies. Whereas in *Mémoires d'un fou* the second narrator appears as surrogate for the first, who had failed to provide adequate grounding for his discourse, and hence plays briefly at distancing himself from that subjective viewpoint before adopting it with renewed didactic fervour, in *Novembre* the second narrator keeps his detachment, helps to establish the authority of the first, and, by judgments which seem to the reader unduly harsh, serves as a foil which directs sympathy back to the other narrator.

'I knew the author of these pages', he begins . . . 'et si quelqu'un, ayant passé, pour arriver jusqu'à cette page, à travers toutes les métaphores, hyperboles et autres figures qui remplissent les précédentes, désire y trouver une fin, qu'il continue; nous allons la lui donner' (I, 272).[26] The posture is that of one not hasty to judge but accepting with good will the task of setting down the truth as he and society see it and determined to preserve his own impartiality so as to arouse some sympathy for his decidedly odd and unhappy acquaintance. The distancing takes place through denigrations of the first narrator's style and character. Nurtured on bad authors, 'as one can see', he was a man 'qui donnait dans le faux, dans l'amphigourique et faisait grand abus d'épithètes' (I, 275).[27] Solitary and fantastical, he held views on social life, set down here with all appearance of fidelity, which were at the least unusual, and he was vain enough to think of himself as a pariah when in fact no one knew him.

There is, in this procedure, a kind of trap for the reader, who has been led, both by the general requirements of the confessional form and the non-dogmatic tone of the first narrator, to that necessary sympathy which enables him to take an interest in the first narrator's plight. And therefore, when a second narrator pronounces, the reader must compare those judgments against his own and, in the interests of consistency but also to secure the pleasure of finding himself more broad-minded than the social discourse which the second narrator proffers, must renew his sympathy for the former. There is no need for the reader to take the initiative in condemnation, even were he so inclined. Moreover, and this is perhaps of greater importance, what the second narrator tells us about the life of the first reinforces our impressions of the latter's sincerity and strengthens the authority with which he spoke.

> J'admire le hasard, qui a voulu que le livre en demeurât là, au moment où il serait devenu meilleur; l'auteur allait entrer dans le monde, il aurait eu mille choses à nous apprendre, mais il s'est, au contraire, livré de plus en plus à une solitude austère, d'où rien ne sortait. Or il jugea convenable de ne plus se plaindre, preuve peut-être qu'il commença réellement à souffrir. Ni dans sa conversation, ni dans ses lettres, ni dans les papiers que j'ai fouillés après sa mort, et où ceci se trouvait, je n'ai saisi rien qui dévoilât l'état de son âme, à partir de l'époque où il cessa d'écrire ses confessions (I, 272-3).[28]

Such a statement offers us a way of integrating the activity of writing with the themes of the confession itself. To write one's confessions is not to step outside time and indulge in the joys of authorship; it is an activity which has a particular role in a history, which can be undermined by the *taedium vitae* it seeks to portray. In short, it is being taken seriously and made part of a life; the first narrator gains authority to speak by virtue of the fact that he stopped when it seemed appropriate. Silence is a more effective posture than self-dramatization.

We find, however, in *Novembre*, just when it appears to have solved the problem of the confessional mode, an exceedingly curious ending, which would seem a definite regression to the authorial mode, did it not offer so tantalizing a critical problem:

> Enfin, au mois de décembre dernier, il mourut, mais lentement, petit à petit, par la seule force de la pensée, sans qu'aucun organe fût malade, comme on meurt de tristesse,—ce qui paraîtra difficile aux gens qui ont beaucoup souffert, mais ce qu'il faut bien tolérer dans un roman, par amour du merveilleux (I, 276).[29]

Sartre argues that this curious final clause is an attempt by

47

Flaubert to conceal the most personal and serious of his thoughts: as a purely passive agent, defined by ideas which come to exercise an almost visceral influence on him, Flaubert believes that the idea of the impossibility of living — a notion which he has not chosen but which seems to have chosen him as victim — will take hold of him and destroy life itself.[30] And hence this passage would be a prefiguration of the false death of 1844 which brought an end to a life like that of the first narrator and inaugurated a life like that of the second.

But another interpretation is possible, and indeed seems preferable if we are concerned with the problem of narrative effects: here we see Flaubert discovering that solving the problem of narrative authority so as to write a well-formed novel is not in fact what he desires. The reader would then know exactly how to take the book, as the representation of an experience, without reflecting on the central fact that it is not life but a novel. Moreover, Flaubert displays, for whatever psychological reasons, a desire to force the reader out of the socially-accepted rationality into which the second narrator had welcomed him: since the stance in the second part of the book has been that of a man able to reach a true and just 'understanding' of a deviant life, what better way to undermine the complicity between narrator and reader and the categories of a social rationality than to expose the narrator as someone who may only be making up a tale and pandering to a love of fantasy. It is as if, having mastered the problems of the confessional form and having presented a history which moves towards a thematic effect, Flaubert had suddenly turned against this project and, by destroying its empirical basis in his penultimate sentence, confronted his readers with the mocking cry: 'So you thought you could grasp this life as a meaningful whole, did you? That only happens in novels.' Successful employment of the confessional form would be a Romantic solution and could not satisfy.

The prophetic stance, the third narrative strategy of the juvenilia, was a permanent temptation for Flaubert, as his obsession with *Saint Antoine* shows. To project a narrator who cannot be defined as an individual in that he sees and knows what no one could, to create a narrator who enters no reciprocal contract with the reader but merely deigns to set forth a vision of the world, was always, in one sense, the simplest of literary strategies and therefore well suited to the direct expression of a theme. Indeed, the prophet's relation to experience was itself a major theme: to see the world as it is one must get outside it and grasp it *sub specie aeternitatis*. So strong was the desire to display the world as a timeless collection of allegorical figures that a theory of art for art, whose demands would be equally absolute, was required if the temptation was to be resisted.

In the juvenilia, however, it is scarcely combatted. *Voyage en enfer*, the earliest of Flaubert's extant compositions, recounts in pseudo-biblical couplets the vision presented to a young narrator who rises above the world and transmutes its activities into allegorical types: Pedantry, Rationality, Absolutism, Civilization, Liberty, Truth. 'Show me your kingdom', he asks Satan, who has served as guide.

> —Le voilà!
> —Comment donc?
> Et Satan répondit:
> —C'est que le monde, c'est l'enfer! (I, 42).[31]

This is the message which the brief tale is designed to carry, and it does so by projecting an innocent narrator exposed to a new mode of prophetic knowledge.

In the next attempt at this genre, *Rêve d'enfer*, there is a strange amalgam of narrative postures, which one might see as an anticipation of the mature works, were it not for the fact that the narrator does not attempt to vanish but repeatedly insists on displaying his angle of vision. The opening paragraphs, which combine a reduction of the world with selection of emblematic details, indicate that we are dealing with a symbolic mode of perception rather than with the writing of the world:

> La terre dormait d'un sommeil léthargique, point de bruit à sa surface, et l'on n'entendait que les eaux de l'océan qui se brisaient en écumant sur les rochers. La chouette faisait entendre son cri dans les cyprès, le lézard baveux se traînait sur les tombes, et le vautour venait s'abattre sur les ossements pourris du champ de bataille (I, 90).[32]

Yet at other times the narrator slips into an empirical mode and identifies himself with humanity: 'He was offended by our habits and instincts . . . Would he have understood our sensual pleasures?' (I, 91). But rather than allow the identity of the narrator to expire in confusion, he stresses, even in the empirical mode, his distinctive perception as source of the narration: 'Il fallait voir cette femme . . .' (you would be as impressed as I was). 'All this was very strange . . .', to me who observed it. 'It was indeed a love inspired by Hell . . . a satanic passion, entirely convulsive and compulsive, so strange as to seem bizarre, so strong as to produce madness' (I, 98), but I can detach myself from it, describe it to you, and judge it. The shifts in perspective do not destroy the narrator because they are firmly marked as modes of perceptions of a personalized narrator. The result is not an efficacious questioning but simple disorder.

The reasons for this compositional confusion are quite evident. The observer raised so far above the world that men become ants may state directly the theme of a creation gone wrong, but that narrative posture is not propitious for the production of a novel or short story, because at this level of abstraction there is little to be said about the world. Hence the narrator must descend to a point where he perceives the thoughts of man or men and can develop a rudimentary history, even if it be, as in this case, the account of a struggle between the Devil and pure mind. And in order to create some measure of interest he must limit his point of view still further to allow reticence and engage the reader in a possible empirical vision: 'you would have been impressed/puzzled/moved, if you had seen this.' The goals are clear but the strategy a failure.

*La Danse des morts* grapples with the same problems but in a different way. The narrator does not present himself as the recipient of an experience; he offers his tale of the encounter between Christ and Satan, their exploration of the world, and their listening to the words of the dead, without suggesting a source. But he tries to anchor his story and arouse the reader's interest by the incongruity of circumstantial details: 'ce jour-là' Satan was bored; Christ passed by and seeing him standing on a comet stopped for a chat. Descending to earth, they sit down on a broken tombstone, 'covered with moss and hung with greenery'. The narrator does not himself become a prophet, endowed with supernatural understanding, but allows his figures of Death, History, the Damned, Lovers, Prostitutes, to utter declamations bearing his thematic offering. We have here a first attempt at the strategy of *Saint Antoine*, but one it is difficult to take seriously.

*Smarh*, the second attempt, is both more ambitious and decidedly more interesting for the problems it poses. Though primarily dialogue, it is introduced in a summarizing discourse which locates the narrator far above petty particularities:

> L'humanité, qui, un moment, avait levé la tête vers le ciel, l'avait reportée sur la terre; elle avait recommencé sa vieille vie, et les empires allaient toujours, avec leurs ruines qui tombent, troublant le silence du temps, dans le calme du néant et de l'éternité.
>
> Les races s'étaient prises d'une lèpre à l'âme, tout s'était fait vil.
>
> On riait, mais ce rire avait de l'angoisse, les hommes étaient faibles et méchants, le monde était fou . . . il allait se mourir (I,186–7).[33]

The totalizing vision states the theme of emptiness and degradation, which is primarily a condition but which can also be interpreted, for the needs of the story, as an end which will come.

The history is dramatized in a temptation. Consider Smarh, the most saintly of men, says Satan to the Archangel. 'Watch me plunge him into evil and then tell me if virtue still exists on earth and whether my Hell has not long ago melted this old ice-cube which cooled its fires' (I, 187). The basic structure is thus that of a dramatized history which both represents a more inclusive history working itself out and is created to prove that this history has already taken place. The paradox is inescapable: to write a story to show that all is nothing, one must create a tale which shows that all comes to nothing and simultaneously deny that story as development by claiming that coming to nothing is the same as being nothing. The prophetic mode must both produce a history which can serve as allegory and deny that it is a history. The only way to succeed in this enterprise is to become, like Blake, a consummate myth-maker, so that one's tale does not depend for its force on its momentary status as history in time. But this, as yet, is beyond Flaubert's genius.

Satan tempts Smarh with knowledge leading to despair, plunging him into the infinite, leading him to doubt God, and calling on Yuk, God of the Grotesque, to teach him about life, 'for the God of the grotesque is an excellent interpreter for explaining the world' (I, 199). Yuk's exposition takes the form of a series of tableaux, from the noble savage who discovers in himself, by this diabolical agency, Romantic *Weltschmerz*, through a monarch destroying himself and his kingdom through vice, to a series of scenes of family life which end badly. Smarh himself finally succumbs, though not before formulating many hopes which are disappointed, and weeps bitter tears, 'each of which was a curse upon the earth, a bit of the heart falling away into nothingness, the death-rattle of hope, faith, love, beauty; all this was dying, fleeing, wafting away for eternity . . .' (I, 217). But in the final struggle over Smarh Satan is defeated and Yuk triumphs, proving his own claims to superior immortality: 'I am the true, the eternal, the ridiculous, the grotesque, the ugly, I tell you. I am that which is, that which has been, and that which shall be' (I, 213).

In fact, Yuk is really the God of Language, which is both grotesque and creative, the true form of immortality in that nothing exists outside it. For Yuk's power is all in speech. He opens his mouth and out come 'calumnies, lies, poetry, chimera, religions, parodies,' which expand, interact, amalgamate, 'enter ears, take root and sprout, construct and destroy, bury and unearth, raise up and bring low' (I, 202). To ground the vanity of the world in the grotesque autonomy of language will become a familiar theme in Flaubert, but at the moment it is still subordinate to a direct attack on experience; indeed, the relations between the two have yet to be worked out. A *Conte fantastique* cannot disparage language without undermining its own basis, for the effectiveness of the mythological machinery depends on the power of language to evoke what is not while relating it to what is.

What, Sartre enquires, is the relationship of the imagined world of prophetic vision to the real world which the vision attacks? And he concludes that Flaubert, knowing the unreality of the former, still asserts its identity with the latter.[34] This is certainly the implication of the narrative posture; rising above the world, the narrator tells us that to one endowed with supernatural knowledge it appears in *this* way, and hence grounds his tale on an idea of the world made thematically explicit. But Flaubert clearly realized the dangers of such a procedure, which makes the narrator himself the source of authority and exposes the tale to criticism as a distorted subjective vision. In a note appended to his text a year later he observes, in the guise of a disinterested third party, that such direct thematic assertion is ineffective: a tale of this sort must be based on *ideas*, and those you thought so splendid a year ago now seem very bad indeed. 'One can do something wretched now and then, but not of this stamp.' To assert an idea is to make oneself vulnerable.

This is, of course, a risk youth always runs, but it is an especial danger in the narrative modes Flaubert has chosen. A personalized narrator, whether he be prophet, author, or a confessing character, who takes upon himself the presentation of a particular view of the world, always runs the risk of uttering what soon may seem stupidities. 'What form must one adopt', Flaubert asks much later, 'to express one's opinion about things of the world without exposing oneself to appearing an idiot later on. That is a formidable problem' (v, 347). And the solution, as he recognized then, in 1867 when he had already found it, was to eschew the pleasure of giving the opinion an author or bearer, to forgo seeking admiration for what one thinks, and to insinuate one's view into a description which will be read as 'objective': 'I think the best thing is to depict, quite frankly, the things that exasperate you.' 'Disséquer est une vengeance' (v, 347). Realism is a mode of self-protection: 'I never pose as a man of experience; that would be too foolish; but I observe a great deal and never conclude — an infallible way of avoiding error' (i, 337).

For the moment, however, solutions elude him, and his attempts to adapt various narrative postures all suffer from the same basic problem: the presence of the narrators in or behind the stories troubles the representational project. The narrators attempt to establish their authority by asserting that the world presented is the world of experience, but by so doing they draw the readers' attention to these assertions, which can be read by the sceptic as subjective and tendentious, and pose the problem of their own authority. The reader is allowed, as it were, to hold the story at arm's length, reading it in an experimental way, while he decides whether to grant the narrator the prerogatives of vision that he claims. The difficulties, of course, are a direct consequence of the devaluation of history which, I have suggested, was implicit both in the literary situation Flaubert inherited and in his own early projects. To narrate the failure of a single love or the destruction of one individual's hopes would not prove that all is vanity and so seems scarcely worth doing. Far better to create a narrator who, from a position above the world, can assert that all is vanity and cite brief *exempla*.

The strategy is deliberately proposed in a passage from a notebook:

> Climb a tower so high that noise does not reach you and men appear little; if from there you see one man kill another you will scarcely be moved, certainly less moved than if the blood spattered you. Imagine a higher tower and more massive indifference —a giant contemplating myrmidons, like grains of sand at the foot of a pyramid; and imagine the myrmidons slaying one another, the grains of sand moving; what does that matter to the giant? Now you can compare Nature, God, or, in a word, omniscience, with this giant, . . . and reflect after this on the pettiness of our virtues and crimes, our 'grandeur' and baseness.[35]

Effective distancing requires, in one sense, a lack of imagination; if one is to remain unmoved, on one's tower, by the spectacle of men killing one another, one must treat it simply as a visual scene and abandon any tendency to imagine the detail of their quarrels. If one plays the giant for whom the affairs of myrmidons are of no consequence, one will be inclined to dismiss them impatiently and ill-disposed to reconstruct the causal history of the slayings. This is what weakens the juvenilia: a distancing and detemporalizing optic which is not coupled with effective myth-making. Or perhaps one should say, rather, that since the tales are presented not as myth but as representative experience, they cannot succeed when the narrator moves so impatiently away from empirical history to visionary theme. Analysis of the juvenilia is essentially an investigation of the forms of impatience.

To see the problem in another light, one might consider Flaubert's treatment of discontinuity and incoherence. Romantic literature had expended considerable energy in transcending discontinuities as it presented them, unifying the disparate through thematic syntheses. It is not simply, as Hazlitt says, that a puddle is filled with preternatural faces, or that everything which we see reflected in 'this vegetable glass of nature' is related to the permanent forms of an eternal world. It is rather that the evocation of diversity is usually accompanied by an immediate transcendence of diversity towards some common if abstract principle. Thus, Wordsworth's famous description of the Bartholomew Fair in Book Seven of *The Prelude* is swiftly recuperated lest the presentation of the inchoate have demoralizing effects:

> Oh, blank confusion! true epitome
> Of what the mighty City is herself,
> To thousands upon thousands of her sons,
> Living amid the same perpetual whirl
> Of trivial objects, melted and reduced
> To one identity, by differences
> That have no law, no meaning, and no end.

Pure difference, without meaning, is not allowed to stand. Analogously, though in a totally different mode, Lamartine's 'Le Lac' lifts us away from the potential chaos of nature which threatens to make itself felt in any concrete description, and makes the diversity and activity of nature a stay against time. 'Preserve the memory of that night, O Nature!'

> Qu'il soit dans le zéphyr qui frémit et qui passe,
> Dans les bruits de tes bords par tes bords répétés,
> Dans l'astre au front d'argent qui blanchit ta surface
> De ses molles clartés![36]

Rather than pick a single silent object which might serve more easily as repository of permanence, he cites a rudimentary catalogue of nature's elements, hinting at that secret longing for the chaos lying hidden in the womb of orderly creation that Schlegel saw as the hallmark of Romanticism. But explicit synthesis tempers the chaotic possibilities of catalogues.

In Flaubert's early works the same tendencies can be observed; indeed, it is quite striking how easily negative and pessimistic syntheses can be substituted for positive. In *Smarh*, at a moment when everything seems splendid, one finds a traditional pantheistic catalogue of nature's diversity and unity:

Tout ce qui chantait, volait, palpitait, rayonnait, les oiseaux dans les bois, les feuilles qui tremblent au vent, les fleuves qui coulent dans les prairies émaillées, rochers arides, tempêtes, orages, vagues écumeuses, sable embaumant, feuilles d'automne qui tombent, neiges sur les tombeaux, rayons de soleil, clairs de lune, tous les chants, toutes les voix, tous les parfums, toutes ces choses qui forment la vaste harmonie qu'on nomme nature, poésie, Dieu, résonnaient dans son âme . . . (I, 215).[37]

But, retaining many of the same terms, he can turn such a catalogue to another purpose:

pour celui qui regarde les feuilles trembler au souffle du vent, les rivières serpenter dans les prés, la vie se tourmenter et tourbillonner dans les choses, les hommes vivre, faire le bien et le mal, la mer rouler ses flots et le ciel dérouler ses lumières, et qui se demande: 'Pourquoi ces feuilles? pourquoi l'eau coule-t-elle? . . . pourquoi la tempête? pourquoi le ciel si pur et la terre si infâme?' —ces questions mènent à des ténèbres d'où l'on ne sort pas (I, 243–4).[38]

Diversity is quickly recuperated in one way or another: items in the series are cited as examples of a theme explicitly announced. And even when the theme bears directly on diversity rather than on general futility, the series is taken up by a summarizing discourse:

elle regarda la foule qui s'engouffrait dans les spectacles et les cafés, et tout ce monde de laquais et de grands seigneurs qui s'étale, comme un manteau de couleur au jour de parade. Tout cela lui parut un immense spectacle, un vaste théâtre, avec ses palais de pierre, ses magasins allumés, ses habits de parade, ses ridicules, ses sceptres de carton et ses royautés d'un jour. Là, le carrosse de la danseuse éclabousse le peuple, et là, l'homme se meurt de faim, envoyant des tas d'or derrière les vitres; partout le rire et les larmes, partout la richesse et la misère, partout le vice qui insulte la vertu . . . (I, 119).[39]

Shortly afterwards we are told that 'le bruit du monde lui parut une musique discordante et infernale', and this type of summary — the fact that the world can be contained by a single phrase — undercuts the thematic drive which, citing its incompatibilities, calls it discord. The world does not seem incoherent but rather too effectively structured: excess on your right hand, starvation on your left, cleverly arranged to counterpoint one another. The semantic organization of the discourse prevents the scene from dissolving into fragments which would be simply and gratuitously there.

Elsewhere the relationship between coherence and incoherence may be somewhat different, but the general effect is much the same. A passage from a notebook describes a ball:

J'y ai vu des fillettes en robe bleue ou en robes blanches, des épaules couvertes de boutons, des omoplates saillantes, des mines de lapin, de belette, de fouine, de chien, de chat, d'imbécile à coup sûr—et tout cela babillait, jacassait, dansait et suait—un tas de gens plus vides que le son d'une botte sur le pavé m'entouraient . . .[40]

Parts are disengaged from wholes with no attempt to be exhaustive — this will later become one of the major devices of incoherence — but the animal series suggests an order of species as well as a confused menagerie, the parallel sequence of verbs provides a grammatical order in the absence of any other kind, and the 'tout cela' recomposes whatever had been dispersed as the sentence moves towards the coherence of the final thematic summary: 'un tas de gens plus vide . . .' In later works Flaubert will give us more heterogeneous details strung together in sentences which burst at the seams because of the incommensurability of the contexts they try to knit together. But as yet the sentence undergoes no strain and, if anything, offers, in the series of imperfects, its own easy and excessive elaborations.

In a discussion of 'Flaubert's Preoccupation with Incoherence in his Early Work', Roger Huss argues that Flaubert's development in his juvenilia displays an attempt to overcome incoherence and that this is largely successful in the first *Education sentimentale*.[41] But it would be more apposite to invert his formula and say that in the earlier works incoherence is controlled, in that it is a constant theme and the details cited as instances are at once made coherent by the thematic structures which recuperate them; before incoherence can establish itself in its own right, the narrator draws us back to a coherent theme. It is only later that incoherence will be truly displayed.

The first *Education sentimentale* is incontestably the best of the juvenilia, the only song of triumph, as Sartre says, that Flaubert was ever to permit himself; and it comes close to solving, in its way, the problems of narrative strategy which the earlier works display. The narrator still makes direct appearances as a man of the world whose knowledge is superior to that of his readers and characters and who can offer whatever explanations are necessary and some that are not, but he no longer allows delight in his narrative role to thrust him into so prominent a position as to steal attention from his characters. He attempts, in short, to prevent himself from becoming an object which readers observe and judge. He must remain a subject and to that end create characters who are sufficiently compelling as subjects of experience to engage the readers' attention and who will not become collapsible cardboard figures as soon as they are treated with detachment: objects for both narrator and reader. This, presumably, was the project. Henry was to be the representative figure, whose failure would display the impossibility of living, and Jules would serve as his foil. If, in the end, Henry collapses and the ridiculously effete Jules blossoms into a superman, that is a matter of some biographical interest which, for our purposes, is best ignored. The interest lies, one might say, in the narrative techniques which present the interaction between the world and a hero, whatever his name.

The opening sections of the book show considerable progress in the construction of deadening, petrifying sentences. The hero, we are told, arrived in Paris one October morning 'avec un coeur de dix-huit ans et un diplôme de bachelier ès-lettres'. He entered the city by the Porte Saint-Denis, 'dont il put admirer la belle architecture;'

> il vit dans les rues des voitures de fumier traînées par un cheval et un âne, des charrettes de boulanger tirées à bras d'homme, des laitières qui vendaient leur lait, des portières qui balayaient le ruisseau (I, 278).[42]

'Cela', we are told 'faisait beaucoup de bruit. Notre homme, la tête à la portière de la diligence, [the interrupting phrase set off by commas to break the flow] regardait les passants et lisait les enseignes.' Flaubert was to become, of course, a master of opening paragraphs, but this must rank as one of his best, equalled only, perhaps, by the brilliant bathos of *Bouvard et Pécuchet*. The opening sentence suggests a relationship between 'un coeur de dix-huit ans et un diplôme de bachelier ès-lettres' as possessions, but offering none it creates an initial awkwardness that attaches both to an ordering discourse and to the hero himself. Manure carts are drawn by a horse and an ass and bakers' carts by men, but that too is a parallel allowing little development (to say that men are like beasts seems excessive and could lead the reader to feel that the language is mocking him), and the absence of connection only asserts the resistent and 'factual' nature of the details. 'Dont il put admirer la belle architecture' is glaringly and disconcertingly ambiguous, especially since one feels that the choice between irony or praise is of no consequence; 'des laitières vendaient leur lait' presents a tautology, as if mocking what counts as fact, and if one then expects the symmetry of 'portières qui balayaient leurs portes' one is disappointed by the arbitrary substitution of 'le ruisseau'. We are quietly told that 'there was a lot of noise', with no attempt at evocation, and the whole scene is simply laid before the hero, who 'regardait les passants et lisait les enseignes' with no attempt at interpretation.

This is not to imply that the paragraph must be read with such attention and self-consciousness. On the contrary, it offers nothing very odd or striking, does not require deciphering, and is easily passed over. It is precisely the silence of the text, the blankness of a self-sufficient narrative surface, which makes one's interrogation of it seem somewhat gratuitous and there-'ore the more fascinating. The easy and traditional questions — fwho is speaking here? what sort of man is he? how does he view the world? whence comes his authority?' — find no answer and seem, indeed, irrelevant. In the phrase, 'il put admirer la belle architecture', for example, the effect is of a constituent ambiguity of language which is on display rather than of a positive signifying intention on the part of a narrator which the reader must recover. One is, in short, more interested in the fact that such flat praise seems inevitably ambiguous than in trying to reconstruct and characterize a speaker so as to determine what he meant. There are, then, only two ways to treat this text: one takes it as a self-sufficient and unrevealing piece of description and passes swiftly on, or one hovers over it, worrying its blankness, to discover the complex structures that do the work of deadening and petrifying. The move back through language to a persona, whose character is both the origin of the discourse and determinant of its truth, seems proscribed. We have, in short, a *text*, an example of *writing*.

This level of achievement is not sustained, but Flaubert does experience some success in making the world a text which offers no easy holds to interpretation: 'Les poignets sur les cuisses, les yeux tout grands ouverts, il contemplait d'un air stupide les quatre pieds de cuivre d'une vieille commode en acajou plaqué qui se trouvait là' (I, 278).[43] That characteristic gaze makes contact with objects not as functional items involved in human activities but as singular and isolated parcels of dead matter. And if Paris itself is not dead matter, it is at least a disordered spectacle with which the young man has difficulty in making effective contact: 'he wandered about the streets, the squares, the gardens, he went to the Tuileries, the Luxembourg gardens, he sat on a bench and watched children play or swans glide across the water.' The disjunction (*ou bien*) decomposes a scene which might easily have been composed, and we seem, with this and the following sentence, to be entering the realm of clichés that provide alternative activities: 'He visited the botanical gardens and fed Martin the bear; he strolled in the Palais Royal and heard the pistol shot at noon.' And then again in the mode of passive visual contact, 'il regardait les devantures des boutiques de nouveautés et des marchands d'estampes, il admirait le gaz et les affiches. Le soir, il allait sur les boulevards pour voir les catins, ce qui l'amusa beaucoup les premiers jours, car il n'y avait rien de pareil dans sa province' (I, 279).[44] '*Admiring* the gas lights and posters' is a particularly nice touch, for not only is the sentence itself singularly lacking in admiration, devaluing the hero's reactions by its refusal to sketch them more fully; it reduces his contact to that of detached reverie.

Paris escapes his understanding; he can stand before it but cannot *comprehend* it, take it in and make it his own. He does make efforts, of course, and like one of Balzac's provincials he would distinguish the inhabitants by their species: 'il se faisait transporter en omnibus d'un quartier de Paris à l'autre, et il regardait toutes les figures que l'on prenait et qu'on laissait en route, établissant entre elles des rapprochements et des antithèses' (I, 279).[45] But the text immediately moves on to another subject, isolating this feeble attempt at interpretation, telling us nothing of what might have been learned, and suggesting by its own detachment that such attempts are artificial and gratuitous modes of imposing meaning on recalcitrant matter.

There are here the beginnings of an ironic style, but Flaubert has not yet mastered the complex dialectic of speech and silence nor the modes of anti-climax which will later distinguish his prose. 'Les dames ne disaient rien ou causaient littérature, ce qui [and this an unfortunate ending] est la même chose.' Or, 'on se passa les verres de main en main, vivement, pêle-mêle; la mousse tombait sur la nappe et sur les doigts, les dames riaient; il y a ainsi des bonheurs infaillibles.' Less awkward, but still less successful than the sentences which, in later works, will drag to a diminished close, is the description of a Parisian worthy: 'M. Renaud obéit à sa femme, il fit la révérence à tout le monde, s'inquiéta de la santé de chacun, offrit des sièges à la société, donna des tabourets aux dames, des tapis aux messieurs; il fut obséquieux et léger, il glissait, il volait' (I, 286).[46] The Flaubertian 'chute de phrase' has not yet been developed and his prose remains at times almost Dickensian.

Moreover, the narrator still, from time to time, shows a desire to display his own sophistication and to enter the story, not in the authorial, confessional, or prophetic mode, but as an authority who feels at ease with his audience and assumes that they share his view of the heroes' activities. He can recount brief anecdotes — 'I knew a man once who . . .' — to illustrate a point being made or reflect with kindly irony on the mania for writing love letters and their facile charms. And occasionally he allows himself to emphasize points which he thinks the reader might not have noticed. But above all he enjoys shifting the point of view, though he does it without skill and to little effect: shifting into the present tense to offer some rather artificial drama; pretending, for a moment, to be only an observer who didn't happen to notice what people were wearing; withdrawing at another point to the persona of an observer who describes in the present tense an encounter in the street between two men whom he does not know but who are in fact Henry and M. Renaud; and even, for part of one scene, adopting dramatic form, complete with stage directions. Some shifts of these kinds, more subtly employed, will be important in the later works, but here the only one used to good purpose is the adoption, for a single paragraph, of a particular kind of 'respectful' discourse, here articulated with some irony:

Madame avait sa bourse particulière et son tiroir secret; Monsieur grondait rarement et depuis bien longtemps déjà ne faisait plus couche commune avec Madame. Madame lisait très tard le soir dans son lit; Monsieur s'endormait de suite et ne rêvait presque jamais, si ce n'est quand il s'était un peu grisé, ce qui lui arrivait quelquefois (I, 282).[47]

In the latter part of the novel, however, these acrobatics cease, and the famous encounter between Jules and the dog, which occupies Chapter XXVI, is narrated with unusual assurance and consistency. Jules' thoughts and reactions in the recent past are recounted, at first with some distancing judgments but shortly afterwards in a *style indirect libre* which is in no way the vehicle of irony, so compelling is Jules' encounter with and reaction to the mangy, limping dog that attaches itself to him. Readers agree that this is the most effective chapter of the book, and indeed the incident exercises a fascination on critics, who are drawn back to it to offer their explications. If one tries to define the reasons for this signal success, it becomes clear that Flaubert's narrative strategy plays a large role, for the suggestion that the incident is of the highest importance is strengthened by a striking gap in the narrative. Having fled the dog and returned to his house, Jules begins to meditate on what has happened to him, and from the combination of attraction and repulsion there emerges the desire to see the dog again, 'pour tenter le vertige, pour voir s'il y serait plus fort'. Feeling that the dog is awaiting him below, because of the sense of expectancy that is mixed with his own horror, he descends the stairs and opens the door: 'le chien était couché sur le seuil.'

Full stop. End of chapter. One turns the page and Chapter XXVII begins: 'Ce fut son dernier jour de pathétique; depuis, il se corrigea de ses peurs superstitieuses et ne s'effraya pas de rencontrer des chiens galeux dans la campagne' (I, 354).[48] And he begins a program of self-instruction. We are told that an important change has taken place, but the final crisis, the wrestling with the angel, is not described; and insofar as the change involves abandoning superstitious fears, it is almost as if upon opening the door he had found no dog there. But if we think about the incident in an empirical mode we can, as Sartre says, imagine almost anything happening on his seeing the dog, except his calmly closing the door.[49] If we try to fill up the blank we may well find ourselves following Sartre and placing there the epileptic fit at Pont l'Evêque which brought one life to an end and inaugurated another and which, one year later, is still too painful to describe, even in another form. We may imagine Jules fainting and awakening another man, or perhaps even staring the dog down until it slinks off to the nether realms from which it emerged. The blank might seem to welcome various alternatives.

It is curious then, that this is not the question critics ask; they do not, for the most part, try to explain what happened; their efforts are directed almost entirely on the problem of the dog as symbol. What does he represent? That this should be the question asked tells us something both about the success of Flaubert's narrative strategy and about the blindness of certain critical procedures. To have left the moment of crisis a blank is both a powerful representation and a suggestion that we need not try to formulate what happens there, that whatever versions we might invent would only falsify by particularizing; and we feel this strongly enough not to enquire what might have happened, unless like Satre we have a particular biographical argument to present. We take from the crisis, as it is presented, only a sense of mystery and importance which we transfer to the dog itself. And then, as critics whose job is one of naming, we attempt an interpretation. What is the dog? A symbol to be named, and once he is given a name, the assumption must run, something will have been gained. The dog, we can say, is Jules' past, with which he must come to terms; the lost passion he was in danger of forgetting; reality, which must be accepted, for all its running sores; the meaning of experience, which transcends the problems of a purely personal existence; his own soul, which he must face; death, which cannot be escaped by jejeune pantheism. Choose your name and make out a case for it; the conventions permit the citation of evidence not only from this chapter but from encounters with dogs in other novels, references to dogs in the letters, and hypnotic encounters elsewhere that serve as crises.

Such interpretations are all attempts to recuperate the dog, to make him something comprehensible by giving him a name which will take its place in a discourse that tames, to reduce him to a noun that we can put in our sentences. Once this is accomplished, he is no longer something strange, hypnotic, and compelling. And one's complaint is not simply that he is no longer what Jules has encountered, but that he is not even what the reader has encountered, if he found the chapter sufficiently worrying to undertake interpretive labours. Nor am I simply attacking such readings from a general anti-interpretive bias. For the fact is that such recuperative processes are undermined by the text itself in its presentation of the scene. Jules too, after all, experienced reader and artist that he is, attempts several interpretations. The first does not rise to a symbolic level but is a purely empirical and classificatory naming: 'one of those dogs who have lost their master and who are always chased away, wandering haphazardly around the countryside, until they are found dead at the side of the road' (I, 351). This is reasonable and in accordance with the evidence, but soon it proves inadequate. Jules cannot chase him away; perhaps there is a particular historical bond between them. 'Was it not Fox, perchance? the spaniel he had once given Lucinda?' As a poet he knows what to do with that and brings forth his memories of a love now lost. But perhaps the dog is not Fox after all; he doesn't look like him, and a retrospective melancholy proves an inadequate reaction. He feels 'an infinite compassion for this inferior being who was looking at him with so much love', but this does not work; the dog still threatens; he exceeds the role Jules had tried to assign him. Then, as the dog leads him to the river bank, uttering 'ces sons furieux, plaintifs et frénétiques tout ensemble', he strives to interpret the dog's language, to read in it a message addressed to him:

il usait cependant toutes les forces de son esprit à tâcher de les comprendre, et il implorait au hasard une puissance inattendue, qui puisse le mettre en rapport avec les secrets révélés par cette voix et l'initier à ce language, plus muet pour lui qu'une porte fermée. Mais rien ne se fit, rien n'arriva, malgré les soubresauts de son intelligence pour descendre dans cet abîme; le vent soufflait, le vent bruissait, le chien hurlait (I, 353).[50]

It is not his intellectual powers that will permit decipherment; that door is firmly closed, and when he does offer another interpretation it is sparked by an exterior circumstance and a memory: he had once contemplated suicide at this place; perhaps the dog wants to remind him of that, to force him to come to terms with his past, or perhaps someone else has committed suicide. 'N'était-ce pas Lucinde? grand Dieu! était-ce elle? serait-ce elle, noyée, perdue sous le torrent? si jeune! si belle! morte! morte!' And he is off again, imagining her body floating downstream towards him, her long blond hair wafted on the waters. But this reading fails also; the dog is not a simple harbinger of tragedy or an admonition. His eyes flame and grow to the size of mirrors: 'ils se confrontaient tous deux, se demandant l'un à l'autre ce qu'on ne dit pas. Tressaillant à ce contact mutuel, ils s'en épouvantaient tous deux, ils se faisaient peur; l'homme tremblait sous le regard de la bête, où il croyait voir une âme, et la bête tremblait au regard de l'homme, où elle voyait peut-être un dieu' (I, 353).[51]

That too is an interpretation of sorts, but it is a more empty name than the others, and when Jules finally struggles back to his room and reflects on his experience he avoids specific names altogether:

Il était sûr pourtant qu'il n'avait pas rêvé, qu'il avait vraiment vu ce qu'il avait vu, ce qui l'amenait à douter de la réalité de la vie, car, dans ce qui s'était passé entre lui et le monstre, dans tout ce qui se rattachait à cette aventure, il y avait quelque chose de si intime, de si profond, de si net en même temps, qu'il fallait bien reconnaître une réalité d'une autre espèce et aussi réelle que la vulgaire cependant, tout en semblant la contredire. Or ce que l'existence offre de tangible, de sensible, disparaissait à sa pensée, comme secondaire et inutile, et comme une illusion qui n'en est que la superficie (I, 354).[52]

The process of interpreting the dog, as Jules' case itself shows, is full of pitfalls opened by wishful thinking and premature foreclosure. Indeed, the dog could almost be defined, in terms of his role in the scene, as a dialectical excess, as that which always exceeds the interpretations which it provokes. It is precisely in this that he is both fantastic and highly realistic: something which is still there in all his concreteness, as a *signifiant* calling for meaning, however much one tries to attach to it a *signifié* which will integrate it in a discourse. These modes of discourse, on which Jules tries to draw, are defined as *pathétique*, as something one must go beyond. But it seems very much as if it were only through surfeit that one may go beyond: one must face directly that greatest of Romantic clichés, the inexpressible thoughts and indefinable feelings of hierophantic moments, and pass beyond them by recognizing that they can only be defined negatively, as 'ce qui ne se dit pas', as the forever unfilled *signifié* of a *signifiant* that can appear only as excess. Whether the intimations be of a divine order or of 'le Néant du monde' does not matter greatly. This is why we need not worry whether Jules' discovery is positive or negative, or whether *Saint Antoine* ends with the discovery of divine order or monstrous disorder. In either case the moment of supreme 'Romantic synthesis' which takes one beyond the *pathétique* grants a sense of another reality to be grasped in the excess of the concrete itself and not statable except as an absence dialectically created by this presence.

To say all this, of course, is to offer an interpretation of one's own, but it differs from other symbolic interpretations in that it requires a quite literal reading of the scene: Jules encountered a dog which he could not place; he was frightened by that very fact, but facing the fear and encountering the dog again allowed him to accept his inability to place him as part of the scheme of things, and henceforth, as our narrator tells us, 'he was no longer afraid of encountering mangy dogs in the countryside'.

At this level the text is quite self-sufficient, and in that it resembles the opening paragraph of the novel. One can take it in this way, without postulating a positive secret which lies behind it and generates it. And when one does dwell on it at greater length and investigate the source of its effects, this takes one not to a level of symbolic patterns but to an allegorical drama of reading and writing played out in the sentences themselves.

These two passages are, of course, extremely different, and the interaction of imposed form and resistant material takes place in different ways in each case; but that, if anything, strengthens the point which can be drawn from them and which, as I shall argue later, proves valid for most of Flaubert's mature works. At one level the text can be justified and read as a self-sufficient representation, an attempt at what we have come to call realism, which need pose no problems, though it may be somewhat lacking in interest if read in that way. When one tries to go beyond that to a symbolic synthesis, lifting details away from a realistic function and using them as the motivating bases of a symbolic thematic pattern, one finds that this can be accomplished only in a state of critical blindness which ignores the ways in which the text mocks and undercuts such interpretive processes. But this mocking and undercutting activity carries one to a level of interpretation which may be called allegorical rather than symbolic, where Flaubert's activity is indeed, as he hoped it might be, a matter of writing sentences and where possible themes emerge as versions of the problems of composition and interpretation. And one should say further that the move to this level is not to be justified simply by the convention that modernist literature is always, ultimately, about literature, but rather by the fact that the self-awareness which is created at this level and obscured at others — awareness of what one does when trying to come to terms with the world in languages that determine the forms of that encounter — seems the only moral value sufficiently formal and comprehensive to subsume whatever more restricted goals and values might be cited in support of other types of reading.

This pattern of two levels which exclude, as their middle term, a level of symbolic interpretation becomes possible, as I have suggested, when certain narrative techniques are adopted. The prophetic and authorial stances, and even the confessional stance as Flaubert uses it, fail because they themselves immediately take up whatever the text offers in the way of an empirical surface and dispose it in thematic patterns. As long as the narrator remains a major figure in the work or a source of authority, his vision and personality will be made the determinant of the story and the truth to which it must be related. And this, at least in Flaubert's hands, produces failure. Success requires that the narrator become less adept at interpretation, that he abandon the attempt to express his conviction that all comes to naught, and that he content himself with displaying, under the guise of a realistic project, a recognizable world, whose negativity appears only in the interstices of sentences.

Jules, after his conversion, is on his way to becoming such an artist. Undertaking a program of universal education not unlike that of Bouvard and Pécuchet, he experiences none of their frustrations because he is more detached: attempting none of their practical experiments, he grasps ideas not as means of operating in the world whose efficacy and truth would therefore concern him but as truths of the world: beliefs which play a role in it and which he can set down with detachment. This detachment must, however, be accompanied by sympathy: without enthusiasm or hatred 'he participates in the prayer of the priest, the defeat of the conquered, the fury of conquerers': 'he becomes one with colour and substances, materializes spirit, and spiritualizes matter.' Identification is a means of representation rather than a step towards synthesis; it is an aesthetic attitude: 'il lui a fallu que la vie entrât en lui, sans qu'il entrât en elle, et qu'il pût la ruminer à loisir, pour dire ensuite les saveurs qui la composent' (I, 369).[53] Noting the flavours, numbering the streaks of the tulip will be his project — this in a 'concise', 'mordant', and 'supple' style.

Jules has become the ideal artist, and therefore the ending poses a problem. There is simply no way to go on, for Jules would have to live and thus become a character like any other. All Flaubert can do is to have Jules imagine his great works. Then, stepping back to his authorial persona, he suddenly assures the reader that he is about to finish his tale and speaks of the pleasure he has taken in 'blackening all this paper'. The song of triumph finds no appropriate form; there is no way to end it successfully, and this no doubt is why it will have no progeny.

## C. 'Beyond' Romanticism

In a letter of 1846, meditating on the roads to artistic glory, Flaubert divides writers into two classes: the greatest, the true masters, 'encompass all humanity; without concentrating on themselves or their own passions they reproduce the universe'; others can be harmonious when crying out in pain and remain eternal when writing about themselves. Byron, says Flaubert, is of the latter company, and one is often tempted to follow his example and to convince oneself that it suffices the artist to say what he thinks and feels (i, 385–6). But Flaubert had learned that this did not suffice. As a youth he had not only played with the repertoire of Romantic themes but also run the gamut of Romantic narrative strategies and found them wanting. He had not the patience to create a temporal history which would gradually reveal truths about the universe, because he knew those truths already. And consequently, when he adopted the confessional or prophetic modes, which required such temporal development if they were to succeed, he found himself impatient with their demands and inclined to move too quickly towards explicit thematic statements which devalue the proposed illustrations and expose the narrator to judgment as an object. His own self-consciousness, which is linked with a knowledge of earlier literature, led him to shun, though occasionally after the fact, 'la boursouflure romantique' as a form of self-display which made one much too vulnerable now that it lacked originality; and he had therefore to face what, as Geoffrey Hartman says, was a basic problem of Romantic literature: whether the mind can find an unselfconscious medium for itself.[54] The poet as seer cherishes the individuality of his vision, as that which defines his own soul, but knows that its value lies precisely in the extent to which it can be made to transcend the solipsistic and subjective; yet to make large claims for that vision is to expose himself to the irony of his own and the readers' reflective gaze. What is to be done?

A return to innocence is not, of course, possible, and even the 'organized innocence' of which Blake speaks seems denied Flaubert, unless one interpret it in a peculiar and Hegelian way, as the state of a spirit without a self to be true to, in that it has annulled, preserved and transcended (*aufgehoben*) its alienation and become objective to itself. This would be not precisely the condition of Rameau's nephew, whom Hegel cites as a case of freedom in and through alienation, but of a dialectical successor who can mimic without playing the buffoon, who is not himself present in every objectification, and who therefore is defined only as an absence which lies behind the forms that are presented. Moving through knowledge to a recovery of a new kind of innocence and freedom would be for Flaubert, as the incident of the dog shows, a passage through a sense of the negative determination of everything in the universe — a determination which cannot be expressed — to a consciousness which does not define itself by taking a position but tries to receive everything into itself by, as he says, describing it. This is, to be sure, something that Flaubert never accomplished, and indeed the very abstractness of the terms makes it unclear how one would know whether it had been accomplished or even whether such accomplishment were possible; but one may at least try to identify Flaubert's movement towards the later novels as an overcoming of self-conscious alienation by incorporating the problems of self-consciousness in the writing itself rather than in a persona.

One might even hazard a comparison with Goethe, who has come to figure in our literary mythology as the last 'unfallen' man who could take in the entire universe, in order to suggest both the extent to which Flaubert's passage beyond Romanticism was an aspiration to an earlier condition and the differences in the resulting forms. In *Werther* Goethe creates and cites, in the form of letters, the kind of Romantic language which Flaubert would later cite as worn and trivialized clichés; but, above all, the ending of *Werther* achieves the combination of distance and potential sympathy, the relating of details which in their very emptiness and irrelevance suggest absent depths, for which Flaubert was later to strive.

> From the blood on the arm of the chair one could infer that he had shot himself while sitting in front of the desk and then had slumped down, twisted himself convulsively out of the chair. He lay collapsed on his back by the window, was fully dressed in his blue coat and yellow waistcoat, with his boots on.

The curious, almost clinical details, asserting their reality and thereby deflecting attention from the theme of the suicide, would not be out of place in Flaubert. But he could not have written the magnificent conclusion:

> Um zwölfe mittags starb er. Die Gegenwart des Amtmannes und seine Anstalten tuschten einen Auflauf. Nachts gegen Eilfe liess er ihn an die Stätte begraben, die er sich erwählt hatte. Der Alte folgte der Leiche und die Söhne, Albert vermocht's nicht. Man fürchtete für Lottens Leben. Handwerker trugen ihn. Kein Geistlicher hat ihn begleitet.[55]

> (Towards noon he died. The judge's presence and precautions smothered any outcry. At about eleven that night he had him buried in the spot he had chosen himself. The old man followed the coffin, and the sons; Albert could not bring himself to it. There were fears for Lotte's life. Workmen bore him. No priest attended him.)

If one compares this with Emma Bovary's funeral one sees at once a difference in Flaubert's greater willingness to allow irrelevance, as if the impossibility of having funerals which are properly summed up in eight words adds to the tragedy.

> Le drap noir, semé de larmes blanches, se levait de temps à autre en découvrant la bière. Les porteurs fatigués se ralentissaient; et elle

avançait par saccades continues, comme une chaloupe qui tangue
à chaque flot.
   On arriva.
   ... tandis que le prêtre parlait, la terre rouge, rejetée sur les
bords, coulait, par les coins, sans bruit, continuellement (I, 688).[56]

The passages share a rejection of sentimentality, and an apparent refusal on the part of the narrator to do anything more
than give an account of the facts. But in Goethe the sense of
repression is much stronger. The short flat sentences are
designed to stand as a stoical facade, whose exaggerated in-
sufficiency is to be read as an indication of deep feeling.
Werther's death, the suggestion seems to be, is as tragically
powerful as he would have desired, and the narrator who kept
his distance before is now joined in mourning. In Flaubert,
however, irrelevant details prevent precisely this kind of positive silence. What lies behind the writing that reports is rather
a silence of emptiness. The difference, in short, is that when
reading the ending of *Werther* we may well have recourse to a
narrator, whom we make the source of the sentences in order
to produce a suitably thematized emotion, whereas no purpose
is served by trying to imagine, in this portion of *Madame Bovary*,
who speaks. No one speaks; it is written. One cannot return to
the self-assurance of Goethe's narration. That would require a
faith in the dignity of human order and its relation to the
divine.
   Sartre sees a nostalgia of this kind as one of the basic determinants of Flaubert's project: the establishment of a diabolical
order as revenge for the loss the divine. If style is, as Flaubert
says, 'une manière absolue de voir les choses', this means a way
of seeing things from the point of view of the Absolute, as if
they were produced by the Absolute ('Création en vue du Mal
radical'). Instead of saying, 'the world is hell,' which is too
abstract to have an effect, he must make the proposition haunt
each word through his style. Flaubert tells us, by Sartre's
account:

volez lelangage aux hommes, détournez-le de ses fins pratiques,
asservissez sa matière à rendre par elle-même des imaginaires
inarticulables et vous aurez incarné dans vos phrases le pôle de
toute imagination, le Beau ou le Mal radical, en faisant sentir à

propos du langage que le monde est produit et soutenu par une liberté maligne. Le style c'est le silence du discours, le silence dans le discours, le but imaginaire et secret de la parole écrite.[57]

Sartre, of course, cannot think of Flaubert as having attained any kind of freedom and must conceive of his project in pathological terms. The novels are ingenious attempts to present a limited and neurotic view of the world, and Sartre is quick to spot a malignant *metteur en scene* behind any text. He tends, in short, still to regard the text as expression of a narrator's attitude, however indirect such expression may be. But when he comes to explain how this is done, even in the programmatic statement quoted above, his language betrays another way of viewing the matter. To speak of 'the silence of discourse, the silence in discourse, the negative and secret goal of written language' suggests that we are dealing with properties of language itself, not with goals that Flaubert uses language to attain nor secret attitudes of a narrator which the silences express. The concept of a vituperative author brooding over his texts and chuckling over the slow destruction they wreak is useful as an organizing device — this will be sufficiently clear in Chapter II — and as a way of naming a single unifying project, but it is perhaps best bracketed when we want to observe the operation of the texts themselves, much of whose achievement, as was suggested in the comparison with Goethe, lies in the extent to which they render irrelevant the process of identifying narrators and attributing themes to them.

Sartre would see Flaubert as one who adopted realistic modes in order to achieve, indirectly, the ends of Romantic Satanism, but there is a point at which means so preponderant become ends in themselves, especially if the former end is recognized as inarticulable. The incident of the dog may be read as a conversion of this kind, in which the glimpse of what cannot be stated but is no doubt monstrous frees one from thematic ends formerly proposed and now characterized as *pathétiques*, but also, and this is perhaps more important, offers one no new themes to express but only steels one for the tasks of a detached *travail du langage* in which the writer, 'nothing himself, beholds/Nothing that is not there and the nothing that is'.

One must, as Stevens says, have a mind of winter to observe

in detail one's surroundings, the boughs of the pinetrees, the junipers shagged with ice;

> and not to think
> Of any misery in the sound of the wind,
> In the sound of a few leaves,
> Which is the sound of the land
> Full of the same wind
> That is blowing in the same bare place
> For the listener, who listens in the snow,
> And, nothing himself, beholds
> Nothing that is not there and the nothing that is.[58]

He is quite right; it would require a very special cast of mind indeed 'not to think of any misery', but what one can do — and Flaubert may well have aspired to be the original Snow Man — is to deny that misery and, by the rejection of this simple pathetic fallacy, to allow a far more comprehensive version of misery to enter the poem: the same wind blowing in the same bare place, given, in its full nakedness, as nothing but that same bare wind, not even a metaphor for something else. And in recording this scrupulous bareness the listener is nothing himself — not the purveyor of Romantic *Naturphilosophie* nor even the source of a theme that he casts in symbolic form — but only the space in which is inscribed nothing that is not there (and whose lack is thereby suggested) and the nothing that is.

This nothingness cannot be articulated — not because it is so profound an experience but because it is defined precisely in those formal and dialectical terms: as the emptiness of any presence. But we can name some of the forms it takes. It is, for example, the *signifiant* without *signifié*: matter taken as a sign but which offers emptiness in place of meaning. It may also be called profundity, the quality of objects which prove inexhaustible and before which the mind exhausts itself. The type of profundity is perhaps the monstrous: excess which attracts. 'Sa stupidité m'attire', says Saint Antoine, confronted with the monstrous Catoblépas (I, 570), providing another name. Stupidity, as Chapter III will show, is closely related to profundity: the materiality and opaqueness of things divorced from any practical function or, inversely, so completely determined by a practical function that their existence at other moments is an excess. But stupidity is also a quality of language itself, whose order is factitious and empty.

Nothingness, in short, is the absence every presence supposes. To call it Hell is already a positive determination, and so rather than place a saint on a mountain and have demons torture him — one would have to explain, after all, what that meant — far better for Flaubert to take as his subject a country doctor and his adulterous wife or two aging autodidacts. Readers will be enjoined to recognize the scenes he presents, to find them natural, so that the malice of any destructive project may be concealed behind the fatality of the real. He can blow through the world like that hail-storm which descended on Rouen one Saturday, destroying crops and breaking windows. Though he suffered a good hundred francs' damage it was not without pleasure, Gustave writes, that he saw his espaliers destroyed, his flowers cut to pieces, the vegetable garden overturned.

> En contemplant tous ces petits arrangements factices de l'homme que cinq minutes de la nature ont suffi pour bousculer, j'admirais le vrai ordre se rétablissant dans le faux ordre . . . Il y a là un caractère de *grande farce* qui nous enfonce. Y-a-t-il rien de plus bête que des cloches à melon? Aussi ces pauvres cloches à melon en ont vu de belles! . . . On croit un peu trop généralement que le soleil n'a d'autre but ici-bas que de faire pousser les choux. Il faut replacer de temps à autres le bon Dieu sur son piédestal. Aussi se charge-t-il de nous le rappeler en nous envoyant par-ci par-là quelque peste, choléra, bouleversement inattendu et autres manifestations de la Règle, à savoirle Mal-contingent, qui n'est peut-être pas le Bien-nécessaire, mais qui est l'Etre enfin (iii, 275–6).[89]

There is a strong temptation to go through the world destroying melon covers, establishing, as the negation of what exists, the true order. This order, the law of existence, is not a necessary evil, not the manifestation of a firm diabolical synthesis, but only contingent evil, which is the more demoralizing for its arbitrariness. In displaying this order has one become a vengeful God who plays tricks or is one merely a youthful vandal? It is in any case a criminal role, for which Flaubert was well-suited by temperament and situation. The succeeding chapters chart his progress in crime and the techniques that made him a master criminal.

# 2
# The Perfect Crime: The Novel

> Ecco svaniro a un punto
> E figurato è il mondo in breve carta;
> Ecco tutto è simile, e discoprendo,
> Solo il nulla s'accresce.
>
> LEOPARDI

## A. *Opportunities*

At the beginning of Part II of *Madame Bovary* we encounter a description of Yonville-l'Abbaye which brings us down from the hill, across the bridge, to the first houses standing in court-yards enclosed by hedges and full of scattered out-buildings. It is an unremarkable scene, and one might expect to find something quite comparable in any description of a village undertaken by Flaubert's predecessors: Stendhal's Verrières, Balzac's Blagny and Couches. But there follow two sentences unlike any to be found in those authors, which might well stand as touchstones of Flaubert's revolutionary achievement:

Les toits de chaume, comme des bonnets de fourrure rabattus sur des yeux, descendent jusqu'au tiers à peu près des fenêtres basses, dont les gros verres bombés sont garnis d'un noeud dans le milieu, à la façon des culs de bouteilles. Sur le mur de plâtre, que traversent en diagonale des lambourdes noires, s'accroche parfois quelque maigre poirier, et les rez-de-chaussée ont a leur porte une petite barrière tournante pour les défendre des poussins, qui viennent picorer, sur le seuil, des miettes de pain bis trempé de cidre (I, 598).[1]

In one sense there is nothing remarkable about them; they present a series of details which the reader may take as realistic 'filler' and pass over quickly. But if he does Flaubert the honour of considering his sentences more closely, he cannot but find them decidedly odd. In the first place, they violate basic principles of composition. A sentence, we are told, is essentially a proposition, composed of a subject and a predicate which makes a statement about that subject. Therein lies its coherence. And subordinate clauses amplify, explain, or restrict the main proposition. But in Flaubert's first sentence, for example, it is the mention of the windows in the main proposition which leads on to the glass, and that to a comparison of its central boss with the bottoms of wine bottles. The point of arrival has nothing to do with the point of departure. In the second sentence, as if, having run down, one had caught one's breath and set off again, we begin with the plaster wall, but the main clause describes what is only sometimes the case, while the subordinate clause offers the principal description; and then, in the second half of the sentence, we are led, as if by association, from the swinging gate to the chicks, to their activities, to what they eat. It is not simply that each sentence appears to fritter itself away, as it runs down towards the minute and trivial; that is almost a by-product of the spectacle mounted by a prose style determined to show how grammatical devices enable it to link together a set of disparate and trivial facts. If one reads the sentences deliberately, pausing on the numerous commas, one is tempted to laugh at the spectacle of this elegant prose straining to hold itself together — and to no obvious thematic purpose.

That is the second curious feature. The sentences have no apparent function. They are not dealing in recognized categories or characteristics which would 'place' the village for us and tell us something about it that we need know. Nor do they offer fertile terrain for the cultivators of symbols: to say that the inhabitants are, like the houses, one-third blinded or, like the chicks, seekers of scattered and ineffectually forbidden pleasures, is to take a great deal upon oneself, since one could in this way recuperate practically any detail whatsoever. A rather more obvious function is that which the swifter reader assigns them: fleshing out the village and signifying, 'this is reality'. In so doing they reveal one of the basic conventions of post-seventeenth-century European culture: that 'reality' is opposed to meaning. It consists of discrete concrete objects and events prior to any interpretation, and therefore to give a sense of 'the real' one must offer details which have no meaning.[2]

Finally, the sentences display a curious mode of narration. Since the paragraph had begun with the road 'which leads you in a straight line to the first houses' one might expect what follows to be an account of what someone entering the town would see, presented by a narrator who has himself done this.

Such passages are frequent in Stendhal and Balzac and are marked by their references to what would be found *notable*. Flaubert's first metaphor might be read in this way: thatched roofs, 'like fur caps pulled down over the eyes' is a purely visual impression which leads nowhere but suggests a disinterested and bemused observer, taking an aesthetic attitude towards the scene. The second metaphor, however, is somewhat different. Less gratuitous than the first, it implies a communicative relation between the narrator and a reader who requires explanations if he is to identify what is being described. And the second sentence, with its strange mixture of singulars and plurals, presents details which are difficult to attribute to a casual observer: he might well speak of 'plaster walls with black beams showing', but it is difficult to imagine precisely who might say, 'On the plaster wall, which black beam-joists traverse diagonally, a withered pear tree sometimes clings'. The degree of detail clashes oddly with the typifying singular on the one hand and the mild quantifier on the other, and towards the end of the sentence we move from a careful observer to a speaker with precise knowledge: at each of these houses chicks 'come to pick up, on the threshold, bits of wholemeal bread dipped in cider'. The particularity suggests a single scene, but the mode is one of generalization; and the result is simply that we do not know who speaks or from where. The narrator is depersonalized, in that we cannot give him a character which would explain and hold together the moments of his discourse. We have, in short, a written text, which stands before us cut off from a speaker.

This passage, trivial and limited though it is, might serve as an example of the type of impersonality and 'objectivity' which Flaubert achieves. If we take this as part of an 'objective' description of Yonville, it is not, of course, because of our knowledge of the referent but because of a specific effect of language. Objectivity is the absence of other determinations. The sentences do not prove anything about Yonville; they do not thrust themselves forward as material for symbolic organization; they do not tell us anything of a character's predilections; nor are they observations which characterize a particular speaker. Their objectivity is a direct result of the difficulty of identifying a point of view from which they might be proffered; they appear, as if from nowhere, which is to say, as language without an author and, by their lack of functionality in the novel, signify 'we are the real'.

If we approach the matter in this way, through the activities of reading, it is clear that Flaubert's much-discussed 'impersonality' has relatively little to do with the expression of opinions or judgments. Critics have expended much time in pointing out the occasions on which opinions are expressed or on which some narrator does make his presence felt. But impersonality involves, rather, the desire to prevent the text from being recuperated as the speech of a characterizable narrator, to prevent it, that is to say, from being read as the vision of someone who becomes an object that the reader can judge. The language of the text will organize the world, select details, offer judgments, shift its perspectives, adopt momentarily various modes of discourse and types of speech that can be identified, but it does not create for us a personality whom we feel we know. We can say a great deal about the created narrator who speaks in *La Chartreuse de Parme* or *Le Père Goriot*, but if we try to talk about the narrator of *L'Education sentimentale* we discover so little evidence to work on that we have recourse almost immediately to discussing Flaubert and citing his correspondence.

'Steal language from men' is Sartre's paraphrase of Flaubert's project, and indeed it is here that the secret of impersonality lies. One should always be in a position to claim that a description fell off a lorry. One may offer it for consumption along with other objects stolen from different owners, but one has no personal connection with them. They are, as it were, instances of languages working themselves out. Champfleury, of whom Flaubert disapproved but whose book on realism appeared at the same time as *Madame Bovary*, defined the 'romancier impersonnel' as a Proteus: supple, multiform, able to adopt the role of the priest or the magistrate, the naïveté of the people, or the stupidity of the petit-bourgeois.[3] And to adopt these roles in a novel one may adopt their language, not simply to cite it with withering effect, but to embed it in other languages of slightly differing sources and so create a text which stands alone, upheld not by its speaker but by the tensions among its styles.

'If ever I take an active role in the world,' wrote Flaubert to Ernest Chevalier, 'it will be as thinker and demoralizer. I will only tell the truth, but it will be horrible, naked, and cruel' (i, 41). He does not yet know what he will say, but he knows the effects desired: the readers are to be demoralized. The Romantic Satanism of the juvenilia was a preliminary sally, but it had proved a failure because the narrators could be caught in *flagrant délit* and their crimes imputed to distorted views of the world which had nothing to do with readers themselves. To try again he must move to a different narrative mode, one which offers more solid alibis, and the letters suggest a possible approach: 'When will things be transcribed from the point of view of a *cosmic joke*, that is to say, as God sees them from on high?' (iii, 37). The italics are Flaubert's and the emphasis they provide indicates it is not so much God's objectivity he desires as his absence: the world will be totalized in a negative fashion, its order shown to be that of an ironic joke, but the author of that joke will be as difficult to pin down as the God who for so many centuries managed to escape, with the aid of his theologians, his obvious responsibility for the world's evil. And just as this evil without an author convinced men that they were themselves guilty of an original sin, Flaubert's 'cosmic joke' (*'blague supérieure'*) should have a thoroughly demoralizing effect which men would take as a correlate of their objective condition.

For success in this project three things must be done, which though inseparable in the final achievement might well have failed independently of one another. If the reader is to receive the impression of objectivity, there must be, first of all, a compulsion to identify the text with a world conventionally regarded as real. This is done through what Barthes has called the referential illusion: the signs used must appear to derive their meaning from their referents rather than from their place in a system of functional relations within the text. Secondly, and this is again a device for the creation of objectivity, the language of the text must be isolated from any definable narrator, and this is perhaps most easily done through irony. As Kierkegaard says, 'if what is said is not my meaning, or the opposite of my meaning, then I am free both in relation to others and in relation to myself.'[4] And the language itself is left free, as matter through which no determinate communicative intention emerges. Ambiguity displays itself as a property of a language resisting communicative functions it might have been assigned. But finally, and perhaps most important, demoralization is produced by undermining the conventions of reading, hampering the operations which readers are accustomed to perform on texts so as to 'make sense' of them, but hampering these operations with sufficient subtlety that readers will not throw down the books in a moment of outraged frustration. To see how this is accomplished and what it involves we must try to formulate the theory of reading presupposed by the pre-Flaubertian tradition of the novel.

The basic enabling convention of the novel as genre is confidence in the transparency and representative power of language. When Madame de Lafayette writes of the Comte de Tende that, upon learning that his wife was pregnant by a lover, 'he first thought everything it was natural to think in such a situation,'[5] she displays immense confidence both in her language and in her readers. The Lockean theory of a language in which words are but tokens that stand for objects or states of affairs could not be more blatantly assumed. The sentence presupposes a state of affairs lying behind the text, its similarity to situations with which readers are already familiar, and its availability as an object towards which the language of the sentence need merely gesture. The text might continue in the same mode by saying, 'he then did what was natural and the inevitable result followed,' and thus become an extreme and of course parodistic example of language reduced to the function of pointing at what is already known.

If language is not often brought to this pass it is not so much because it is assigned a different function as because the world contains a variety of objects, courses of actions, and thoughts, and the author's language must indicate which of these he has in mind. Thus, though in one sense an immense distance separates the sparse descriptions of Madame Lafayette, which rely so much on her readers' knowledge of, for example, what kind of furnishings count as magnificent, from the flood of details that Balzac offers, the two approaches use the same kind of linguistic gesture: 'Au milieu se trouve une table ronde, . . . décorée de ce cabaret en porcelaine blanche ornée de filets d'or effacés à demi, que l'on rencontre partout aujourd'hui.' Or, 'La façade de la pension donne sur un jardinet, en sorte que la façade tombe à l'angle droit sur la rue Neuve-Sainte-Geneviève, où vous la voyez coupée dans sa profondeur.'[6] The reader is supposed to pass through the language of the text to a reality that he recognizes and to which it refers. And the composition of a novel, to put it extremely crudely, is a matter first of selecting and developing one's story in all its circumstances and only then of transcribing it.

This is not to imply, of course, that novelists before Flaubert did not *work* on their language. On the contrary, the confidence in the representational function of language, the assurance that referents would always serve as *signifiés* for any *signifiant*, allowed considerable freedom in the actual writing of sentences. This freedom is reflected in the possibility of debates about language and rhetoric. One can argue about the 'bienséance' of certain expressions because there are a variety of ways of saying the same thing, some of which may be accepted and others proscribed. Preciosity, for example, must be defined not as love of recherché expressions but as an attempt to use such expressions as names. 'Le conseiller des grâces' is *précieux* because it is thought of not as a metaphor which presents an object in a new light but as a name: it denotes a mirror.[7] Rhetorical figures are ornamental detours which do not trouble the representative function of language. Locke and Hobbes, dreaming of a perfectly transparent and unambiguous language, feared that rhetoric would actually conceal thoughts and hence deceive, but such fears seem to have had little currency in France: ornament is purely decorative and not deceptive. 'A fine mind', writes La Rochefoucauld, 'produces with ease things which are clear, agreeable, and natural; he presents them in their best light and decorates them with all the ornaments appropriate to them.'[8] *Convenance* is a social value; some forms of expression are inappropriate not because they involve distorted vision or thoughts but because they are socially unacceptable ornaments.

Hence we find in so many novelists what ought to be called a rhetoric, if that term may be used without derogation: particular modes of expression which are explicitly separated from the representative function. Many of what now seem the most curious effects in Stendhal are the result of this separation. At first glance the elaborate strategies of the ironic narrator, proliferating judgments which we do not know quite how to take, laughing in turn at his characters, the French, the Italians, those who laugh at his characters, or at the French or the Italians — these strategies ought, it seems, to create situations of such indeterminacy that we no longer know what is true. But of course this is not the case; the narrator is always anxious to emphasize what did in fact happen and usually what the character in fact thought or felt. Thus, the superb passage in *La Chartreuse de Parme*, which begins with ironic intimations of Fabrice's stupidity and hypocrisy in not considering himself guilty of simony, which moves on to an attack on the Jesuits for the education they had given him, and which suggests that a Frenchman could in good faith accuse Fabrice of hypocrisy, ends, in its final clause, by assuring us that 'our hero was opening his heart to God with the greatest sincerity and most profound emotion.'[9] Quoted thus, it still seems ironic, but in context its position as a subordinate clause identifying what is happening at the moment in the story assures us of its status as fact.

Ezra Pound was not wrong to note in Stendhal 'a sort of solidity which Flaubert hasn't. A trust in the thing more than the word.'[10] The fascinating narrative posturing leaves a residue of event, feeling, and object untouched, and part of the reason is simply that with his faith in the representational powers of language he need not strive to make his language rise to the occasion. He refuses, as Jean Starobinski says, to grant the slightest value to verbal intensity,[11] and consequently his descriptions of those rural scenes whose beauty brings bliss to his characters make no attempt to be evocative; nor is there any attempt to recreate moments of sexual ecstasy. He is quite content to use his language simply to refer, as when he skips over Fabrice's three years of happiness with Clélia in a phrase which, amazingly, bears no trace of irony: 'Après ces trois années de bonheur divin.'

On the surface few narrators could be more different from Stendhal's than Balzac's. The latter's rhetoric consists of a proliferation of manichean metaphors, a drive towards abstract antitheses, and a linguistic exuberance which becomes at times a mode of autonomous progression: one word, phrase, or image determining the next. But Balzac is careful to isolate this linguistic activity as something not affecting his story. At the beginning of *Le Père Goriot*, for example, he moves into what is explicitly a reflection on his tale, and no sooner has the image of 'the chariot of civilization' led to an appropriate metaphorical development, running over hearts, breaking them, and continuing its 'glorious march', than we are assured that the story itself contains no exaggeration: 'Sachez-le: ce drame n'est ni une fiction, ni un roman. *All is true*.' And a few pages later, having produced a Dickensian description of *l'odeur de pension* — 'elle sent le renfermé, le moisi, le rance; elle donne froid, elle est humide au nez, elle pénètre les vêtements; elle a le goût d'une salle où l'on a dîné; elle pue le service, l'office, l'hospice' — in which syntax and rhyme have taken over, he swiftly abandons this language and assures us of the reality and indescribability of his referent: 'Peut-être pourrait-elle se décrire si l'on inventait un procédé pour évaluer les quantités élémentaires et nauséabondes qu'y jettent les atmosphères catarrhales et *sui generis* de chaque pensionnaire, jeune ou vieux.'[12] Do not be deceived by my language, he seems to be saying. Whatever its elaborations it is still only a gesture to refer you to the reality in question.

Such novels make an internal distinction between their *discours* and their *histoire*, and the former is not allowed to contaminate the latter. Whatever its other functions — and they are legion, especially since our present modes of reading are focused here — the self-consciously presented discourse is a rhetoric which must not trouble the representational function of language. This assumption, that the truth of language lies in its referents, is of capital importance, not only because of the diverse narrative modes to which it ministers, but because of the strategy of reading it entails. To read the text is to identify the world to which it refers. To read is to recognize.

Hence the fundamental convention is a pact of community between author and reader, signalled in various ways by the narrative language. The narrator is more knowledgeable than the reader, perhaps, but basically they are presumed to share the same world and to be capable of agreement. The recurrent stylistic tics of Balzacian prose are almost all means of evoking and solidifying the contract with the reader. The demonstratives followed by relative clauses ('she was one of those women who . . .' 'on one of those days when . . .' 'the façade is painted that yellow colour which gives Parisian houses . . .') create categories while pretending that the reader knows them already. The hypostatized observers act as personae of the reader and suggest how he would have reacted to the spectacle that is being presented: 'From that aura which wealth acquired in commerce gives retired shopkeepers *one could recognize* the Parisian elected official, at the very least a former assistant mayor of his borough.' Or, 'From the way he accepted the coachman's assistance to alight from the carriage, *one could have told* he was fifty years old.'[13] Such constructions imply that the meaning extracted from the scene is the common property of reader and narrator, as do the references, surprisingly frequent, to 'readings' of a face, scene, or object: 'The captain advanced towards the steps of the house with *an air which said* . . .' Or, 'From the look of the goatskin shoes, *whose craftsmanship told* of a fourth-rate shoemaker . . .'[14] Moreover, the complicity between reader and narrator is reinforced by the ways in which deviance from the *vraisemblable* is announced, labelled, and then naturalized. 'This may appear strange to those who are not thoroughly familiar with this particular social milieu', Balzac will say, but when you understand the background you will see its appropriateness.[15] Appealing to shared notions of explanation, showing that he finds strangeness precisely where the reader does, the narrator strengthens the ties that bind them together.

Similarly, though with less intensity, Mérimée's bourgeois narrators 'naturalize' tales set in foreign and exotic climes by offering as the basis of the contract with the reader an image of what he himself might see and think in such situations. And if Stendhal's narrators are more wily and playful, they do at least, by suggesting what some readers might think and then sneering at them for doing so, or by telling the reader what he is *not* to think, implicitly provide models of plausible interpretation at various levels of sophistication, reassuring the reader that one set of responses is natural while inviting him to accede to the grace of a higher level. The citation of public interpretive processes is an important manifestation of the convention on which the novel is based.

Brought into a relation of community with the narrator, the reader feels that he knows what to do with the text before him. One might say that all claims made for the novel as a humanizing influence, as a purveyor of vicarious experience, as a tool for refining and extending our awareness of the possibilities of life, assume a cyclical movement on the reader's part between text and world. The first step takes him from text to that of which it speaks. He must identify in the world the referents towards which the text gestures. Then, having given meaning to the signs of its *histoire*, he can move back and read its *discours* as a commentary on what he has recognized. Thus the attribution of meanings which the text performs, its attempts to distinguish, explore, and interpret, are applied to objects which the reader has identified in his own world, 'dans son coeur peut–être'.[16]

The moment of recognition, the sense that the novel refers to a world we had hitherto thought private, is one of the great pleasures of novel-reading and responsible for the most obvious cases of popular success. But more lasting achievements seem to depend on the second moment of contact, when the novel becomes an instrument for creating meaning, and it is here that critics usually locate a novel's value. Whether, in a Balzacian attempt at natural history, it propose a zoological classification that distinguishes the species of men and charts the laws of their behaviour, or whether it merely display with the clarity of example alternative courses of action and sentiment open to a single character, the novel must offer paradigms of organization. It can be a vehicle for understanding the world because it displays the modes of understanding and invites us, if we would enrich our perception, to read our own lives as novels. To make one's own life a novel is to name its elements in the terms those models provide and compose them into a legible text. And here, of course, lies the opportunity that attracts someone aspiring to the role of demoralizer. What if, when readers had composed their lives as novels, they found them unintelligible? What if, instead of learning how to unify their dispersed selves into a personality and the disparate events of their lives into a meaningful destiny, they found that when put together according to novelistic models things still did not fit together? The prospect might well tantalize literary minds of vituperative bent.

That it tantalized Flaubert there can be little doubt. He speaks with glee of a projected preface to the *Dictionnaire des idées reçues* 'où l'on indiquerait comme quoi l'ouvrage a été fait dans le but de rattacher le public à la tradition, à l'ordre, à la convention générale, et arrangée de telle manière que le lecteur ne sache pas si on se fout de lui, oui ou non' (ii, 237–8).[17] To present false bibliographical references in *Bouvard et Pécuchet* strikes him as a joke of considerable potential,[18] and when planning a novel on the Second Empire, which he never got down to writing, he decided to put at the heads of chapters titles 'which give the moral, which indicate to the reader what he should think' and which would have been another source of mystification and misdirection.[19] It too, one may imagine, would have been 'un livre de vengeance'.

One could, of course, set out to demoralize the reader by blocking the process of recognition, making him read the text as an autonomous verbal object governed by its own laws, and preventing him from moving through the text to a world for which it stands. *Finnegans Wake*, most of the works of Roussel, Beckett's *Comment c'est*, and various examples of the *nouveau roman* operate in this way, though their strategies differ. The simplest technique may be the introduction of uncertainties within a supposedly representational context, as in Robbe-Grillet's famous description of the tomato slice, which tells us first that it is perfect and then that it is flawed, thus lifting us away from the object to the process of writing.[20] This is something Flaubert does not do, and for good reason. Recognition must take place; the first move from text to world must not be blocked; for only if the reader has identified the world described as his own will he be prevented from pulling back when demoralization sets in.

It is rather the move back from world to text, the attempt to compose and give meaning to an identified experience, that must be troubled. If this process is undermined and put on display then the reader will be left with flawed and incomplete meanings which are still applied to his own life by virtue of the prior recognition. Accustomed to finding novels better organized and more replete with meaningful discriminations than his own world, he will experience some kind of dismay if a novel resists his attempts to discover meaning and organization. And if the processes by which novels invite him to construct meaning are shown to be factitious and distorting, he will gain, as Flaubert might have wished, some sense of the nothingness at the heart of existence.

For convenience of discussion one might identify four levels at which the conventions of novel-reading permit the production of meaning and hence four strongholds at which attacks might be directed. In each case the novelist must take for granted what readers will try to do with his text and devise ways of undermining that activity, preventing it from reaching satisfactory completion, for insofar as the reader can succeed in making the novel into what he expects to find, he is not really challenged or upset.

There is first of all the level of description. In the classic novel a basic article of the contract between narrator and reader is that the former speaks to the latter and what he tells him can be presumed relevant. Whenever the time of the story is momentarily arrested and the narration lingers over a given scene, character, or event, the reader is allowed an elementary presumption: that these details are in some way necessary and that he must do something with them. And to do something with them is to give them a meaning in terms of their function in the text. The conventions of novel-reading provide two basic operations which may be performed: these might be called *empirical* and *symbolic recuperation* in that they are based, respectively, on the construction of causal and symbolic relations. If, for example, a character's appearance is described, we may give meaning to these details either by calling on social theories of personality which, in their clichéd way, tell us that if someone is elegantly dressed it is *because* he is a dandy or that if she is beautiful she will, *as a result*, be admired and pursued; or we may, in the absence of causal connections, establish a sign relation between the details and the meanings our symbolic codes permit us to give them: we would be unwilling to assume a causal connection between perfect or blemished complexions and perfect or blemished moral character, but the symbolic codes permit such associative operations. To process descriptions is to collect details and perform such semantic transformations on them.

Novelists like Balzac, of course, not only invite such treatment but do much of the reader's work for him by developing in explicit fashion causal theories of the relationship between environment or appearance and personality or atmosphere. Phrenology offers ways of reading physical characteristics, and the 'zoological' theory of national and social types establishes causal connections between initial description and social behaviour. Balzac's prose is an omnivorous machine which can take in anything and give it a meaning. The world is fundamentally intelligible; everything obeys some law, though it may cost an effort to discover it. And therefore the reader's course of action is clear. Presented with the description of the *Pension Vauquer* he must try to see how everything about it displays its essential misery and petty economy, how the very dress of the owner 'résume le salon, la salle à manger, le jardinet, annonce la cuisine et fait pressentir les pensionnaires'.[21] And where causal connections cannot be established, one must pursue possible symbolic relations, as in the description of Bette's neighbourhood which quickly moves from the crumbling façades and the narrow, almost subterranean streets to metaphors of ghosts and tombs. This *quartier* has no doubt been allowed to remain next to the Louvre, we are told, because of 'the need to symbolize in the heart of Paris the intimate connection between misery and splendour which characterizes the Queen of capitals.'[22] Recuperation is a process of making details into *signifiants* and naming their *signifiés*. The drive towards meaning on the reader's part is extremely powerful, and, as we shall see, the ubiquity of the cultural models and symbolic codes which guide it makes it a difficult process to disrupt.

The second level at which meaning can be produced is that of narration itself. The convention that in a text the narrator speaks to his readers acts as support to interpretive operations for dealing with anything that might otherwise remain without significance. Insofar as the novel is, as George Eliot said, 'a faithful account of men and things as they have mirrored themselves in my mind', anything the reader encounters and to which he can ascribe no other function may be put down as an effect of the narrator's vision or cast of mind. The world is fundamentally intelligible. So much so, that any potential disorder or irrelevance can be read as the symptom of a particular individual's ordering of experience. This is especially important in the case of novels narrated in the first person, which are so common in the eighteenth and early nineteenth centuries, where anything whose strict functional relevance cannot be discovered may be read as an excess which displays the narrator's individuality and used to develop a theory of his obsessions. Anything in the text can be given the function of revealing character if the narrator makes himself felt as a character.

Moreover, the same convention can be made to apply, though in a slightly different way, to novels with no well-defined narrator. The theory of limited point of view, developed by Henry James and his critical followers, offers the reader a strategy for discovering meaning in scenes which resist other types of interpretation. If he can think of no other function served by the details presented, he may try to read them as those things noticed by a major character who happened to be present at the time. The scene, he can say, is narrated from the point of view of that character and hence the details serve to characterize him by revealing his predilections and general cast of mind. This has become a particularly important strategy for reading Flaubert, and we shall have to investigate how far the texts resist this type of recuperation.

The next level is that of character. Most defences of the novel as a humanizing influence come to rest here, and quite rightly so, for the conception of personality which the novel fosters — and one can also say, conversely, the conventions concerning personality on which the reading of novels is based — is the major device by which we come to invest our own experience with meaning. To interpret our own lives is to consider them, with a degree of detachment, according to the models we have encountered in novels. To see those who surround us as characters in novels is to attempt to penetrate their opaque surfaces, to endow them with a complexity, richness, and yet coherence, which are more obviously the attributes of novelistic characters than of our acquaintances. The basic convention, at least for readers of the post-Rousseau and pre-Joyce novel, is that of coherence. However we think of individuals we actually encounter, it is clear that the way in which we read novels depends on the assumption that a character is a centre of coherence, though that coherence may be a balance of conflicting tendencies. As we proceed through the text we collect details relating to characters, notice the actions they perform, and attempt to dispose these items in classes which we can name as character traits. And this whole interpretive process is guided by the assumption that the final result must be a set of interrelated qualities. Were this not the case, interpretation would be much more haphazard than it is, for any particular action as described in a text would permit one to postulate a wide range of motives, and if we did not assume coherence we would have little reason to pick one rather than another. The novel makes the world intelligible for us by leading us to discover how everything about a character flows from a definable personality. The drive towards coherence at this level is one of the major activities that assigns meaning to details.

The second basic convention governing the production of

meaning at the level of character is the requirement that characters themselves be significant. They must, that is to say, be in some way exemplary, and therefore we attempt, in reading a novel, to set characters one against another and name the tendencies which they represent. We seek, in constructing characters from the novelist's data, certain kinds of clarity and particularly prize cases where characters are too complex to be named as the representatives of single forces or qualities but where two or more complex sets of characteristics attain an individuation by being set against one another. Hence the importance of contrasts between characters becomes a basic convention for the reading of novels: given two heroes or heroines we immediately begin to look for differences in their moral constitution and approach to experience so as to derive meaning from their respective successes and failures without reducing them to mere personifications. The drive towards meaning at this level once again seems very strong, but the writer can attempt to undermine and frustrate it by proffering oppositions and contrasts which seem thematically unproductive and by posing obstacles to the search for coherence.

Finally, one might speak of a 'thematic' level, though it would be difficult to draw a line between this and the third. It is here that Flaubert most explicitly attacks, in his statements on fiction, the novels of his predecessors and contemporaries: novels should not conclude, should not offer a moral, should not, one might say, lose their character as texts by becoming *means* of expression which can be effaced as soon as communication has been effected. On this count Flaubert's practice and that of his successors have brought about a modification in the conventions of reading: despite the desire for coherence which drives readers and critics on, we are rather less inclined than we once might have been to regard the statement of a moral as the natural culmination of work on a novel. But it may be only that our goals are now clothed in more sophisticated styles, for we still believe, I think, that everything should contribute to some thematic end and would only require that the statement of that end be sufficiently complex to protect us against accusations of simple-mindedness. One can undercut thematic synthesis in one way by making it a problem explicitly confronted in the novel and displaying the factitiousness and deleterious effects of novelistic syntheses, but this, in the modern critical climate, poses little threat to readers, who can make this destructive process the subject of thematic synthesis. Even so, the hesitations and critical acrobatics which the novelist's texts enforce upon his readers may serve as an indication of his success as 'thinker and demoralizer'.

## B. Description and Meaning

The desire for meaning is perhaps the defining characteristic of the life of the mind, and readers are not to be easily thwarted in their attempts to make things signify. It is not possible, for example, simply to quote a passage from a text and assert that it is meaningless in context, for the agile mind can always find something to do with it. One must therefore argue about interpretive strategies, the kinds of success that they may encounter and the varieties of blindness that they encourage. In looking at Flaubert's descriptive techniques, therefore, I shall suggest that while there are ways of reading descriptive passages which achieve a measure of thematic and symbolic integration, these strategies tend to blind one to the differences between Flaubert and other novelists who ask to be read in these ways, to make one neglect other sources of delight in the text, and generally to render Flaubert much less interesting than he potentially is.

One might take, as a preliminary example, the famous description of Charles Bovary's cap at the beginning of *Madame Bovary*.

C'était une de ces coiffures d'ordre composite, où l'on retrouve les éléments du bonnet à poil, du chapska, du chapeau rond, de la casquette de loutre et du bonnet de coton, une de ces pauvres choses, enfin, dont la laideur muette a des profondeurs d'expression comme le visage d'un imbécile. Ovoïde et renflée de baleines, elle commençait par trois boudins circulaires; puis s'alternaient, séparés par une bande rouge, des losanges de velours et de poils de lapin; venait ensuite une façon de sac qui se terminait par un polygone cartonné, couvert d'une broderie en soutache compliquée, et d'où pendait, au bout d'un long cordon trop mince, un petit croisillon de fils d'or, en manière de gland. Elle était neuve; la visière brillait (I, 575).[23]

For most critics this is the traditional symbolic object; by describing it at such length the narrator assures us of its significance, and we cannot rest until we have given it a meaning by describing it in terms which are applicable to Charles or his world. The cap, says Thibaudet, 'already contains all of Yonville-l'Abbaye'; it sums up, argues Brombert, 'in its tiers and superstructures, the layers and monumentality of the wearer's unintelligence.'[24] For Martin Turnell, it does a great many different things at once. The military elements in the cap are an allusion to Charles' father; the progression from busby to nightcap 'points to the moral and material decline of father and son'. The hat itself is, on the one hand, 'a stupid and shapeless muddle like the wearer and the society in which he lives' but on the other 'suggests a society constructed in layers where each layer exemplifies its particular kind of stupidity'. Nor, he continues, 'should we overlook the point of the "trois boudins circulaires", for the novel is in a sense a widening circle'. And the cord with a cross at the end 'is probably intended to suggest a clown's hat and looks forward to Charles' failure as a doctor'.[25]

This fascinating explanation displays only too clearly Flaubert's success in provoking a parody of symbolic reading. If meaning is to be produced by taking any word used in the description and applying it to something else, then we can go on indefinitely: 'boudin' tells us that Charles or Yonville is as mushy as pudding; the 'cordon trop mince' with a tassel attached indicates tenuous attachment to frivolity, the 'losange' prefigures Charles' medical career and 'velours' the garments on which Emma will spend his income. The description forces symbolic reading to take place at such a distance from the text that anything becomes possible, and this ought, one feels, to make the reader realize that he is being tricked, either by the narrator or the critic. At the empirical level we can say little more than that a silly hat denotes a silly wearer, and at the symbolic level we are led into arbitrary extravagance by the sheer excess of detail. The cap, one might say, is, in its excessiveness, a parody of a symbolic object, in that by throwing down a challenge it calls into play interpretive operations that are inadequate to the task it appears to set.

'It was one of those caps,' begins the narrator in a Balzacian mode. But clearly we have never seen anything like it before, and its grotesqueness depends on its uniqueness. 'Its mute ugliness has the depths of expressiveness of an imbecile's face.' Such expressiveness is at least suspect, for the depths are mute, and fill them as one may with a description which swiftly takes on the character of linguistic desperation before the complex materiality of its object, the hat will not speak. The attempt at precision gets us nowhere, and the hat becomes increasingly stupid as we progress because it takes so long to describe. The discrepancy between the prose and its object grows, displaying the ludicrousness of language spinning itself out in clauses piled one on the other, all in an attempt to comprehend an unworthy hat. Finally the sentence collapses, gasping out two last facts: 'It was new; the peak shone.'

It is as if the exuberant narrator, still characterized as a youth engaged in mocking the new boy, had set out to reveal 'depths of expressiveness' and been defeated by his run-away prose, and the critic who seeks the comfort of a world in which everything signifies must avert his eyes from this defeat and treat the object as a sign whose *signifié* is Charles. But if he eschews this kind of blindness and enjoys the spectacle that the sentences themselves provide, he discovers another case of what might be called symbolic exclusion, where the passage signifies, at one level, 'this is reality, in all its grotesque particularity', and offers at a second level an allegory of reading and writing in which we follow the adventures of a language attempting to capture the world and make it signify but experiencing defeat before the particularity of an object about which one could go on and on without getting anywhere. The middle level of ordinary symbolic interpretation seems excluded by the *excess* which, whatever semantic features are extracted for symbolic construction, will remain behind, mocking us for our inability to deal with it.

Readings of this kind work in the case of Balzac, for whom there is a nice fit between the world and language and for whom, therefore, the visual is always material for knowledge, a flesh that can be made word through his mediation. Everything is subject to thematic elaboration and nothing need escape him. But here in Flaubert we can witness the escape; flesh made word is singularly grotesque, with all the flaws of incomplete metamorphosis. There is none of the existential cosiness, derived from a faith in the intelligibility of the world, which reassures the readers of Balzac's descriptions: only an emptiness, in the guise of lingustic despair.

The inappropriateness of subjecting Flaubert's descriptions to empirical and symbolic recuperation becomes clear if one reads them against analogous passages in Balzac, for the latter invite and indeed explicitly perform such operations, and to treat Flaubert in the same way is to obscure the differences which are not only obvious but the marks of Flaubert's individual achievement. Brombert notes, for instance, that the masked ball in *L'Education sentimentale* 'recalls the famous Taillefer orgy in Balzac's *La Peau de chagrin*: the same display of available carnality, the same specter of disease and death, the same garish couplings of the lascivious and the macabre. Only Flaubert is not concerned with sheer pyrotechnics.'[26] But it is not difficult to show that beyond a similarity of manifest content resemblances are produced only by a recuperation of Flaubert which reduces and ignores all that resists it.

Both passages begin on a note of surprise: a moment of silence when the characters simply stand before the spectacle that confronts them. 'Frédéric fut d'abord ébloui par les lumières,' begins the Flaubert passage, but the ensuing phrase — 'il n'aperçut que de la soie . . .' emphasizes that this is a fact about vision and forces us to suspend, at least for the moment, our attempts to offer a moral and symbolic interpretation. But in Balzac the opening sentence states a theme which will immediately be taken up and developed. After the men have risen from the dinner table the doors of the salon are thrown open: 'The whole company remained for a moment immobile and charmed on the threshold.' They are immobile because they are charmed, and the next sentence tells us why: 'The excessive pleasures of the feast paled before the tempting spectacle that the host offered to the most voluptuous of their senses.' The meaning of the scene has been established; details which follow become illustrations and justifications. Nor is this the only respect in which the passage is orchestrated with a view to meaning. Former pleasures, we are told, paled in the light of those to follow, and therefore the image complex of dazzling light is used to give the passage a metaphorical coherence: 'beneath the sparkling candles of a golden chandelier' are the assembled women, 'dazzling beauties' who eclipse the splendours of the room, with eyes like 'torrents of light', wearing rubies and sapphires or silk scarves 'like the flames of beacons'. And even the syntax becomes a device for enforcing coherence of a type that would have appalled Flaubert: 'Riches étaient les parures, mais plus riches encore étaient ces beautés . . .'[27]

There is nothing like this in Flaubert, no attempt at coherent orchestration. We can justify the choice of details in the first paragraph by saying that they are what Frédéric sees, but that gives them only a factitious unity.

> Frédéric fut d'abord ébloui par les lumières; il n'aperçut que de la soie, du velours, des épaules nues, une masse de couleurs qui se balançait aux sons d'un orchestre caché par les verdures, entre des murailles tendues de soie jaune, avec des portraits au pastel, çà et là, et des torchères de cristal en style Louis XVI (II, 49).[28]

Nothing is illustrated. The sentence leads us from one thing to another, taking contiguity rather than similarity as its law. We can do little with the details themselves, which show neither the magnificence nor the tawdriness of the gathering. The reader seeking to unify, to grasp the sense and function of this scene, has as yet little to work on. And in the second sentence, as so often in Flaubert, the very precision of the writing acts to defer meaning.

> De hautes lampes, dont les globes dépolis ressemblaient à des boules de neige, dominaient des corbeilles de fleurs, posées sur des consoles, dans les coins;—et, en face, après une seconde pièce plus petite, on distinguait, dans une troisième, un lit à colonnes torses, ayant une glace de Venise à son chevet.[29]

The objects are united by the sentence only as 'things which might be seen'; there is no other principle of coherence. It seems for a moment as though the main verb, *dominaient*, might offer semantic features which one could use in establishing some kind of thematic relationship or proposition, but one can do little with the notion of superiority and is forced to fall back on the literal, purely positional meaning. *Dominaient* merely allows the sentence to weave itself around juxtaposed objects, moving jerkily, over commas, from position to position. Having worked itself into corners, it starts out again, in its laboured progression, with an '*et*' *de mouvement*. We wait, passing over commas, moving through the second room, for the subject to appear but discover only the neutral *on distinguait* which defers expectation and focuses attention on the end of the sentence; but that, in turn, yields only a bed with, at its head, a mirror that mocks our pursuit.

The reader may, of course, attempt to exercise his symbolic imagination, finding in the twisted columns of the bed a suggestive juxtaposition and in the mirror a hint of narcissism; but if he tries to integrate in a thematic pattern the snowballs of the first metaphor and the flowers which they overhang or dominate, the arbitrariness of his procedure will be revealed by the fact that he must decide whether the interior speaks of a twisted and narcissistic sexuality in which natural flowers are smothered by snow or whether it promises a passage beyond the dominance of chilling repression to the bed of polymorphous pleasure. Such decisions seem arbitrary if not ridiculous. The text has not marked its objects as extraordinary in any way that invites such elaboration; it has suggested, rather, by the construction of its sentences, that it has led us towards indifferent details which turn out to be dead ends.

Balzac is not a man of dead ends, and once he has established that the spectacle is dazzling in its splendour he proceeds in the next paragraph to tell us in what its attractions consist. Diversity, he announces, something for every taste: 'Ce sérail offrait des séductions pour tous les yeux, des voluptés pour tous les caprices.' This is once again an explicit instruction to the synthesizing reader: read what follows as a catalogue of the various types of women as classified by the social analyst, and you shall see that there was indeed something for everyone. This is, of course, exactly what we find. First, four types of provocativeness: the overtly voluptuous, barely clothed; those who reveal momentarily the odd limb; then 'vierges factices' who excite by their look of innocence; and finally regal and indolent aristocratic beauties. From the moral we pass to national and regional types: the pale, chaste and melancholy English girl, the *Parisienne*, graceful but heartless; placid Italians, strapping Norman wenches, and black-haired beauties of the Midi. 'You would have said', the narrator tells us by way of summary, 'the beauties of Versailles assembled by Lebel', who could cater to any royal desire. Moreover, what might have been seen by a spectator is already converted to knowledge by the time it reaches the page in the sentences of a knowledgeable narrator generalizing from an analytical experience:

La Parisienne, dont toute la beauté gît dans une grâce indescriptible, vaine de sa toilette et de son esprit, armée de sa toute-puissante faiblesse, souple et dure, sirène sans coeur et sans passion, mais qui sait artificieusement créer les trésors de la passion et contrefaire les accents du coeur, ne manquait pas à cette périlleuse assemblée.[30]

Her presence, it seems, is of minor importance. Interest is focused on the semantic patterns constructed: the coupling (vain in dress and mind), the oppositions (all-powerful weakness, supple and hard, without heart or passion but able to simulate the effects of heart and passion), which unify the passage as knowledge.

There is no such principle of coherence in Flaubert's description. The dancers, we are told in one of those single-sentence paragraphs which isolates a fact as though no more of interest were to be said, 'étaient une soixantaine environ, les femmes pour la plupart en villageoises ou en marquises, et les hommes, presque tous d'âge mûr, en costumes de roulier, de débardeur ou de matelot' (II, 50).[31] Illustrating this statement would be a rather feeble function for the ensuing paragraph, but it does not even do that, much less organize the dancers into types according to their differences and similarities. Heterogeneity, incongruity and parody seem the only governing principles:

Un vieux beau, vêtu, comme un doge vénitien, d'une longue simmare de soie pourpre, dansait avec Mme Rosanette, qui portait un habit vert, une culotte de tricot et des bottes molles à éperons d'or. Le couple en face se composait d'un Arnaute chargé de yatagans et d'une Suissesse aux yeux bleus, blanche comme du lait, potelée comme une caille, en manches de chemise et corset rouge.[32]

And we move, in similar fashion, from cavewoman through missionary, shepherd, bacchante, Pole, choir boy, Spanish dancer, to medieval baron in full armour. 'Il y avait aussi un ange, un glaive d'or à la main, deux ailes de cygne dans le dos, et qui, allant, venant, perdant à toute minute son cavalier, un Louis XIV, ne comprenait rien aux figures et embarrassait la contredanse' (II, 50).[33]

We could, of course, appeal to these figures in deploring the debasing and frivolous exoticism of this culture, but that scarcely seems the point. Nor is there much to be made of the particular partnerships, except in noting general incongruities.

The description connotes only a frenetic and meaningless human activity, oppressive in its facticity. 'Frédéric, en regardant ces personnes,' we are told, 'éprouvait un sentiment d'abandon, un malaise.' When he does succeed in organizing and interpreting the scene it is in a passage which seems very much a parody of the interpretive process as displayed in Balzac:

> ce mouvement giratoire, de plus en plus vif et régulier, vertigi-neux, communiquant à sa pensée une sorte d'ivresse, y faisait surgir d'autres images, tandis que toutes passaient dans le même éblouissement, et chacune avait une excitation particulière selon le genre de sa beauté (II, 51).

It is Frédéric's reading of the scene that is presented, and instead of a knowledgeable analysis of the types of beauty, we are offered categories that are so many Romantic clichés:

> La Polonaise, qui s'abandonnait d'une façon langoureuse, lui inspirait l'envie de la tenir contre son coeur, en filant tous les deux dans un traîneau sur une plaine couverte de neige. Des horizons de volupté tranquille, au bord d'un lac, dans un chalet, se déroulaient sous les pas de la Suissesse, qui valsait le torse droit et les paupières baissées. Puis, tout à coup, la Bacchante penchant en arrière sa tête brune, le faisait rêver à des caresses dévoratrices, dans les bois de lauriers-roses, par un temps d'orage, au bruit confus des tambourins (II, 51).[34]

And so on for a series of figures. The unnecessary commas, which fragment his visions into their elements, help to make the particularizing descriptions weapons of irony, which give his reveries an air of misplaced concreteness. Desire is shown manifesting itself in images whose concreteness and irrelevance trivialize it. And since the categories evoked are but the result of so many clichés, the irony cannot avoid attaching, in some degree, to anyone who attempts analogous readings of 'the varieties of voluptuousness', for the cliché is nothing other than a socially-defined category of the real. If Balzac's categories seem less vulnerable to irony than Frédéric's, it is only because in his case the characters seem generated by the clichés them-selves, whereas in Frédéric's we can see the clichés being applied to women whom we expect would prove unworthy of the honour done them.

But perhaps the greatest contrast between the two passages lies in what might be called their synoptic moments. Although at one point Frédéric stands watching the dancers and 'breathing in the soft smells of women, which circulated like an immense distended kiss' (II, 50), the only sustained panoramic view comes when the company are at table: 'With a rustling of cloth the women, arranging their skirts, their sleeves, and their stoles, sat down next to one another; the men, standing, occupied the corners' and the general atmosphere is described:

> Une horloge allemande, munie d'un coq, carillonnant deux heurs, provoqua sur le coucou force plaisanteries. Toutes sortes de propos s'ensuivirent: calembours, anecdotes, vantardises, gageures, mensonges tenus pour vrais, assertions improbables, un tumulte de paroles qui bientôt s'éparpilla en conversations particulières. Les vins circulaient, les plats se succédaient, le docteur découpait. On se lançait de loin une orange, un bouchon; on quittait sa place pour causer avec quelqu'un (II, 53).[35]

Aside from a sense of factitious gaiety there is little to be drawn from such a passage. The throwing of an orange or of a cork is an act which signifies only its own nullity. But when Balzac draws back and offers a panoramic view of the salon we get a determined attempt at thematizing organization: 'The salons at this moment presented an advance view of Milton's Pandemonium.' The mythic reference provides a goal towards which metaphors of the ensuing description can strive. With the point of arrival already established, we scarcely balk at metaphors which seem to start at some distance from their objects: 'Les flammes bleues du punch coloraient d'un teint infernal les visages de ceux qui pouvaient boire encore' or 'Jonchés de morts et de mourants, le boudoir et un petit salon offraient l'image d'un champ de bataille.'[36] The language lifts away with amazing swiftness from an empirical scene; we start not with drunken revellers but with the dead and move from there to a battlefield which we are invited to compare with the burning plain on which the infernal host lay defeated. If Flaubert were to put on display in this fashion a synthesizing Romantic sensibility transforming the real before even presenting it, he would do so in an ironic mode quite different from Balzac's. But the latter is convinced of the intelligibility even of disorder itself:

L'ivresse, l'amour, le délire, l'oubli du monde, étaient dans les coeurs, sur les visages, écrits sur le tapis, exprimés par le désordre, et jetaient sur tous les regards de légers voiles qui faisaient voir dans l'air des vapeurs enivrantes.[37]

The scene, he assures us, can and will be read. Everything in it may be processed, its meaning extracted and used in the construction of thematic patterns. In Flaubert not only is the production of meaning delayed or arrested, but the ironic distancing repeatedly suggests that such interpretive operations are made possible only by codes constructed of social clichés and empty imaginative syntheses.

If one approaches Flaubert in this frame of mind, determined to give full value to those aspects of his prose which differentiate him from a Balzac and striving always to be aware of anything in the text which might mock one's attempts at symbolic recuperation, it is not difficult to see that even scenes renowned for their symbolic import contain elements of self-parody. One such is Frédéric's famous 'idyll' with Rosanette in the forest of Fontainebleau. Retiring from the turmoil of a Paris in revolution to the tranquility of the countryside, Frédéric and Rosanette visit the Palace, admire the ceilings, and discover an historical nostalgia. Visiting the forest in an open carriage, they observe, under the coachman's guidance, famous sites, climb the Aspremont heights and drink a lemonade. The next day they wander through the variegated light of the forest, admire the patriarchal trees, whose majestic and twisted forms are described at length, and the silent sand dunes. Nature exercises its influence on them and Frédéric 'did not doubt that he was happy for the rest of his days'.

The purpose of the scene, Sherrington argues, is to show the effects of nature on the couple.[38] But others would subject it to a symbolic reading which gives it much greater importance. 'The underlying structural unity of the book,' writes Brombert, 'the functional value of all the episodes — even those which at first may appear digressive and gratuitous — are perhaps nowhere more evident than in the pages describing Frédéric's and Rosanette's excursion to Fontainebleau.' The episode is not merely an 'escape from the battle-torn capital . . . it also replaces this tragedy in the larger context of a metaphysical meditation.' Frédéric gains a sense of human history in the château and of natural history in the woods.

Quite clearly, the details of the episode are dramatically and thematically relevant. There is irony in those trees which, on the one hand, join each other high up in the air like immense triumphal arches, and on the other seem to be 'falling columns' . . . The political revolution is measured against the geological 'revolutions'. The 'immobilized Titans' remind us, in their angry pose, of the revolutionary fervour. But they also point up the insignificance of all human endeavor in the face of eternal change and death. The Fontainebleau landscape assumes an apocalyptic grandeur which further underlines the futility of 'human' events. It is an almost religious awe which the 'gravity' of the forest inspires.[39]

The curious feature of Brombert's reading is that he goes on to observations about the effect of the scene which seem thoroughly correct: 'the very proliferation of phenomena and their immutable profusion cause a feeling of numbness and torpor' and we end in a 'contemplation of universal nothingness.'[40] It is as if he had responded to the scene in ways which seem wholly appropriate but had no other critical procedures for dealing with the text except those of symbolic interpretation. But it is not difficult to show that it is precisely through its resistance to the critical operations Brombert applies that the text produces the effects which he discerns.

When Frédéric and Rosanette set out on their tour of the natural beauties which critics are tempted to read as instances of a majesty dwarfing human pretentions, of the slow time-cycle of true order, or simply of apocalyptic grandeur, they are accompanied already by one mode of interpretive discourse:

Les arbres devinrent plus grands; et le cocher de temps à autre disait: 'Voici les Frères-Siamois, le Pharamond, le Bouquet-du-Roi . . .', n'oubliant aucun des cites célèbres, parfois même s'arrêtant pour les faire admirer (II, 125).[41]

The recitation, as Peter Cortland says in criticism of the passage, 'is too irritating for us easily to draw any conclusion therefrom.'[42] And when we move into the forest itself and watch Frédéric and Rosanette admiring the trees we find that though the guide is silent a voice in the text still interprets Nature as a spectacle:

Quelques-uns, d'une altitude démesurée, avaient des airs de patriarches et d'empereurs, ou, se touchant par le bout, formaient avec leurs longs fûts comme des arcs de triomphe; d'autres, poussés dès le bas obliquement, semblaient des colonnes près de tomber. . . . La diversité des arbres faisait un spectacle changeant (II, 126).[43]

If the point of the metaphors were simply to describe the trees more precisely there would be no grounds for uneasiness, but if they do function as interpretations — and this is what, for Brombert, justifies a symbolic reading of the trees against a political background — then one must attend to the incoherence produced by this type of reading. Is political revolution an act of desecration like chopping down monarchical trees or destroying the Empire's monuments, or does the very posture of trees which look like columns about to fall offer a natural analogue which refutes the former suggestion? To discover irony Brombert must conflate the two different types of tree and suggest that the triumphal arches are also (really?) falling columns, but even so the thrust of that irony is scarcely clear since he cannot decide whether analogy with nature shows the tragic seriousness of political revolution or its triviality and insignificance.

The changing spectacle of the trees includes birches 'bent in elegaic attitudes', pines 'symmetrical as organ-pipes', and oaks,

rugueux, énormes, qui se convulsaient, s'étiraient du sol, s'étreignaient les uns les autres, et, fermes sur leurs troncs, pareils à des torses, se lançaient avec leurs bras nus des appels de désespoir, des menaces furibondes, comme un group de Titans immobilisés dans leur colère (II, 126).[44]

It is clear that everything can be interpreted but not what is the significance of such interpretations. And when we are told that on the edge of ponds, over which a feverish langour broods, the moss, where wolves come to drink, is sulphur-coloured, burnt, as by the footsteps of witches, we are fully prepared for Frédéric's reading of a plain full of rocks: 'la furie même de leur chaos fait plutôt rêver à des volcans, à des déluges, aux grands cataclysmes ignorés. Frédéric disait qu'ils étaient là depuis le commencement du monde et resteraient ainsi jusqu'à la fin' (II, 127).[45] It is a matter of producing meaning according to those banal cultural models which facilitate symbolic interpretation and not worrying about the consequences or bases of such associations. Nature provides starting points, and there is pleasure in playing with it, especially if one has an innocent faith in the results. But the reader, who after all is at a certain distance from Frédéric, may find it difficult to enjoy such naïveté; he encounters sentences which report interpretive activities in ways which should confirm their gratuitousness. Like Polonius reading clouds, Frédéric can see rocks as animals: 'çà et là, telles que des promontoires sur le lit desséché d'un océan, se levaient des roches ayant de vagues formes d'animaux, tortues avançant la tête, phoques qui rampent, hippopotames et ours' (II, 127).[46] These comparisons undercut the grotesque menagerie of those that follow.

Nor does there seem much difference, except in degree of vulgarity, between the reactions of Frédéric and Rosanette. Wandering among the pines and rocks in a wild corner of the forest, the one finds his source of pleasure: 'One dreams of hermits, companions of the great stags bearing flaming crosses between their horns, who used to receive with fatherly smiles the good kings of France, who knelt before their caverns.' The other, less taken by this mythological furniture so confidently reported, is delighted to find, 'beneath a roof made of branches, a kind of tavern where woodcarvings were sold. She drank a bottle of lemonade, bought herself a holly stick' and enjoys herself in ways as much prescribed by cultural codes as are Frédéric's. And earlier, when they visit the palace, though Rosanette is not moved to the vague historical reverie which Frédéric's better education inspires, she does find a way of reading the scene in terms of her own preoccupations: in the room where Christine had Mondaleschi assassinated 'Rosanette listened attentively to this story, then, turning to Frédéric: 'It was from jealousy, I imagine. Look out for yourself!' (II, 125) This is not far from Frédéric's reading of the paintings of Diane de Poitiers: 'Frédéric fut pris par une concupiscence rétrospective et inexprimable. Afin de distraire son désir, il se mit à considérer tendrement Rosanette' (II, 125).[47] Neither can serve as a model for a process of symbolic interpretation which pretends to any degree of critical self-awareness.

The problem in which the text is immersed is the familiar one so thoroughly and self-consciously explored by Baudelaire. A literature which aspires to a portrayal of the emotional life must, if it is to secure any power to move, employ images which can be related to the world and thereby offers an interpretation of the world. But insofar as the experience conveyed is in any way interesting and particular, the self-conscious poet will be aware of his images as interpretations, of his words not as the furniture of the world but as devices which, at least for the moment of this particular perspective, are being used to communicative ends.

> L'un t'éclaire avec son ardeur,
> L'autre en toi met son deuil, Nature![48]

One cannot avoid doing one or the other, and one thereby exposes oneself both to external criticism and self-reflective irony:

> N'est-ce pas grand' pitié de voir ce bon vivant,
> Ce gueux, cet histrion en vacances, ce drôle,
> Parce qu'il sait jouer artistement son rôle,
> Vouloir intéresser au chant de ses douleurs
> Les aigles, les grillons, les ruisseaux et les fleurs . . .[49]

The solution is either to use one's images in self-conscious rhetorical play, as in the *Spleen* poems, never allowing them to compose themselves into a scene from the world, or else explicitly to incorporate references to the poetic process in the poem, as in *Un Voyage à Cythère*, where the vision of a disembowelled corpse on a gibbet is explored in gruesome detail and then recognized as a creation of the poetic mind:

> Le Ciel était charmant, la mer était unie;
> Pour moi tout était noir et sanglant désormais,
> Hélas! et j'avais, comme en un suaire épais,
> Le coeur enseveli dans cette allégerie.
> Dans ten île, ê Vénus! je n'ai trouvé debout
> Qu'un gibet symbolique où pendait mon image . . .[50]

Horror is located in the interpretive process rather than in the images themselves. Seeing the world in these terms, the poem tells us, is a horrifying thing; and thus it takes as its subject the tension between the concrete and powerful images required if a state of mind is to be effectively represented and the disengagement of a mind fully aware of the final arbitrariness of its images.

For Flaubert, who is operating in a different mode, the same problem arises though he enters it at a different point. Whereas in Baudelaire the desire to express a particular state of mind and posture before the world leads to the production of images which offer interpretations from which the narrator must distance himself, in Flaubert the starting point seems to be the writing of sentences rather than a particular expressive project. He composes scenes which can be related to an external world. That world is of interest only when interpreted, but to treat one's interpretations as natural meanings is to enter a realm of illusion and disappointment. The only solution is to produce interpretive images but to cut them loose, as it were, from justifiable motivations. The sentences must display within themselves the gap between a supposed world and its potential meanings; and consequently Flaubert's novels come to take as their subject the tension between the need to read and interpret the world as one is accustomed to read a text and the irony that undercuts possible readings.

Seldom is this tension better displayed than in the bathetic climax to the Fontainebleau episode when, as we are told in one of those flat, one-sentence paragraphs which drop a fact before us in a splendid isolation which prevents anything from being done with it,

> Avant de repartir, ils allèrent se promener le long de la berge.
> Le ciel d'un bleu tendre, arrondi comme un dôme, s'appuyait à l'horizon sur la dentelure des bois. En face, au bout de la prairie, il y avait un clocher dans un village; et, plus loin, à gauche, le toit d'une maison faisait une tache rouge sur la rivière, qui semblait immobile dans toute la longueur de sa sinuosité. Des joncs se penchaient pourtant, et l'eau secouait légèrement des perches plantées au bord pour tenir des filets; une nasse d'osier, deux ou trois vieilles chaloupes étaient là. Près de l'auberge, une fille en chapeau de paille tirait des seaux d'un puits;—chaque fois qu'ils remontaient, Frédéric écoutait avec une jouissance inexprimable le grincement de la chaîne.
> Il ne doutait pas qu'il ne fût heureux pour jusqu'à la fin de ses jours, tant son bonheur lui paraissait naturel, inhérent à sa vie et à la personne de cette femme (II, 127).[51]

We have here, Cortland says, one of those moments of bliss which are the goal of all romantic literature.[52] But this impression of bliss is something which floats above the paragraph, as a general and amorphous connotation; it does not seem embedded in the particular details. The gentle movement of reeds in the river is perhaps the one exception, but in other sentences the careful positioning of objects ('facing them, at the end of the meadow'; 'further off, on the left') and the verbs which simply note the presence of certain objects ('there was a steeple in a village'; 'an eel-trap, two or three old launches were there') prevent the scene from becoming directly evocative. And that what Frédéric hears with 'inexpressible pleasure' should be the grating of a chain emphasizes the distance between scene and response.

But this distance is characteristic of moments of epiphany. Proust's madeleine, after all, is a trivial object; and the old man of *Resolution and Independence* has not much to say for himself. No reader of literature can presume to decide in general terms what situations or objects justify intimations of order and bliss. Distance cannot be equated with irony, and one might accept the scene as a perfectly proper occasion for a sense of peace and harmony, were it not for the sentence which follows. But since we know or can guess that Frédéric has not found eternal happiness and that his reasons (happiness seems *natural* to his situation, *inherent* in his life with Rosanette) are precisely the wrong ones, we cannot avoid the possibility that his reaction to the scene is also an unjustified extrapolation, an interpretation which swings clear of its occasion. The tension between the need to interpret and the awareness of the arbitrariness of interpretation is very strong here, and one can only express surprise that critics who are quick to point out Frédéric's 'illusions' in his reading of the scene can themselves immediately offer another synthetic and symbolic reading which differs from his only in that the terms are drawn from models other than romantic novels: 'The scene in this particular paragraph is loaded with phallic symbolism, such as "dôme", "clocher dans un village", and more distantly the drawing of the water from the well . . . The bending of the reeds and the sticks holding nets are perfect Freudian dream material.'[53] The desire to produce coherence is very powerful: even stronger in critics than in Frédéric.

The descriptive passages so far discussed have all been cases where critics are tempted to perform synthesizing interpretive operations which the text resists or undermines. But there are in Flaubert many passages in which details seem subject to no particular thematic determination and in which the interpretive process never even gets under way. There seem neither causal nor symbolic connections to be made. Such is the case, for example, in the description of the scene which confronts Bouvard and Pécuchet when, on the first morning at their newly-acquired 'château' they arise and gaze out the windows:

On avait en face de soi les champs, à droite une grange, avec le clocher de l'église; et à gauche un rideau de peupliers.
Deux allées principales, formant la croix, divisaient le jardin en quatre morceaux. Les légumes étaient compris dans les plates-bandes, où se dressaient, de place en place, des cyprès nains et des quenouilles. D'un côté une tonnelle aboutissait à un vigneau; de l'autre un mur soutenait les espaliers; et une claire-voie, dans le fond, donnait sur la campagne. Il y avait au delà du mur un verger, après la charmille, un bosquet; derrière la claire-voie, un petit chemin (II, 208).[54]

The description covers the terrain in a fashion rather rigidly systematic: the three boundary elements are listed and then we are told that on the other side of the wall there lay an orchard, beyond the arbour a thicket, and behind the lattice fence a small track. 'I am doing my best to organize all this', the syntax asserts. But it is, in the end, to no avail. Matter thus organized becomes closed in on itself in an autonomous system which offers the reader no hold. This description, for example, suggests neither that the garden is splendid and a cause for joy nor that it is mediocre and unworthy of the proprietors' attention. It is simply there. The sentences lead us through it and reveal, at the end of their adventure, only an orchard, a thicket, a small track. As Jean Levaillant puts it, discussing description in *L'Education sentimentale*, 'in place of the living and synthesizing consciousness of the perceiving subject there is substituted the analytic and dissociating consciousness of an author.' Flaubert's organization of scenes produces an 'autarky of matter', unlike Balzac, whose descriptions

are caught up in the same dynamic movement as the story itself and are part of the same system of narration as the events. Here, on the contrary, the majority of descriptions have lost their property of analogy; they form an objective and separate discourse; instead of advancing the story they slow it down or suspend it.[55]

Matter becomes the 'opposite' of the story, its 'other', thrown up as a block to the readers' activity of synthesis. Flaubert has mastered what Barthes calls the indirect language of literature, which produces *signifiants* without filling in the *signifiés*:

> the best way for a language to be indirect is to refer as constantly as possible to things themselves rather than to their concepts, for the meaning of an object always flickers, but not that of the concept.[56]

A mode of writing that seeks to question the concepts by which we organize the world may well adopt this way of resisting recuperation: Pretend to take the referential function of language seriously. Construct descriptions which appear determined only by the desire for objectivity (best suggested by words of position: left, right, in front of, etc.). Write flat sentences which struggle over commas and around off-set prepositional phrases. The world created will seem real but there will be nothing to be done with it. The appearance of these sentences in the novel will imply that they can be taken up and given a meaning as well as a referent, but that meaning will remain empty. Since, however, both a world and a text of this sort will be of little interest, change your strategy from time to time and name meanings which appear to fill the empty space of the *signifié*. But in so doing make these meanings sufficiently detached from their objects that the arbitrariness of the connection will be evident. Make them the stuff of illusion. Display their inadequacy by the consequent misfortunes of characters who try to live by them. Make meaning problematic: either difficult to find or offered too freely and too gratuitously. Create, in other words, arbitrary and unmotivated signs, so that neither reader nor character may experience the solace of organic synthesis or of 'natural' significance. 'Le sens', as Sartre says,

> apparaîtra au lecteur à partir du travail pratique qu'on le sollicitera d'entreprendre et qu'il poursuivra d'un bout à l'autre de sa lecture mais qui s'effondrera sous ses yeux *malgré lui*, en montrant de lui-même son inanité.[57]

The readers attempting to motivate signs and produce a natural meaning from the text will find they have been made fools of, and those who are more wary will be, perhaps, 'demoralized' by the emptiness of signs and arbitrariness of their meanings — unless they find consolation in the opportunity to write about them.

Various forms of this basic strategy will be investigated in other sections, especially in the discussions of stupidity (a property of objects presenting a blank and inexhaustible face to the world) and irony (which undermines interpretive syntheses). For the moment one should simply take note of the ways in which the Flaubertian text defeats readers' expectations: the ways in which, shall we say, it is written *against* the novel as institution.

## C. *The Elusive Narrator*

Nineteenth-century fiction, Sartre observes, is told from the viewpoint of experience and wisdom and listened to from the viewpoint of order. Order is everywhere. The narrator evokes the spectacle of a past disorder, but it cannot cause uneasiness because he has understood it and will bring his audience to understand also. [58] Sartre's paradigm is the narrator seated of an evening midst friends, in surroundings which affirm the presence and reality of the social order, and recounting the vicissitudes of his own or another's past. The experience, as presented, has an order; its essence has been distilled; emotion is recollected in tranquillity and named from the viewpoint of tranquillity; so that the tale offers a moral, or at least a psychological law. The narrator has mastered the world, whether in the role of social historian or of an individual who looks back, all passion spent.

This kind of narration should be opposed to that which gives a taste of the primacy yet indeterminacy of moments, the uncertainty of effort, the real oppressiveness of choice, the dispersal of activity, the zones of mystery and opacity, which we take to be features of experience as lived. And for that, we might say, a limited point of view is preferable: a narrator who does not yet have the benefit of wisdom, whose order is what the novel itself attempts to investigate and construct, who recounts the impressions of a moment and may thereby become 'unreliable'. But whatever the virtues of this narrative technique, the concept of 'limited point of view' now has so long and distinguished a critical history that it can no longer be viewed as a revolt against order. In fact, the function of the concept, especially when applied to the more radical works of the past hundred years, is to enable us to order them. Anything, however fragmented or incoherent, any details, however odd they may seem, can be recuperated, justified, and given a meaning by the hypothesis that the text is the product of a narrator who is demented, schizophrenic, hallucinatory, or a congenital liar. The notion of limited point of view, one might say, artificially prolonged the life of the characterizable narrator by inviting us to attempt to discover *who* is speaking in any text whatsoever; and in that sense it is still very much a device of order.

What then is the alternative? How can one avoid an order based on the narrator's position? The answer might be found in a possible interpretation of Flaubert's doctrine of impersonality: a text in which no one speaks; a text which is simply *written*; a series of sentences which pass before the reader and which, if he tries to determine who speaks in each, baffle him by the variety of answers he finds. In these terms a text can, as Flaubert wished, be impersonal while conveying judgments of characters or events. Impersonality depends not on what is said but on the fact that no identifiable narrator speaks. And hence the efforts of critics to undermine Flaubert's doctrine of impersonality by citing all the instances where opinions are expressed seem to miss the point. What is rejected is a consistency in point of view which could lead to the identification of a knowledgeable Balzacian narrator or a series of narrators limited in their points of view and characterizable by those very limitations. The result is a strange and complex amalgam.

The absence of a controlling narrator, speaking from the viewpoint of order, is clear enough from the novels themselves. But most critics have not noticed that the *process* of rejection is displayed in those opening pages of *Madame Bovary* which they have found puzzling. Why does Flaubert begin in the first-person plural — 'We were all at prep, when the Headmaster came in, followed by a new boy . . .' — and describe Charles as seen by his schoolfellows, only to abandon this perspective after a few pages? Enid Starkie, in what is a typical comment, notes that the opening scene is vivid but

> different in tone from the rest of the novel, and the first-person narrator takes from the impersonality of the book, while the transition to the third person, without any warning, is somewhat

clumsy, and one cannot help feeling that there has been here an error in technique — though it is certainly presumptuous, and probably incorrect, to accuse so meticulous an artist of error. It is, however, difficult to discover what has been the gain from this method.[59]

Brombert also finds the point of view 'puzzling', since this personal voice is soon displaced, yet 'it seems hardly conceivable that so careful a craftsman as Flaubert should not have noticed the discrepancy, and that the curiously oblique approach should be the result of inadvertance'.[60] And Sartre's explanation, that Flaubert says *we* 'in order to put himself on the side of the mockers and present his character from outside in all his opacity'[61], is not much better, since the literary effect of opacity could have been achieved in other ways and the choice of means is put down to Flaubert's personal pathology.

This puzzlement seems a result of the *seriousness* which incapacitates so much Flaubert criticism: an attitude which induces reverence before the work of art and a refusal to entertain the possibility that it may be engaged in parody and obfuscation. For that is clearly what these first few pages do. Flaubert has made no attempt to smooth the transition by presenting the opening as the dramatized reminiscence of one who has since followed Charles' career ('I remember very well the first time I saw him; we were in class and . . . After leaving school he . . .') The first narrator presents Charles from the outside, deducing facts about him rather than calling upon knowledge acquired, judging him by the standards of the schoolroom. And when the text turns to an account of his family history, in the best manner of traditional novels, the whole tone changes. We no longer find the adolescent enthusiasm and attempt at Homeric evocation ('There was an uproar let loose, which rose in a crescendo, with loud shrieks. We shouted, we howled, we leapt for joy, repeating, *Charbovari! Charbovari!*') but a detached and knowledgeable discourse, picking out and juxtaposing details: Charles' father was 'A handsome chap, a braggart who made his spurs jingle, his whiskers meeting his moustache, his fingers always adorned with rings, and dressed in bright colours'; and his mother — 'once blithe, expansive and full of affection, she had become, with advancing years . . . more querulous, shrewish, nervous' (I, 576). And then following hard upon this synoptic account we have a sentence which throws the discrepancy in the reader's face: 'Il serait maintenant impossible à aucun de nous de se rien rappeler de lui.' None of us, who were in school with him, would be able to remember anything about him. Who then has narrated this passage? Who has recounted the details of his family and upbringing?

Léon Bopp, in his commentary on *Madame Bovary*, notes, his sentence and is somewhat demoralized by it. One cannot the avers, avoid including the author in this 'we', but thent he assertion 'is belied not only by all the precise details about Charles that Flaubert has already given . . . but also by those which he adds in the lines that follow. Do we have here a new lapse on the novelist's part?' Perhaps, he adds, grasping at straws, Flaubert is trying to excuse the brevity of his account, or suggest that Charles is unremarkable, but 'whatever the case, the statement in question would be more acceptable in an attenuated form'.[62] One is grateful to such critics for revealing so nicely the effectiveness of this *piège à cons* and for providing evidence about the ways in which the Flaubertian text can demoralize. For that is clearly the point of the sentence. It undermines the narrative convention whereby the observer recounts what he has experienced, adding background information where required for the edification of readers. Having allowed us to enter this novel in the traditional way and to set about identifying the narrator who speaks, the text stops us short by telling us that the narrator we have identified knows nothing about the events in question, can remember nothing about the character whose history we have taken him to be recounting. There may be a suggestion that most novels are unrealistic in the amount of detail the narrators are supposed to recall, but that is very much incidental to the main point: that the text is not narrated by anyone and that the attempt to read it as if it were can lead only to confusion.

Given that point of departure, we are better equipped to appreciate the complexity, not of the narrator, but of *narration* in Flaubert. R. J. Sherrington, in the fullest study of the subject, argues that the complexity of the mature works is the result of his use of limited points of view:

> First, it is no longer just occasional descriptions, but nearly all scenes and actions, which are now seen through the eyes of the

characters; secondly, *only* scenes and actions which can be seen through the eyes of the characters, and which are of importance to them, are now presented . . .[63]

Though narrated in the third person, descriptions of scenes include only what a particular character would notice, and hence, for Sherrington, Flaubert's technique is that of shifting from one identifiable narrator to another.

There are, it seems to me, three basic criticisms to be levelled at such an approach. First of all, in order to show the pervasiveness of limited points of view, one is led to create narrators who do not appear as characters in the story if one is to account for the way in which many scenes are described, and soon one has so many narrators that it seems far simpler to invert one's perspective and take the shifts in narrative distance as the primary phenomenon. Secondly, in undertaking to demonstrate the pervasiveness of limited points of view, one neglects the fact that under this rubric may be grouped procedures whose differences are far more crucial to narrative effect than their similarities. Even if a scene is described in relation to a particular character it matters considerably whether the description takes the form of a direct report of his thoughts and reactions or a report cast in *style indirect libre*, whether it summarizes and offers an organized synthesis or whether it passes from detail to detail in an impressionistic way. There are shifts within 'limited points of view' which are part of a general strategy of narrative discontinuity and which must not be ignored.

Finally, though this objection takes us to another level, emphasis on limited point of view can have a pernicious effect on the reading of novels because of the kind of recuperation it encourages. It suggests that the details of every description are justified and given a function by virtue of the fact that someone noticed them. It denatures strangeness by personalizing it, making it a function of a particular optic. Now it is certainly true that some descriptions do function in this way, but it is equally true that if we are to garner information about the cast of mind of a particular character we must have some sense of the 'real' scene which he is distorting; so that it is not limited point of view in itself which enables us to understand a character but rather discrepancies within the text or shifts out of that limited perspective. Thus, to say that everything in the account of a given scene is something Charles might have observed does not in fact give those elements a function unless the text move outside of Charles' vision and show what he would not have noticed, enabling us to grasp the peculiarities of his modes of perception. Where this does not happen, where the description of a scene does not effectively distinguish one point of view from other possible perspectives, then the concept of limited point of view serves little justificatory purpose. It becomes, in fact, simply another version of the representational justification which no sophisticated reader of novels would allow himself to employ today: that a particular passage is justified because it describes the world as it is. This is so weak a determination — an infinite set of descriptions of rooms becomes, by that criterion, equally justified — that it has fallen out of serious use; but the notion of limited point of view — the description is as it is because that is what the character noticed; we know that this is what he noticed because the description is as it is — offers a determination which is almost equally weak but more pernicious as it sounds rather more sophisticated.

It is not difficult to show the circularity of arguments by which critics and readers recuperate and naturalize passages which they take as instances of this sort. Sherrington's first example is Charles' visits to Les Bertaux, where he meets Emma: 'only details which force themselves upon Charles' awareness are mentioned.' Entering the kitchen, he notices that the shutters are closed; 'naturally, this fact draws attention to the patterns of light filtering through the shutters and coming down the chimney to strike the ashes in the fireplace.' Since Emma is standing near the fireplace he then sees her, but Sherrington offers no explanation of why, in the midst of the description of the light, before coming to Emma, we are offered a sentence which displays considerable interest in the behaviour of flies: 'Des mouches, sur la table, montaient le long des verres qui avaient servi, et bourdonnaient en se noyant au fond, dans le cidre resté' (I, 581). There seems no particular reason to believe that Charles' cast of mind causes him to observe flies drowning themselves, and to discover what they are drowning in, before noticing Emma. 'Then he sees Emma and notices only one thing about her: "sur ses épaules nues de petites gouttes de sueur".' How characteristic of Charles! Full of admiration for Flaubert's artistry in recounting just what

Charles noticed, Sherrington agrees with Jean Rousset that Flaubert substituted this last detail for 'ses épaules blanches étaient roses' because 'such an observation would be beyond Charles limited sensibility'. Yet Charles is supposed to notice that the light which came down the chimney 'veloutant la suie de la plaque, bleuissait un peu les cendres froides.'[64] It is clear that the critic knows 'what Charles would have noticed' only from what is actually written. He is unable to tell us what this passage shows us of Charles' character or what is gained by the pretence that it is narrated from his point of view. There is selection of unconnected details and there seems no reason to try to connect them by attributing them to Charles' sensibility.

Let us now turn to an example of a somewhat different kind. In his review of Salammbô Sainte-Beuve was particularly critical of the passage describing Hamilcar's return to his palace. The storehouses and all the riches they contain are described in considerable detail. The narrator, he complained, seems to be an appraiser who is amusing himself amid all these fantastic objects: 'It's overdoing it and showing the cloven hoof of the mystificatory dilettante'.[65] In reply, Flaubert can argue only that the description is background (II, 753), but the modern critic, of whom Sherrington is a capable example, can offer other justifications. The section is presented from Hamilcar's point of view, and since he has been away for a long time he is naturally anxious to check his possessions.

> Seen in this light, the apparently tiresome detail begins to have some psychological validity. A person of Hamilcar's character, in a situation of such vital concern to him, would not let the tiniest detail escape him, and conversely, one so acute would have to be such a character in such a situation.[66]

The circularity of argument is apparent, but more important, it is simply not true that the entire scene is presented from Hamilcar's point of view. The opening sentences are proffered by one who takes his distance from Hamilcar: 'Le Suffète se promena d'abord à grands pas rapides; il respirait bruyamment, il frappait la terre du talon, il se passait la main sur le front comme un homme harcelé par les mouches' (I, 735).[67] Hamilcar is rendered comic by this detached and purely external description, and later, as he listens to reports from his various subalterns, their thoughts and reactions are presented: 'the chief of farm-lettings was so afraid of speaking . . .', 'Abdalonim hesitated, surprised at this generosity', 'when he came upon the workmen, Abdalonim, in order to deflect anger from himself, tried to arouse him against them by muttering complaints about their work. Hamilcar passed on, paying no attention'. This is not Hamilcar's view of the scene, nor is he likely to have dwelt on the hair, fingernails, and mode of attachment of a prisoner who cries out for mercy as he passes but receives no reply. And further on, in a gallery where piles of riches are stacked on the floor, 'The Suffete brushed them in passing with his robe, without even looking at the huge blocks of amber, a nearly divine substance formed by the rays of the sun' (I, 738). Sherrington cites this as an instance of 'Hamilcar's acceptance of Carthaginian myths and traditions, implied by his point of view', but that is clearly specious, since the phrase about amber is tacked on as a note about something which Hamilcar does not even glance at, much less reflect on. It is offered as a flat statement from nowhere in particular.

What we have in this scene, then, is extremely agile narration, restricting itself for a moment and then withdrawing, darting in and out to adopt first one perspective and then another. And the passage of which Sainte-Beuve particularly complained, when Hamilcar contemplates his treasures and is pleased, as the text informs us, less by the spectacle itself than by conscious-ness of his wealth, need not emanate from Hamilcar but can be read simply as the discourse of that society:

> c'étaient des callaïs arrachées des montagnes à coups de fronde, des escarboucles formées par l'urine des lynx, des glossopètres tombés de la lune, des tyanos, des diamants, des sandastrum, des béryls, avec les trois espèces de rubis, les quatre espèces de saphir et les douze espèces d'émeraudes . . . Il y avaient des topazes du mont Zabarca pour prévenir les terreurs, des opales de la Bactriane qui empêchent les avortements, et des cornes d'Ammon que l'on place sous les lits afin d'avoir des songes (I, 737).[68]

Hamilcar would have no incentive to explain the uses of these objects, and it seems more appropriate to read this passage as a repertoire of citations from that discourse by which the ancients created sacred and talismanic objects. The carbuncles formed from lynxes' urine are to be found in Theophrastus, and the other sources could no doubt be identified. To the question, 'who tells us that opals prevent miscarriages?' the only answer the text gives is that 'it is written'. The passage displays the exotic in all its excess and heterogeneity, and to say that the catalogue's function is to reveal the character of Hamilcar is to dismiss the sense of oppressive strangeness which such a description provokes in the reader.

Sherrington applies the same strategy to *L'Education sentimentale*, arguing that seventy per cent of the book is narrated from Frédéric's point of view. But once again one must ask whether anything is gained by attempting to recuperate so many passages as instances of Frédéric's vision. The evening at the Alhambra, for example, is occasionally described in terms which might relate Frédéric's impressions, but there are other moments where one is confronted with a kind of cosmic impressionism which has nothing to do with him:

> Puis on causa de Delmas, qui pourrait, comme mime, avoir des succès au théâtre; et il s'ensuivit une discussion, où l'on mêla Shakespeare, la Censure, le Style, le Peuple, les recettes de la Porte-Saint-Martin, Alexandre Dumas, Victor Hugo, et Dumersan. Arnoux avait connu plusieurs actrices célèbres; les jeunes gens se penchaient pour l'écouter. Mais ses paroles étaient couvertes par le tapage de la musique; et, sitôt le quadrille ou la polka terminés, tous s'abattaient sur les tables, appelaient le garçon, riaient; les bouteilles de bière et de limonade gazeuse détonaient dans les feuillages, des femmes criaient comme des poules; quelquefois, deux messieurs voulaient se battre; un voleur fut arrêté (II, 35).[69]

The curious combination of proximity and distance, of impressions of a moment and generalizations, prevents us from identifying a narrator here. We seem at first to be observing a particular event, but then the disjunction (quadrille *or* polka) and the plural participle move us back and imply a general view of what happens after each dance. The *quelquefois* comes from someone who has seen the whole evening, and after this confusion the final fact, 'un voleur fut arrêté', seems thoroughly detemporalized. The passage moves back and forth from ironic summary, as of the conversation, to momentary impression; and the effect of the passage is falsified if one tries to compose it by claiming that it derives coherence from the personality of an observing Frédéric.

Indeed, the most interesting narrative effects in Flaubert involve, almost invariably, rapid shifts of perspective which prevent one from determining who speaks or from where. One cannot compose a perspective which would make clear the salient features of the scene, their relation to one another, and their importance. The wedding scene in *Madame Bovary*, for example, begins with a reductive overview: 'Les conviés arrivèrent de bonne heure dans des voitures, carrioles à un cheval, chars à bancs à deux roues, vieux cabriolets sans capote, tapissières à rideaux de cuir . . .' But it immediately dips down to dwell on a particular scene, which, however, is presented in the plural: 'et les jeunes gens des villages les plus voisins dans des charrettes où ils se tenaient debout, en rang, les mains appuyées sur les ridelles pour ne pas tomber, allant au trot et secoués dur' (I, 583).[70] Then a position is identified; we are told what 'on entendait' and 'on voyait' as the guests arrived at the farm, but in this description limited knowledge (boys 'seemed uncomfortable in their new clothes') is juxtaposed with other information ('many were even christening that day the first pair of boots they'd had in their lives').

> L'on voyait à côté d'eux, ne soufflant mot dans la robe blanche de sa première communion rallongée pour la circonstance, quelque grande fillette de quatorze ou seize ans, leur cousine ou leur soeur aînée sans doute, rougeaude, ahurie, les cheveux gras de pommade à la rose, et ayant bien peur de salir ses gants (I, 583).[71]

Within a single sentence we have both explicit limitation of information ('sans doute') and firm knowledge of feelings and background, both suggestion of a specific perception and devices which render it plural ('quelque', 'leur'). Finally, at the end of the paragraph, the narrator withdraws so that the company becomes simply a mass of 'grosses faces blanches épanouies'.

'The author's attitude in this passage', writes Sherrington, 'is strangely ambivalent', but he both achieves immediacy and 'gives us an objective picture of what is going on'.[72] This seems an excessively strained rationalization. When the narrator hovers over the marriage procession wending its way from the church he achieves neither immediacy nor objectivity in any ordinary sense of the word:

> Le cortège, d'abord uni comme une seule écharpe de couleur, qui ondulait dans la campagne, le long de l'étroit sentier serpentant

entre les blés verts, s'allongea bientôt et se coupa en groupes différents, qui s'attardaient à causer (II, 583).[73]

His failure to say a word about the ceremony itself should make it sufficiently clear that we are dealing with no objective account of a wedding but an incoherent combination of aesthetic detachment, immediate impressionism, and informative explanation. But incoherent, one should add, only for those who attempt to identify its narrator and the position from which he speaks. For those who are willing to follow the narration in ambiguously observing the guests, soaring above the procession but not entering the church, admiring the food but missing the dinner itself, the incoherence lies not in the text itself but in the scene described: a world which refuses to be composed according to ordinary principles of significance.

Shifts in perspective are often designed to undermine one judgment by juxtaposing it with another, as when, having described Bouvard and Pécuchet's enjoyment of vaulting across ditches with a long pole, the text draws back to dehumanize the project it has presented and offers a reductive view: 'La campagne était plate, on les apercevait au loin; et les villageois se demandaient quelles étaient ces deux choses extraordinaires, bondissant à l'horizon' (II, 262).[74] Alternatively, they may knit together an anonymous text of social judgments — ordinary discourse which could be spoken by anyone from a certain social milieu — as in the accounts of Frédéric's mother, the preparations for the Comices agricoles before the ceremony actually begins, and the townspeople's view of Léon, Emma, and others.

All of these techniques are brought together in the account of Charles and Emma's visit to the theatre. Sherrington, of course, sees this as narrated from Emma's point of view, but that is clearly only one of many elements. There is an instance of the unidentified social discourse, which describes their activity before entering the theatre: '*Madame* s'acheta un chapeau, des gants, un bouquet. *Monsieur* craignait beaucoup de manquer le commencement . . .' (my italics). Another ironic look at Charles refers to him differently and calls upon special knowledge: 'Bovary, par prudence, garda les billets à sa main, dans la poche de son pantalon, qu'il appuyait contre son ventre.' Within the theatre itself there are three different modes of discourse. Some descriptions can certainly be taken as what Emma noticed, and her reactions are reported in *style indirect libre*: 'Pourquoi donc n'avait-elle pas, comme celle-là, résisté, supplié', or 'Avec lui, par tous les royaumes de l'Europe, elle aurait voyagé de capitale en capitale, partageant ses fatigues et son orgeuil, ramassant les fleurs qu'on lui jêtait . . .' (I, 650–1).[75] But alongside this there is knowledgeable, analytical narration which tells us that she was 'drawn towards the man by the illusion of the character', that she took a 'childish pleasure' in pushing open the door of the box with her finger, that the actor's reputation as a lover had increased his fame as an artist, and that 'Un bel organe, un imperturbable aplomb, plus de tempérament que d'intelligence et plus d'emphase que de lyrisme, achevaient de rehausser cette admirable nature de charlatan, où il y avait du coiffeur et du toréador' (I, 650).[76]

This is very far indeed from Emma's thoughts, and one's impression is that when Flaubert wants to show how one of his characters perceives and reacts to a scene he makes the project quite plain by setting that discourse against others which provide alternative views of the situation in question. Here, in addition to the judgments which deflate the actor after whom Emma swoons, we have a third type of discourse, impressionistic rather than analytical, which describes the scene with a detachment that makes it appear ridiculous: 'tous les mouchoirs tirés épongeaient des fronts rouges' or

> Dès la première scène il enthousiasma. Il pressait Lucie dans ses bras, il la quittait, il revenait, il semblait désespéré: il avait des éclats de colère, puis des râles élégiaques d'une douceur infinie . . . (I, 650).[77]

This is not Emma's view of the play, for she knows the story and would not think of his actions as arbitrary and unmotivated. It is rather that of a detached spectator who finds the whole thing silly and incomprehensible. The narration has simply drawn back for a moment before moving in on Emma's reactions once again.

But the best example, because it illustrates so well not only the predilection for continually shifting points of view which make us uncertain who is speaking but also the thematic ends to which the elusive narration is manipulated, is the famous *fiacre* scene in *Madame Bovary*. We are privy to Léon's thoughts as he awaits her in the cathedral and to those of the guide, who is indignant that this individual should presume to admire the cathedral on his own. Then we shift to an external impression: 'But a rustle of silk on the stones, the brim of a hat, a black cape' and Léon's 'It was she!' From his thoughts we switch to hers, as she prays 'or rather forced herself to pray' in the Lady chapel, hoping that a sudden resolve will descend from heaven. But this does not quiet the 'tumult in her heart', and as she rises the narrative moves definitively away from her consciousness. As the guide details the beauties of the cathedral we see Emma only from the outside, though we follow the modulations of Léon's impatience, until, pushing Emma into the *fiacre*, he tells the coachman to drive 'wherever he likes'.

At this point, with the single-sentence paragraph, 'Et la lourde machine se mit en route', Léon and Emma vanish and are no longer even referred to by name. The narration offers at least five different kinds of information but eschews any knowledge of who is in the coach: 'Continuez! fit *une voix* qui sortait de l'intérieur' (my italics). The itinerary is given in some detail, as if by an omniscient narrator; the coachman's behaviour at a particular point is described, as if by an observer on the spot; the coachman's thoughts from time to time, his feeling of despair and incomprehension when forced to continue a pointless drive, are set down in ways that imply special knowledge. What miscellaneous townspeople see is described: the coach was seen at x, y, and z and 'les bourgeois ouvraient de grands yeux ébahis devant cette chose si extraordinaire en province . . .' And finally, as though willing to display knowledge of everything except those in the coach, the prose is allowed to dwell on 'les jardins de l'hôpital, où des vieillards en veste noire se promènent au soleil, le long d'une terrasse toute verdie par des lierres' (I, 657).[78]

Nor can this narrative strategy be attributed simply to a desire to be discreet and leave us to imagine what is taking place inside the coach, for the final sentence adopts a distance which that purpose would scarcely require and, refusing even to pronounce the name used when she entered the coach, tells us that 'vers six heures, la voiture s'arrêta dans une ruelle du quartier Beauvoisine, et une femme en descendit qui marchait le voile baissé, sans détourner la tête' (I, 657).[79] There is only a woman, who is denied the sympathy that individuation or even naming might make possible.

Sartre has written some brilliant pages on this scene and the way in which Emma and Léon, who try through the feeble gestures of their language to rise above 'the material level of sexual desire and the copulation which they know is inevitable', are denied the status of subjects and become objects, whose conduct is figured by that of 'la lourde machine.' 'If he were to show the interior of the coach and the two lovers making love, Emma and Léon would have remained human in the same way as the coachman.'[80] Flaubert's 'irrelevant' description of the coach's journey through the town prevents us from seeing their encounter in human terms and renders it absurd. But Sartre judges the episode a failure because the shift in perspective 'refers us to the malignant intention of the author . . . It's the end of dramatic illusion: there are no longer characters, just puppets manipulated by a director.'[81]

It is not a little ironic that Sartre, whose greatness derives from his overpowering theoretical sophistication, should condemn *Madame Bovary* in the name of dramatic illusion and the theory of the novel it implies. For shifts in point of view are Flaubert's staple technique and it was through their use that he discovered, especially in his later work, that dramatic illusion was not necessary to his project. The novel need not pretend to be representing a scene in a neutral prose through which one can look as through a window. The artifice of *Madame Bovary*, *L'Education sentimentale* and *Bouvard et Pécuchet* does not destroy the impression of 'reality' but it does destroy the basis of dramatic illusion by undermining the reader's attempt to determine where he stands to look at the scenes displayed. The thematic projects which Sartre correctly identifies depend, in large measure, on the techniques of displacement and fragmentation which he finds disturbing. The reader would not be demoralized, after all, by a tale told from the point of view of an order which he could identify and adopt as his own.

## D. Weak Vessels

The meaning of an object or event is always the meaning it has for someone, and therefore in novels with elusive narrators characters become especially important as purveyors of meaning or at least as catalysts through and around whom a represented experience can assume shapes. It was Henry James's complaint about Flaubert's characters that they did not assume this function as adequately as one might have hoped, that Emma Bovary is 'really too small an affair' and when associated with Frédéric Moreau forces us to ask why Flaubert chose, 'as special conduits of the life he proposed to depict, such inferior and in the case of Frédéric such abject human specimens?'[82] If he could imagine nothing better than 'such limited reflectors and registers, we are forced to believe it to have been a defect of his mind.' It is not sufficient to answer, as critics have done, that the point was to show the mediocrity of common experience, and that mediocre characters were chosen to that end, for that easy excuse was clearly envisaged by James and his reply was quite simply that 'the purpose itself then shows as inferior'.

The argument, then, must be about the purpose and its validity. That it should have seemed inferior to James will be no cause for surprise. His metaphors of 'reflector and register', of 'conduit' and 'vessel', indicate that the function of characters is to see and to feel, to take in the world of the novel and to invent and reflect on possible responses. That he should praise in *The Golden Bowl* 'the manner in which the whole thing remains subject to the register, ever so closely kept, of the consciousness of but two of the characters' and the way in which Maggie, as a finely polished reflector, becomes a compositional resource as well as a source of moral richness, may indicate only an awareness of what is, after all, the main interest of that work. But the assumption that in writing *What Maisie Knew* 'the small expanding consciousness would have to be saved, have to become *presentable* as a register of impressions', indicates the force of the obsession.[83] The possibility that a child-hero might offer a supremely obtuse and hence ironic point of view seems scarcely to have been entertained.

What James could do with a child, Flaubert should have done with his adults: make them presentable, vehicles of a perceptiveness and understanding sufficiently complex to interest the discriminating reader. To say that James solved the problem by enforcing his own large conception of what children might understand would be to mistake the subtlety of the achievement, for though, as he says, 'it is her relation, her activity of spirit, that determines all our own concern', the narrator takes advantage of these better than she herself. The alternative, which Flaubert and James reject with equal alacrity, would be the combination of a limited reflector and a separate knowledgeable commentary. And it is no doubt because they take the same line here, because both are committed to the strategy of presenting the character's awareness in a language that is not his, that James feels his reproach to be just.

But the value to which his scheme particularly ministers, the quality to which it so ruthlessly subordinates other possible concerns, is one which never held special appeal for Flaubert: intelligence. Though he may remark on his own intelligence more frequently than on his stupidity — and even that would be a close-run thing — it is usually by way of contrast with the stupidity of others, especially the intelligent classes. The notion that fineness of perception, intricacy of experiential imagination, might be the touchstones by which his novels could eventually come to be judged would both have astounded and appalled him, but he would have recognized the coherence of James's condemnation. Indeed, the weak vessels, the poor reflectors, are not simply, as James would have it, lapses or failures of judgment. The opportunities for sensitivity, for probing feelings and discriminating among possible moral reactions are not simply missed; they are deliberately and brutally missed, for specific narrative effects.

A single example, but so awkwardly and voluntarily obvious as to prove the point, comes at a crucial dramatic moment in *L'Education sentimentale*: a scene which James would have finely exploited had it not seemed too blatant an occasion for his tastes. After considerable absence and infidelity Frédéric calls on Mme Arnoux, and for once they go beyond politeness, with Frédéric strongly denying his love for Rosanette, and end in one another's arms:

> Un sanglot de tendresse l'avait soulevée. Ses bras s'écartèrent; et ils s'étreignirent debout, dans un long baiser.
> Un craquement se fit sur le parquet. Une femme était près d'eux, Rosanette (II, 138).[84]

Too melodramatic, perhaps, but it provides an occasion, at

least, for the investigation of some rather complex reactions —
combinations and permutations of guilt, anger, fear, attachment to real and idealized pasts — on the part of Frédéric.
But narrative attention turns on Mme Arnoux:

> Mme Arnoux l'avait reconnue; ses yeux, ouverts démesurément,
> l'examinaient, tout pleins de surprise et d'indignation. Enfin
> Rosanette lui dit:
> — Je viens parler à M. Arnoux, pour affaires.
> — Il n'y est pas, vous le voyez.
> — Ah! c'est vrai! reprit la Maréchale, votre bonne avait raison!
> Mille excuses!
> Et, se tournant vers Frédéric:
> — Te voilà ici, toi! (II, 138).[85]

This is the dramatic moment. Our attention turns on Frédéric,
but not the narrator's: 'Ce tutoiement, donné devant elle, fit
rougir Mme Arnoux, comme un soufflet en plein visage'; she
repeats that her husband is not there; at which point La
Maréchale says calmly: 'Rentrons-nous? J'ai un fiacre, en bas.'
    What is Frédéric's reaction to this, what kind of sensibility
and moral character does he display? None. Or at least none
that we are allowed to glimpse. 'He pretended not to hear',
but Rosanette simply repeats, 'Let's go, come along,' and with
Mme Arnoux's 'Ah! oui! c'est une occasion! Partez! partez!',
'Ils sortirent.' Not a word about Frédéric. Mechanically, like
a robot obeying orders, he exits. Mme Arnoux, watching them
go down the staircase, lets out 'un rire aigu, déchirant' but
Frédéric gets into the coach and speaks not a word.
    Here is not just a missed occasion — and this is said with no
regrets — but a deliberate refusal to explore and exploit
Frédéric's potential as register, reflector, centre of consciousness. There may be several reasons for it, but one cannot argue
that it is pure representational realism in that Frédéric in fact
feels nothing. It seems, rather, that Frédéric has been put in
an exceedingly awkward spot, with which most of us would
not know how to deal, and whatever his reaction, we would be
unlikely to condemn it as stupid. We would, in fact, feel considerable sympathy for him, even if he felt unable to act and
could only allow himself to be led docilely away by the nose,
realizing the futility of protest and fearing the interview with
Mme Arnoux if he tried to stay. Whereas when the reaction is

not reported until afterwards — 'he felt both shame at his humiliation and regret for the happiness snatched from him. He would have liked to strangle Rosanette' — Frédéric is rendered faintly ridiculous. He vanishes from our sight at the crucial moment and surfaces, muttering curses, only after events have settled themselves.

Shifting away from characters at the moment when they might, through their reaction, become interesting or at least profoundly human, is a common technique. During the revolutionary uprising, for example, Frédéric, to whom it has so far been a kind of unreal spectacle, is in the crowds in front of the Palais Royal:

> Frédéric sentit sous son pied quelque chose de mou; c'était la main d'un sergent en capote grise, couché la face dans le ruisseau. Des bandes nouvelles de peuple arrivaient toujours, poussant les combattants sur le poste. La fusillade devenait plus pressée. Les marchands de vin étaient ouverts; on allait de temps à autre y fumer une pipe, boire une chope, puis on retournait se battre. Un chien perdu hurlait. Cela faisait rire (II, 113).[86]

Though there is irony in this passage it is not the irony of Fabrice at the battle of Waterloo; it is not a matter of placing an innocent consciousness before scattered details which it is unable to compose. There is, rather, a deliberate refusal to use Frédéric as reflector and register, for one may suppose that anyone treading on the hand of a dead man before the Palais Royal would have some kind of reaction which could be reported. If the scene seems grotesque, stupid, fragmented, it is largely because of the refusal to work through Frédéric in order to invest it with meaning.

Nor is the technique simply one of silence, for James also has moments of silence or reticence, which play a very different function. Milly, we are told in *The Wings of the Dove*, is not 'easy to know'; she may be dying of an unspecified illness but that is, as Kate says, 'a matter in which I don't want knowledge'. The reticence on this point is full rather than empty, an invitation to supposition, an exfoliating reticence. The lack of understanding is allowed to loom quite oppressively as a suggestion of unexplored depths. The effect depends, of course, on the fact that depths are sometimes explored. Densher is introduced to Lord Mark:

'Oh!' said the other party, while Densher said nothing — occupied as he mainly was on the spot with weighing the sound in question. He recognized it in a moment as less imponderable than it might have appeared, as having indeed positive claims. It wasn't, that is, he knew, the 'Oh!' of the idiot, however great the superficial resemblance: it was that of the clever, the accomplished man; it was the very speciality of the speaker, and a great deal of expensive training and experience had gone to producing it. Densher felt somehow that, as a thing of value accidentally picked up, it would retain an interest of curiosity.[87]

With that kind of suggestive possibility always before us it is scarcely surprising that we find depths in the silences of the text, as indeed the characters themselves are forced to do. 'You're too splendid", says Fanny Assingham to Maggie.

'Splendid?'
'Splendid. Also, you know, you *are* all but "through". You've done it,' said Mrs Assingham.
But Maggie only half took it from her. 'What does it strike you that I've done?'
'What you wanted. They're going.'
Maggie continued to look at her. 'Is that what I wanted?'
'Oh, it wasn't for you to say. That was *his* business.'
'My father's?' Maggie asked after a hesitation.
'Your father's. He has chosen — and now she knows . . .'[88]

We move in a labyrinth born of silences, in which 'knowing' and 'understanding' have no direct objects but suggest the possibility of infinitely finer perceptions, discriminations, and suppositions. One can always go on: 'He was just going to understand and understand without detriment to the feeblest, even, of his passions.'[89] It is that process to which readers are invited. And hence when one of James's characters says 'I see, I see', this thin verbal act contains a richness of possibilities which makes it totally different from anything we find in Flaubert; for it is richer, James's silence implies, than anything which could actually or possibly be *seen*. But if Frédéric were to say 'I see', we should take it as a feeble social gesture, an indication that he had not seen anything at all, and perhaps that there was nothing to be seen. Such is the nature of weak vessels. We approach with the assumption that they contain nothing and do not allow silence to figure profundity.

Emma's and Frédéric's crudeness of perception cannot be

justified simply by a desire to portray crudeness; but the fact that the strategies of presentation seem designed to suggest that there is nothing to understand, to open up abysses so different from those in which James's characters and readers are wont to sport, suggests a preoccupation so alien to James that it may explain both his criticism and our admiration. There are, one might say, three ways of dealing with characters and their feelings. The first is to imply depths that can be investigated and to offer, from time to time and by way of guarantee, a proliferation of distinctions and nuances. In this James is at one with Proust, for whom the variety of explanations and comparisons which the exfoliating imagination can produce is limited only by the willingness of publishers to accept interpolations in proof. On the other hand, one may attempt to suggest depths which lie beyond language, which are defined by their indescribability. One might cite here Stendhal, Constant, and Madame de Lafayette. Unlike James, who is committed to convincing us that the range of our experience can, in fact, be as great as the possibilities of our language, they insist that our representational language can only gesture towards the finer states of mind and deeper states of feeling. 'Oh charms of love, once experienced you cannot be described.' 'The feelings of men are murky and complex . . . and language, always too crude and abstract, may serve to designate them but can never define them.'[90] Both these approaches are opposed to the Flaubertian mode, which offers neither perspectives of infinite elaboration (except in disembodied reverie), nor assurances of a reality beyond language, but only an emptiness:

'Quand tout fut fini au cimetière, Charles rentra chez lui. Il ne trouva personne en bas; il monta au premier, dans la chambre, vit sa robe encore accrochée au pied de l'alcôve; alors, s'appuyant contre le secrétaire, il resta jusqu'au soir perdu dans une rêverie douloureuse. Elle l'avait aimé, après tout' (I, 581).[91]

There is no more to be said. In this case Charles, as is invariably the case for Frédéric, is not allowed to react to the stimulus of events which might justify any meanings he could draw from them. The elaborations of his sensibility take place under little pressure from the outside world and float free as gratuitous constructions which reveal the futility of the constructing mechanisms and the triviality of the cultural models employed.

Once again we discover, in different guise, the technique of breaking any 'natural' connection between meaning and the world. Silence serves as a barrier, on the other side of which arbitrary and insubstantial constructions may be erected. Flaubert's characters are poor reflectors in that they do not compose the world for us, do not organize it in ways that reveal new possibilities of feeling and perception. When they do attempt to order it they do so in ways which are undercut by the obviousness of the cultural models they are using or by the failure of their images of the world when they try to live in accordance with them.

In the case of *Madame Bovary* the failure to provide characters who help us to enrich our view of experience is of little moment, for we can read the novel as about Emma and find her pathology sufficiently fascinating to demand no more of the book. But in later works the characters become less rich, less interesting as psychological cases, until finally we reach the extreme existential thinness of Bouvard and Pécuchet. Their characteristic attitude before the world is one of surprise, admiration, disbelief; they offer, thus, a mode of experience which does not affect the world, which does not even order it or assign it meanings, but which takes cognizance of the gap between their intellect or perceptions and the facts which they learn.

'Ce qui les ébahit par-dessus tout, c'est que la terre, comme élément, n'existe pas' (II, 219).
'Le squelette les étonna . . . ils apprirent les divisions de la charpente, en s'ébahissant sur l'épine dorsale. . . . Les métacarpiens désolèrent Bouvard' (II, 220).
'Ils étonnaient que les poissons eussent des nageoires, les oiseaux des ailes, les semences une enveloppe' (II, 226).
'Dans les galeries du Muséum, ils passèrent avec ébahissement devant les quadrupèdes empaillés, avec plaisir devant les papillons, avec indifférence devant les métaux' (II, 204).[92]

All this serves to characterize them, of course, but not to make them figures of any complexity or to make their contact with the world a device for organizing and enriching it. They alternate between enthusiasm and discouragement, both of which are subjective responses which make little contact with the world but which are also devoid of the psychological complexity of Emma's or Frédéric's mythmaking.

Nor does Julien, of 'La Légende de Saint Julien l'Hospitalier', serve as register or reflector. He is assigned various qualities: first a thirst for blood, then humility and horror of his own person; but the narrative remains at a distance from him, never attempting to show how the world might have appeared to one so constituted. Seldom has a version of the Oedipus myth been presented from so anti-psychological a bias. Cover terms such as 'anger' suffice to explain his actions. As with Bouvard and Pécuchet, there is little attempt to construct a plausible psychology by identifying its sources and displaying its effects on experience. Qualities are named, in a parody of the techniques of those unsophisticated novels which introduce characters with static and summary portraits.

But it is not simply that Flaubert refuses to make his characters purveyors of meaning — registers or reflectors of meaning in the Jamesean sense. He also resists the reader's attempt to make them repositories of meaning or objects around which meaning can crystallize. Our expectations lead us to collect evidence about the differences between characters and oppose them to one another as representatives of different attitudes towards the world and strategies for dealing with experience. Flaubert offers us considerable evidence of this kind; indeed, he offers so much evidence that patterns cannot be made to jell unless we blind ourselves to other possibilities. The opening scenes of *Madame Bovary* oppose Charles to the rest of the world, but later he seems to be identified with the rest of Yonville in that both he and other citizens are opposed to Emma. She also opposes Charles to Rodolphe and Léon. And of course we have that vaudeville couple, Homais and Bournisien.

What do these contrasts mean? In Balzac or Dickens oppositions between characters are essential to statements of theme. In order to understand *Hard Times* one must set the members of the 'horse-riding' against the worthies of Coketown, Sissy Jupes against Bitzer; one must contrast Lady Dudley with Henriette de Mortsauf in *Le Lys dans la vallée*, Lucien de Rubempré with David Séchard in *Illusions perdues*, Adeline with Bette and Valérie in *La Cousine Bette*, Vautrin with Victorine Taillefer in *Le Père Goriot*. Set against one another, characters become types: representatives of particular positions or traits. Opposition is a device for the production of meaning

— among the most powerful we have. But in Flaubert, despite the evocation of oppositions, as soon as one attempts to formulate contrasts and give them a thematic reading, a great many appear empty, lacking any firm thematic power. Is not Emma as mediocre as the citizens of Yonville? Does not Charles show himself, by his behaviour after her death, her true husband, as wedded to the forms of romantic nostalgia as she ever was? Is not the opposition between Homais and Bournisien nullified as they fall asleep together over Emma's corpse? What can be drawn from these oppositions if they can be so easily collapsed? It is not merely that contraries meet, in the sense in which love and hatred resemble one another more than either resembles indifference. It is rather that oppositions may themselves prove empty.

*Bouvard et Pécuchet* is, of course, the best example, for, as the title itself announces, it is truly an excercise in binarism. Given two characters, one can rate them as similar or different on any conceivable matter, and the basic structural device of binary opposition thus enables one to carry on writing for as long as one wishes. Whether the differences produced in the process are of any thematic importance is, of course, another question, and this problem is apparent from the very beginning of the novel. After a brief description of the setting, we are told, in a three-word paragraph:

> Deux hommes parurent.
>
> L'un venait de la Bastille, l'autre du Jardin des Plantes. Le plus grand, vêtu de toile, marchait le chapeau en arrière, le gilet déboutonné et sa cravate à la main. Le plus petit, dont le corps disparaissait dans une redingote marron, baissait la tête sous une casquette à visière pointue.
>
> Quand ils furent arrivés au milieu du boulevard, ils s'assirent, à la même minute, sur le même banc.
>
> Pour s'essuyer le front, ils retirèrent leurs coiffures, que chacun posa près de soi; et le petit homme aperçut dans le chapeau de son voisin: Bouvard; pendant que celui-ci distinguait aisément dans la casquette du particulier en redingote le mot: Pécuchet (II, 202).[93]

Though the bathetic ineptness of this beginning is striking enough in itself — a deliberately ridiculous and 'novelistic' way of bringing his two characters together — part of that effect depends on the detailed insistence on what each of the two did, even when they do the same thing. Not only do they sit down at the same moment on the same bench, take off their hats to wipe their faces and reveal their respective names written in their respective hats; we will be told shortly that they have inscribed their names there for the same reason, that they have the same profession, the same age, and a common desire to leave Paris for the country. Against these identities are set differences, since the law of excluded middle seems the basic generative device of the book. As with any pair of individuals, one is the larger and the other the smaller. Moreover, one is dark and the other fair; one has straight and the other curly hair; one respects women and religion, while the other does not.

Even such minor differences count as an explicit invitation to symbolic reading. Confronted with a pair of characters, the reader attempts to divide the world between them, so that every human attribute will belong to one or the other. The model for this procedure is perhaps Don Quioxte and Sancho Panza, who do indubitably represent two markedly different approaches to life. But the power of the assumption that other pairs of characters will function in the same way is really quite amazing, as witness the efforts of critics in recent years to oppose the two tramps of *En Attendant Godot* and make them 'mind' and 'body', 'ego' and 'id', 'optimism' and 'pessimism', etc. But whereas those differences must be deduced from the speech and behaviour of the two characters, Flaubert's text is constructed around the explicit announcement of differences between his two figures. 'L'aspect aimable de Bouvard charma de suite Pécuchet', we are told, almost immediately; whereas, 'L'air sérieux de Pécuchet frappa Bouvard' (II, 202).[94] And this procedure of telling us first about the one, then about the other, is followed even in the most trivial of cases. For their walks in the country 'Pécuchet adopta franchement le bâton de touriste, haut de six pieds, à la longue pointe de fer. Bouvard préférait une canne-parapluie ou parapluie-polybranches' (II, 228).[95] Offering differences, the text invites us to make something of them, but the plethora of distinctions and the insistence with which they are announced might be taken as mocking the recuperative process which readers are assumed to be ready to undertake.

It is especially on the plane of ideas that differences are insisted upon and rendered gratuitous. Collecting shells, 'ils s'élevèrent à des considérations sur l'origine du monde. Bouvard penchait vers le neptunisme; Pécuchet, au contraire, était plutonien' (II, 229). The ease with which such disagreements are stated, as if it were a simple matter of taste, renders them haphazard and unimportant. 'Pécuchet admirait ces idées. Elles faisaient pitié à Bouvard, qui avait lu Augustin Thierry d'abord' (II, 238). 'Bouvard, esprit libéral et coeur sensible, fut constitutionnel, girondin, thermidorien. Pécuchet, bilieux et de tendances autoritaires, se déclara sans culotte et même robespierriste' (II, 239).[96] Such positions, so easily taken up and as easily dropped when they pass on to something else, are offered as characterizing oppositions but seem, by their very presentation, to become neutralized. Their opinions join those of the authors they read in paradigms where all contradict or exclude one another but where choosing one rather than another is an arbitrary enterprise of no avail. And therefore, when in planning the continuation of the text which has come down to us Flaubert proposed to have them give lectures expressing diametrically opposed views, he did not intend this to make them the less inseparable. 'Pécuchet voit l'avenir de l'Humanité en noir', say his notes. 'L'homme moderne est amoindri et devenu une machine.' Whereas, 'Bouvard voit l'avenir de l'Humanité en beau. L'Homme moderne est en progrès' (II, 300–301).[97] But they are still like-minded enough to cherish the same secret desire and eventually to communicate it to one another simultaneously: 'Copier comme autrefois.' It is not that extremes meet; far from it. It is rather that oppositions take one nowhere. The assumption that they should may derive from literary models; it certainly does not, at least to Flaubert's mind, come from the world, in which distinctions are easily adopted but have little consequence.

He tends to think and especially to plan in terms of binary oppositions, but these oppositions are generally neutralized in the actual composition of a novel. The project for a work entitled 'Le Serment des amis' involved two couples: the first, a pair of poets who become one a famous journalist and the other excessively hermetic; the second two republicans who end the one as government minister and the other either on the guillotine or as an office clerk.[98] The original point may well have been that true poets and republicans fail where the false succeed, but one suspects that in the writing heroes and villains would have become as unidentifiable as they are in his other works and that the oppositions of the original plan would have become simply that: oppositions which led no further. As in his other works, readers would have been offered material in the guise of distinctions and contrasts which they might be tempted to process according to the traditional canons of functional oppositions, but the results would have been foolish and artificial.

In respect of characters, then, one may say that Flaubert does not simply fail to use them as reflectors or perceptive devices which create meaning and transmit it to the reader; he fails also to make them repositories of meaning. The functions they serve in other novels, both as subjects of experience and as objects of the reader's experience, are cited and parodied. Readers are defeated not by eccentricity — not by collocations of perceptions or traits which their cultural models do not enable them to hold together within a single coherent character — but by banality. Flaubert's texts display a high degree of organization, but organization which seems to lead nowhere. But that, of course, is a thematic problem.

## E. Thematic Indeterminacy

No novelist, of course, achieves an absence of theme, for the simple reason that disorder is read as signifying disorder and sustained meaninglessness becomes a meaning in its own right. But even with this proviso, if we compare Flaubert with those modern novelists who have declared him their precursor, we find, at the thematic level and elsewhere, differences in degree which ought to qualify as differences in kind. To speak, as Nathalie Sarraute does, of Flaubert's 'books about nothing, almost devoid of subject, rid of characters, plots and all the old accessories', is arrant nonsense when we have the models of Robbe-Grillet and Beckett before us.[99] For one thing, in Flaubert the representational function of language is not troubled. Descriptions are not so modulated as to produce an unreal, phantasmagoric world. We are not so close to objects that they lose all familiarity. Flaubert's language refers to recognizable objects, whatever it may do with them afterwards; so that in the end it is possible to say of one of Flaubert's novels that it signifies, 'this is the world'.

Moreover, Flaubert creates characters. We can discuss the personalities of Emma and Charles, of Frédéric and Deslauriers; and though the psychological material in the later works does become remarkably thin, we are still very far from the empty voice of Beckett's *Comment c'est* or the shifting and confused figures of Sollers' *Le Parc, Drame,* and *Nombres.* Flaubert does not confuse or conflate characters; we know who was involved in any given incident; and even when we are not offered rich psychological portraits, the individuals who figure in the story are named and distinguished.

Finally, and most important because it forms the armature of the 'readable' and intelligible novel, there is plot. By comparison with Balzac and Dickens, Flaubert's novels may contain few events, but their sequence is remarkably clear. Nerval's *Sylvie,* published four years before *Madame Bovary,* was much more radical than anything of Flaubert's in the obstacles it posed to a reconstruction of the plot. The movements back and forth between memory and event or the shifts in tense which do not follow shifts in chronology were certainly techniques available to Flaubert had he wished in *Madame Bovary* to confuse the actual, the imagined, and the remembered. Suppression of the sentences that introduce and label Emma's reveries would have been an easy way of bringing uncertainty into plot, had he wished to undermine the novel in this way.

The ease with which one isolates Flaubert's plots places him firmly within a traditionalist camp and gives each novel a basic thematic unity. For theme, at the most rudimentary level, is an interpretation of the plot's movement from A to B. Given an initial situation and a final situation, theme is a generalized statement of the change which takes one from the former to the latter. We should be hard put, in these terms, to name the theme of *Finnegans Wake* or of Robbe-Grillet's *Les Gommes,* but we can certainly state the themes of Flaubert's major works: *Madame Bovary* is about the frustration of dreams, about the failure of Emma's attempt to find a world ordered to her expectations; *Salammbô* is about the consequences of an attempt to understand the sacred and its relation to the secular; *L'Education sentimentale* is a *Bildungsroman* gone sour, which shows how feeble pursuit encounters not systematic rebuff but an indifference of the world which prevents even tragedy; *La Tentation de Saint Antoine* is about the difficulty of resisting not ordinary temptations but those of stupidity and pantheistic reverie; *Bouvard et Pécuchet* displays the failure of an attempt to master the universe through the mediations of human knowledge. Even if one quarrels with the details of these formulations one can, no doubt, propose alternative statements of theme at roughly this level of generality.

But if there can be no question, in Flaubert's case, of a successful attempt to write 'books about nothing, almost devoid of subject', when one attempts to explore these themes in greater detail one encounters a curious indeterminacy: as if Flaubert had set out to frustrate, by the construction of the novels, the working out of those themes which are explicitly posed and carried by the general movement of the plot. Attention is deflected from the problems which the novels raise and we find ourselves drawn into a puzzling inconclusiveness as soon as we try to take them seriously as thematic statements.

*Salammbô* is a possible exception — the novel which can most plausibly be read as offering a positive conclusion — and it will therefore be discussed in the last chapter where its conclusions are most relevant. But we may briefly examine the problem in the cases of *La Tentation de Saint Antoine* and *Bouvard et Pécuchet* before discussing in greater detail Flaubert's best known works: *Madame Bovary* and *L'Education sentimentale*.

*La Tentation de Saint Antoine* offers the curious spectacle of a book about temptation where it is uncertain whether temptation has been resisted and why many of the apparitions which pass before the Saint should count as temptations. The attractions of wine, women, wealth and knowledge are easily understood, but by the time we reach the catalogues of gods and heresies and the processions of monsters it is no longer clear why the Saint is being tempted or what he is resisting.

There are themes aplenty in the book, of course. Brombert lists as major preoccupations 'Solitude as suffering or joyful redemption; Knowledge as Promethean hope or self-inflicted curse; Time as dynamic force or as principle of disintegration; Nature experienced in hostility or in mystic communion.'[100] But this list indicates something of the thematic dispersal; for in general temptation poses the alternative of accepting or rejecting things which are, simultaneously, attractive and repellent, while Brombert's list implies an alternation between positive and negative themes. Insofar as it contains these themes, the work pulls away from the thematic concentration that the situation of temptation implies. We do not know what Antoine is trying to resist, nor what is at stake in his resistance. His more illustrious predecessor, Faust, is subjected to temptations whose content is dramatically pertinent; but the alternatives for Antoine are not Heaven and Hell — there seems little concern about the state and destination of his soul — nor even two states of mind, so sketchily is his psychology indicated.

We cannot even be sure whether his final desire, 'to become matter', represents triumph or defeat. The conclusion, Brombert admits, 'is one of the most difficult passages in all Flaubert', on which 'hinges the entire meaning of the book.'[101] One might say that this indicates what a sorry thing 'the entire meaning of the book' is, for the hinge is exceedingly creaky. It is not merely that we have two interpretations to choose between: destruction and disintegration of the self in a triumph of infernal materialism or mystical communion with God's universe. It is rather that we construct these alternatives only because we assume that the book is in fact organized as a temptation and that therefore there must be a conclusion to these trials. As soon as we attempt to go beyond the general thematic statement that stupidity and pantheistic reverie have their attractions, we find ourselves embroiled in difficulties. To say, by way of solution, that Flaubert shows resisting and yielding to temptation to be, in the final analysis, indistinguishable is to negate the structural device of the plot which focused attention on this point and forced this particular solution. Thematic indeterminacy could scarcely be clearer — and its forms more obscure — than in this paradoxical result, which will play a major role in the later discussion of stupidity.

*Bouvard et Pécuchet*, that analogous compendium and 'modern parody of *La Tentation*', as Thibaudet called it, poses problems because the theme suggested by its subtitle, 'Du Défaut de méthode dans les sciences' (viii, 336), has seemed insufficient. Surely such energy cannot have been expended, the argument might run, merely to show the unhappy consequences of disorderly self-instruction. On the other hand, if the book attacks culture itself why are its heroes such feeble representatives of human knowledge? 'What is the meaning of this work?' asks Brombert. 'Is it a facetious critique of two inept individuals, a sad commentary on false values, or a more general diagnosis of

137

our sick civilization? Nothing is in fact more elusive than the spirit which animates this strangely repelling and alluring text.'[102]

The text seems untroubled by this problem, occupied as it is with the particularities of its heroes' adventures. We follow their hopes and failures in various realms and, if we would identify the causes of failure, must fasten at times on their own incompetence and incomprehension, at others on the ignorance and contradictory precepts of the best authorities, and at still others on what seems to be a malignant nature that delights to frustrate their attempts to control it. The curious thing, however, is not the diversity itself but the fact that in a book whose theme presumably depends on our decisions about the causes of failure there should be so little attempt to discriminate. When we move beyond the general theme of the failure to master the world through human knowledge and ask the obvious thematic question, 'Why does their attempt fail?', we find that the text manifests a firm disinterest in the question of blame. It does not secrete norms or offer alternatives which might help us to locate responsibility. And consequently, the book becomes, as Flaubert had hoped it might, cause for suspicion and uncertainty: Is the reader being mocked? Are we not in our attempts to discover a unifying and generalizable theme, playing right into the author's hand and showing ourselves as stupid as his 'two idiots' and as stupid as the man who retraced all their steps, read all that they read, in order to write the book? What could reveal more acutely the bathos of our own intelligence than our attempt to make these 'two woodlice' stand for humanity? As they stand, so do we: condemned by our interpretive procedures.

Whereas *Bouvard et Pécuchet*, beneath its general theme of failure, flaunts a randomness of sequence and content, *Madame Bovary* is Flaubert's most 'composed' novel. It is, reports Percy Lubbock, 'a well-made book, — so we have always been told and so we find it to be, pulling it to pieces and putting it together again.'[103] So doing, he finds that the subject — designated by the combination of the title and the subtitle 'Moeurs de province' — 'stands firm and clear' ('the history of a woman like her in just such a world as hers') and that the scenes of the novel are all devoted to the development of this drama, 'distributed and rendered with rare skill', each arising from the one before and steadily directed towards the next.[104]

By comparison with Flaubert's other books *Madame Bovary* certainly deserves this accolade, and since praise of the novel is so closely linked to that reputation it provides something of a test case for showing that compositional skill does not necessarily lead to clarity of purpose but may produce dislocation and frustration of presumptive thematic unity: that the flaw of the book lies precisely in the aspect of its theme which is firmest and most unambiguous, while its greatness derives from those areas of maximum indeterminacy, if not irrelevance.

At the most general level of plot and theme *Madame Bovary* fits very nicely Lukács's definition of the novel as a form based on a *Grunddissonanz*, a fundamental alienation of the hero who finds that the meanings he supposes immanent in the world refuse to penetrate empirical life.[105] The successive episodes of the book record Emma's failure to find a life which accords with her expectations and show how the form of each failure leads to hopes which animate and direct her next attempt at self-fulfilment. To escape life on the farm with her father is to move to a village with a husband; boredom with one village leads to another village; exasperation with Charles makes her desire a more ardent and romantic lover; jilted by Rodolphe, the professional seducer, she seeks to dominate the more innocent and tractable Léon; and her death merely crowns a series of failures. In a world too small for her desires, one is tempted to say, she is fated to disappointment and self-destruction.

This general structure of aspiration and disappointment suggests two major themes which one would expect the novel to illustrate and examine in some detail: that of the heroine's special nature which distinguishes her from others and makes her unable to live, and that of the particular fate which limits her freedom. Insofar as plot, that is to say, is made directly relevant to theme and does not merely offer a development on which thematic explorations might be hung, one would expect, first of all, a rich and perceptive examination of what sets Emma off from other characters and how this distance is to be valued, and secondly, a working out of the causes of failure so that we might gain some sense of what human limitations the novel is exposing, of what is possible and impossible, of how far our freedom extends and where blame is to be laid.

Such expectations are not wrong — indeed, the effect of the novel depends on them — but they are not fulfilled. First of all, though Emma herself is not an ambiguous character, ambiguity arises precisely on the count where clarity is most desired: the value to be attached to her alienation. She is clearly not the Romantic heroine endowed with excessive sensitivity and a vision of the world whose rightness condemns the experience which life offers. She is a foolish woman, but is she foolish woman made tragic heroine or tragic heroine revealed as foolish woman? Her floating anxiety which leads both to passivity and to bursts of activity is not in itself ennobling, though it may be tragic. Nor, on the other hand, do her rebuffs and disappointments illustrate in any convincing way the advantages of an accommodation with reality or convey to the reader that sense of the charms of institutions and of the attractions of everyday life which a recent theorist sees as realism's stock in trade.[106] Emma's dreams of lagoons and palm trees, Swiss chalets and Scottish cottages, of elegant balls and dashing lords, of moonlit rides or promenades beside a waterfall, are not the noble visions of the purer soul; but we are made very uncertain as to how to value them.

On the one hand, Flaubert's *style indirect libre* gives a modicum of objectivity to her dissatisfaction:

> Charles était là. Il avait sa casquette enfoncée sur ses sourcils, et ses deux grosses lèvres tremblotaient, ce qui ajoutait à son visage quelque chose de stupide; son dos même, son dos tranquille était irritant à voir, et elle y trouvait étalée sur la redingote toute la platitude du personnage (I, 6o8).[107]

The final conjunction, implying the dependence of what precedes on a parallel but suppressed verb like *elle remarquait que*, makes this Emma's vision, but the systematic presentation of scenes in this way suggests a measure of truth. Descriptions in other narrative modes are also designed to make the reader feel that boredom and exacerbation are justifiable reactions to a world that can be compassed by such sentences:

> Mais c'était surtout aux heures des repas qu'elle n'en pouvait plus . . . toute l'amertume de l'existence lui semblait servie sur son assiette, et, à la fumée du bouilli, il montait du fond de son âme comme d'autres bouffées d'affadissement. Charles était long à manger; elle grignotait quelques noisettes, ou bien, appuyée du coude, s'amusait, avec la pointe de son couteau, à faire des raies sur la toile cirée (I, 596).[108]

Moreover, the intensity and evocatory force of the writing at moments of exaltation gives a concrete exhilaration to Emma's modes of escape. Sometimes it is a matter of reverie — dreams of 'un pays nouveau' full of fruits and flowers, guitars and fountains (I, 640–41) — while at others it is empirical surroundings that are imbued with an emotional charge. Rodolphe and Emma have just made love for the first time:

Les ombres du soir descendaient; le soleil horizontal, passant entre les branches, lui éblouissait les yeux. Çà et là, tout autour d'elle, dans les feuilles ou par terre, des taches lumineuses tremblaient, comme si des colibris, en volant, eussent éparpillé leurs plumes. Le silence était partout; quelque chose de doux semblait sortir des arbres; elle sentait son coeur, dont les battements recommençaient, et le sang circuler dans sa chair comme un fleuve de lait. Alors, elle entendit tout au loin, au delà du bois, sur les autres collines, un cri vague et prolongé, une voix qui se traînait, et elle l'écoutait silencieusement, se mêlant comme une musique aux dernières vibrations de ses nerfs émus (I, 629).[109]

The ironic possibilities of such passages are not always exploited; here there is little to undermine the vision or to suggest that such moments are not worth having.

Yet on the other hand, while the reader is made to feel the attractions of Emma's vision he is made to see how easily it becomes trivial, vulgar, insubstantial. 'I have a lover! a lover!' she repeats to herself after this scene with Rodolphe, delighting as much in the new image of herself as in the experience. The very concreteness of her desires — she dreams of a lover dressed in a black velvet suit and lace cuffs, of living in a little flat-roofed cottage, in the shade of a palm tree, by a lagoon — makes Emma a more foolish figure, for we know that the realization of these images would not bring happiness. She is destroyed, Leo Bersani writes, 'not only by the unresponsiveness of her world, but also by *our* sense of how easily her superiority can be reduced to the mediocrity of her antagonists.'[110] Irony reduces the particular forms of her desire to clichéd illusions and denies them the status of valuable alternatives to a mediocre world.

Thus the conflict does not set imagination against reality and teach us which aspects of an attempt to transcend reality are valuable. That is what the general thematic structure would lead us to expect, but the novel displaces this conflict from its central position and sets in its place the contrast between aspirations and the triviality of their manifestations. Thus we are no longer directly concerned with where Emma went wrong or with the special qualities of her sensibility but with the general problem of desire and its manifestations, to which attention is deflected by the refusal to define Emma's particular relationship with the world. The case of 'a woman like her in just such a world as hers' is not defined in ways which make it a sustaining object of interest.

The conflict within desire itself is not worked out in formulaic detail, but it would certainly be possible to argue that its richness is the source of the novel's greatness. If we ask what one should do or how one should live we shall tire of staying for an answer, but the novel enables us at least to give form to the problem and produce two stages of some complexity.

First of all, to express desire by an image of possible fulfilment is to make it vulnerable, potentially trivial. The language in which desires take form is a common currency which makes them common. When dreams are cast in forms which could be realized, they can be pricked and deflated by irony; but nothing can be worthy if it cannot withstand the accusation oj triviality. And hence a testing irony which undermines the images that we project upon experience is necessary to the preservation of value. But its effect is to empty desire of its empirical content, which it puts in another light, and to allow it to subsist either as a negation of the actual or as pure aspiration. Purified desire is an empty form whose value is threatened by any realization, whether that realization be the meanings we attempt to read in our experience or the experience we postulate to fit the meanings.

But secondly, the novel in which these problems are explored is itself an ordering and interpreting fiction: an indubitable case of desire. To write a novel which shows that life is not like a novel is an enterprise fraught with perils, but insofar as it can be done it suggests that some images, some posited orders, do have the power to sustain themselves and are not destroyed by irony. One cannot say that they are sustained at the cost of severance from the world, since manifestly the reader must connect them with the world to give them what significance they have. The novel accomplishes some kind of manifestation of desire, through a resolutely self-conscious artifice, whose analogues we must discover and produce. *Madame Bovary* can do no more than adumbrate the problem of the relationship between desire and fictions, for the reader must attempt to integrate in his exploration the indeterminacy of his situation as a reader of novels. The problem remains obscure, but its richness is responsible for one's sense that this is more than a tale of provincial adultery.

The plot also implies an exploration of freedom and fatality. If anything is to be learned from Emma's experience we require some sense of what went wrong, which decisions, if any, were crucial, and what alternatives might have been possible. But these problems receive very little attention. There do not seem to be crucial junctures at which Emma made the wrong decision, or at least any single decision might have been reversed without radically altering the course of her life. Yet Charles' judgment that 'C'est la faute de la fatalité' ('It's the fault of Fate') (I, 692) is very much a cliché, brought out too easily, by one to whom we are not accustomed to grant profundity of mind, for us to accept it as the truth of the novel. Indeed, the function of Charles' pronouncement seems that of making explicit a possible reaction of the reader's and exposing it to the irony that it deserves. Were we tempted to think of Emma's as a tragic fate, we are made to question our reactions by the fact that Charles shares them. And thus the novel poses at least an initial resistance to the easy step of perceiving in every failure the hand of fate.

This final scene between Rodolphe and Charles is one of Flaubert's most effective ironies,

> when the husband acknowledges as a kind of death sentence the fatality which the lover had glibly used as a convenient cliché of love. Even the traditional resolution which man finds in the all-forgiving acceptance of his destiny is sacrificed to the still inexorable demands of Flaubert's realism, and reduced to the level of Charles' mediocre intelligence and Rodolphe's cheap sensitivity.[111]

And thus the reader is prevented, if he wishes to retain his self-respect, from accepting without some kind of deepening modification either Charles' pronouncement or Rodolphe's assumption that Emma's fate was his own doing. Yet we have, as it were, no place to stand in order to hammer the cliché into truth. Other figures in the book do not suggest alternative ways of living or provide norms in terms of which Emma's deviance can be characterized.

Part of the problem is the very absence of drama. If Emma's life were more coherent, with a linear development leading to a peripeteia, if it had a strategy whose failure led directly to her death, then the tragedy would be more obvious and one's sense of an irrevocable fate easier to substantiate. But Emma failed to die when disappointed in love; her vision of God sending angels with wings of fire to bear her up to the heavens or of a withdrawal to a convent where she might live as love's martyr would both have provided satisfactory dramatic closes. But she survives for another affair, and the financial problems that lead to her suicide are only indirectly related to her romantic aspirations. Part of her tragedy is her life's lack of tragic coherence, and the reader's sense of an oppressive tragic destiny comes more from Flaubert's style than from any other form of necessity. One knows Emma's fate, not because one is given to understand that characters like her in such a situation will necessarily meet a tragic end, but because one gains as one reads a knowledge of how the book will treat her aspirations and activities. Emma is fated to be destroyed by the irony of Flaubert's prose.

Such a statement may seem meretricious, a phrase whose air of significance depends on a category mistake. But in fact it rectifies the more pervasive category mistake on which the reading of novels is based: the pretence that language is a medium only and must not be confused with the 'world' that is imitated. Most novels may well rely on such a distinction, but there are others where the fact that they are language and not a series of people and events is important. This is particularly true of *Madame Bovary*, where the discrepancy between language and experience is a major theme and where the tragedy is in some measure that of language itself, unable to make its own unreality suffice, able to sustain itself only as a testing of illusion. And it is not difficult to grasp, it would seem to me, that for the reader there is a greater necessity at work at the level of language than at that of character and plot. If we think of Emma as a person outside of a novel it is not hard to imagine a variety of endings: despair and resignation or escape with a lover more adventurous than Rodolphe. What she is as a character does not produce an inescapable destiny; or, at least, had Flaubert wished to make her life more of an obvious unity he could quite easily have presented her differently and made clear the basis of her fate. He chose indeterminacy at that level because the concept of destiny is precisely one of those problematic novelistic constructs with which we try to structure our lives and because the lack of a destiny is the modern form of the tragic.

Dislocated at one level, destiny is reinstated at another. As we become acclimatized to Flaubert's prose we gain a sense of what is fated to happen: that intensity of aspiration will be given its due but that the particular forms of illusion and aspiration will be cited as phrases and forced to pass through the crucible of irony, which Emma cannot survive. It is no doubt in these terms of style as fatality that one should understand Thorlby's brilliant but somewhat obscure comment, that for Flaubert the problem of freedom and necessity was primarily aesthetic rather than moral and that

> fatality becomes, as a result, the reverse aspect, not so much of any real liberty, as of illusion; while the freedom of the soul is weighed, not so much against any really significant fate, as against the damning effects of realism. Where illusion is strongest, as with Emma and Charles, the force of fatality is most intense; where it is weakest, as with Rodolphe and Lheureux who have few illusions, it has little power to harm; with Homais and Bournisien it is merely playful. It is here that Flaubert's style introduces into what is perhaps the basic form of narrative, the conflict between the hero and his fate, that ambiguous kind of aesthetic contrast which is the distinctive feature of his work.[112]

By turning away from the theme which the plot structure would lead one to expect and making style the source of fatality, Flaubert poses the problem of the relationship between meaning and experience in a particularly complex way, suggesting that the distinction between freedom and necessity may well be a false problem, or at least one with which we are ill-equipped to deal. We cannot simply label Emma as a certain kind of person who must meet a prescribed end but are forced to consider the status of such connections and examine whether the kinds of meanings we derive from a sense of destiny are not produced rather than given: produced by the activity of reading our lives and those of others as novels.

But there is one island of certainty which has so far been neglected — one theme not subjected to irony but stated with as much explicitness as Flaubert allows himself. And it is precisely here that one encounters *Madame Bovary*'s greatest flaw. If there is anything that justifies our finding the novel limited and tendentious it is the seriousness with which Emma's corruption is attributed to novels and romances. If this is an attempt to diagnose Emma's condition, to characterize her alienation, and to explain her fate, it is a singularly feeble one. It limits her case and makes the novel the story of the world's failure to be a romantic novel, which is neither a new nor demanding theme. It is as if Flaubert had allowed a cliché to occupy the centre stage without holding it in the spotlight and subjecting it to any of the critical scrutiny or ironic experimentation which apply in other cases. If Homais had refused to let his daughters Irma and Athalie read novels on the grounds that they would then long for lovers and commit adultery, his speech would no doubt have been treated with some irony, as a sentiment belonging in the *Dictionnaire des idées reçues*; and the reader trained by Flaubert to think in this way can scarcely be blamed if he smile at the master's own lack of self-consciousness.

The theme was, of course, an old one, but the tradition already contained rather more thoughtful and sceptical explorations of it. In *Don Quixote*, though novels corrupt they also create the possibility of a new reality and the Don's life of illusions can both exercise power over others, making them fit in with it, and become a self-sufficient form, as in Part II where he can read and judge the story of his adventures. Rousseau, in the preface to *La Nouvelle Héloïse*, argued in more absolute terms that 'never has a chaste girl read novels' and that any girl who, despite the title and its warning, dared read a single page was 'une fille perdue'. But he did go on to say, primarily in self-defence, to be sure, but also in a rudimentary attempt at analysis, that 'she should not impute her fall to this book, for the harm was already done', and the proof of her prior corruption was her desire to read a love story.

There was also, of course, the possibility of resisting the lure of novels: we are told that Nerval's Sylvie read *La Nouvelle*

*Héloïse* and trembled at the warning in the preface, but continued and came through unscathed ('Cependant, j'ai passé outre, me fiant sur ma raison'). In short, there was no reason for Flaubert to accept in so unquestioning a way the theory of the corrupting novel; if it were to be made a central theme it might at least have been examined in a way which would enable us to discern the limits of its validity. As it is, those who are fond of the book tend to divert their gaze from its one explicit theme, which would so reduce its scope if granted a central place, and explore rather the areas of thematic indeterminacy where more important themes are adumbrated, deflected, turned over, questioned.

*L'Education sentimentale* has no unexamined certainty, no central flaw of this kind. It is also less obviously composed than *Madame Bovary*: lacking the restrictions of character and place and the dramatic ironies which knit together the episodes of *Madame Bovary*. A puzzling and exasperating masterpiece, it is the most striking, most challenging example of thematic indeterminacy. The book is boring because Frédéric is the principal character, wrote Faguet, who would have agreed with Henry James in finding him too weak a vessel to command our attention, yet too privileged to command our sympathy. But it is not merely Frédéric's mediocrity that exasperates the reader; it is rather the obstacle this mediocrity poses to intelligibility. For if Frédéric's mediocrity explains his failure it does so in a way that is peculiarly uninteresting and that closes rather than opens thematic perspectives.

The title tells us that it is a *Bildungsroman*, a story of the youthful hero's contact with the world and education in life and love. The conventions of the genre lead us to expect an opposition between hero and world which will make the plot an intelligible history of resistance and accommodation. Illusions will be destroyed; the world will teach him something, whether or not he choose to accept its lessons; and the conclusion, as the climax of an encounter with the world, will structure that encounter in ways that give it meaning. What happens to the hero will make clear what was learned or not learned, what price must be paid for social integration and whether it is too high.

There is, of course, little learning or social adjustment in *L'Education sentimentale*, but that in itself does not produce indeterminacy. As the story of failure, 'l'histoire morale des hommes de ma génération' (v, 158) who wasted whatever energies they had, it focuses attention on the problem of failure and enjoins us to enquire why dreams have come to nought and whether other types of engagement with the world might have been possible. Frédéric and his friend Deslauriers are presented as a contrasting pair, the one dreaming of love, the other of power. Like René and Rastignac, two models which divide the spectrum of passion and aspiration, they encompass the possible approaches to life of ambitious youth; and one might expect this opposition to produce some meaning. But when both protagonists fail what are we to say? How are we to make sense of this failure?

That is, of course, a question which Frédéric and Deslauriers ask themselves in the last chapter, when they are brought together once more 'par la fatalité de leur nature qui les faisait toujours se rejoindre et s'aimer' (II, 161).[113] That opening sentence might suggest that their lives can be explained only by this kind of tautology: they have come together because their nature fated them always to come together. And indeed we seem scarcely able to break out of that unsatisfying mode. There is nothing approaching analysis. Deslaurier's life is quickly summed up:

> il s'était compromis dans sa préfecture par des excès de zèle gouvernemental. On l'avait destitué. Il avait été, ensuite, chef de colonisation en Algérie, secrétaire d'un pacha, gérant d'un journal, courtier d'annonces, pour être finalement employé au contentieux dans une compagnie industrielle (II, 161).[114]

It is not obvious that such a life is necessarily a failure; one could imagine a similar catalogue being cited to show the interest and variety of one's experiences. It is rather the randomness, the lack of connection, the suppression of the causes which governed the movement from one post to another, which make it an instance of disintegration. The fates of their friends are recounted in one-sentence paragraphs, where once again the problem of distinguishing between success and failure is given no attention. Presumably Martinon, a senator, and Hussonnet, who rules the theatre and the press, must be deemed fortunate, but the other cases are less clear, and it is difficult to construct oppositions from which one might draw conclusions about what is, after all, the ostensible theme of the book.

When they themselves try to draw conclusions from their own cases they make but feeble progress:

> Et ils résumèrent leur vie.
> Ils l'avaient manquée tous les deux, celui qui avait rêvé l'amour, celui qui avait rêvé le pouvoir. Quelle en était la raison?
> — C'est peut-être le défaut de ligne droite, dit Frédéric.
> — Pour toi, cela se peut. Moi, au contraire, j'ai péché par excès de rectitude, sans tenir compte de mille choses secondaires, plus fortes que tout. J'avais trop de logique, et toi de sentiment (II, 162).[115]

Neither explanation stands up very well. There is little evidence for Deslauriers' excess of logic, and in one sense Frédéric's problem has been his reluctance to quit the straight line of devotion to Madame Arnoux. And in any case, there is abdication before 'a thousand minor factors which were all-important'. We are confronted with phrases which might well figure in the *Dictionnaire des idées reçues*, presented as supposed self-scrutiny. 'Puis, ils accusèrent le hasard, les circonstances, l'époque où ils étaient nés.' This one-sentence paragraph, isolated in all its banality, can scarcely advance our under-standing. At the level at which these three phrases are synonymous, or at least interchangeable, they are too vague to count as explanations. There is no attempt to adjudicate between fate and error as possible causes; statements of either position are displayed as stupidities. To choose among such alternatives is as futile as to live them. Not only have Frédéric and Deslauriers learned nothing in this *Bildungsroman*, but the reader can learn little from their example, and that is perhaps the most profound tragedy: that egregious failure brings no compensatory understanding.

'*L'Education*', writes Thibaudet, 'was immediately and is still today criticized for taking part itself, as a work of art, in this wastage, this emptiness, this bankruptcy.'[116] That is certainly the reproach Lukács offers in arguing that Balzac in *Illusions perdues* 'not only created the novel of disillusionment but also exhausted the highest possibilities of this type of novel.'[117] A comparison of the two, however, will show, not that Lukács is necessarily wrong, but that the very qualities which he praises in *Illusions perdues* make it less radical, less disillusioning, than *L'Education sentimentale*.

Balzac's superiority, in Lukács' view, derives from his intelligibility:

> The true necessity in *Illusions perdues* is that Lucien must perish in Paris. Every step, every phase in the rise and decline of his fortunes provide ever more profound social and psychological links in this chain of necessity. The novel is so conceived that every incident is a step towards the same end. . .[118]

Moreover, Balzac grasps clearly the structure of 'objective reality' — that is, a level at which things are informed with their social and historical significance — and does not remain content with 'immediate experience'. He achieves, in the words of his character D'Arthez, 'the greatest possible intensification of the content, the social and human essence of a situation'.[119]

It is certainly true that Balzac is much more of an analyst than Flaubert, more concerned with the reconstruction and statement of causal chains. And it is precisely this analytical bent which makes the world of his novels so much less subject to uncertainty. Society has its laws, which the analyst and the superior individual can understand; to enter society is to accept these laws as the rules of the game, and 'to violate these secret laws is to be dominated by the social system rather than dominate it . . . One is dealing here with the cogs of a machine of gold and iron.'[120] A machine may be cruel but it is comprehensible, and that is why reading Balzac — even the novels of failure — is always an exhilarating experience. A drama of comprehension and mastery is being played out. This is scarcely true of Flaubert, whose sense of fate includes no assumption of order, whose novels conceal or undermine the causal connections which might lead to the formulation of laws. We know how to account for Lucien's failure; Balzac shows us where he failed to understand and where he transgressed the secret laws of the society and by rendering his suicide the effect of definite causes thereby mitigates its horror. The world may be Manichean, may be governed by a diabolical order, but that it is orderly, that one can master it if one studies it properly and acts with sufficient energy, there can be little doubt.

This world is rather less demoralizing than Flaubert's, which refuses to be composed, for while it leaves open the question of whether one should come to terms with society, it is quite clear about how it could be done. *L'Education sentimentale*, on the other hand, denies us the consolation of understanding failure and thereby offers no opportunity to overcome the disorder of an indifferent world where chance and fate are difficult to distinguish. Flaubert's world is a system not in the Balzacian sense — it is not governed by laws which determine how one thing follows another in what one might call syntagmatic sequences. Its system is rather that of an immense paradigm in which everything is equivalent and could replace anything else in the syntagma of chance. It is a more disturbing world because the novel forces the reader to attempt to discover a pattern in the lives of characters and their relations with society and proposes more obstacles than assistance to that process.

But this dicussion has so far neglected the theme which for Frédéric gave order and purpose to his life during most of its course: his experience of sentiment. The concluding sentence of the book, 'c'est là ce que nous avons eu de meilleur', affirms a continuity with the past, a nostalgia for lost innocence, but also nostalgia for a time when love could still propose itself as a project. It suggests, therefore, while carrying in its crystallization around the brothel a kind of disarming self-parody, that Frédéric's romantic aspirations have been a positive good, the only unifying force in his life. But if we are to accept that reading, we must decide what to do with all the time spent with Rosanette: has his relation with her been an ancillary escapade, an opportunity for sexual experience which, in best Victorian fashion, permitted him to cherish, in his precise and delicate way, a purer love for Madame Arnoux without tainting the dream by abortive attempts at action; or is it, as numerous images and descriptions, including this final image of la Turque's brothel, would suggest, a fallen version of the same love? If the former, then the illusion of love as project can be preserved as a value in Frédéric's existence, but at the cost of dividing his life into one series which pursues this project and another which digresses from it. If the latter, then an abstract unity is preserved — Frédéric has always been seeking love in its various guises — but that love, because of the frequency with which it took on tawdry forms, seems weakened as a source of value. Either way, it is difficult to make love both the determinant of his life and a value which gives it meaning.

The problem here is more serious than in *Madame Bovary*. Indeed, it is as though the relatively facile satire of Emma's attempts to fulfill her desires were but preparation for the more skilful presentation, in this work, of the gap between image and action. Emma's desires are admirable only in principle, when purified by an abstracting critical discourse. She, we can say, at least desires something better; but it is at that level only, as formal aspirations, that we can preserve their value. Their concrete figurations both in daydreams and in action are inevitably found wanting and read as ironic reflections on her own mediocrity. But Frédéric, it might seem, is allowed to preserve an ideal intact. The deflation of his love in his affair with Rosanette can be separated from the inflation of it in the vision of Madame Arnoux. As the process of Frédéric's life leads him back and forth between these two poles, we expect to read in this alternation the story of his sentimental education, which will be nothing other than the oft-told tale of the discrepancies between ideals and reality.

But if that is what the book leads us to expect, it goes far beyond those expectations in the penultimate chapter, when Frédéric and Madame Arnoux meet for the last time. More complex than anything in *Madame Bovary*, this scene takes our expectations about possible alternatives and turns them back against us by accomplishing what we, in our sophistication, might have believed impossible.

Critics, who divest themselves of their assumptions less easily than other readers since their assumptions are what enable them to produce discourse of their own, testify by more than a majority to the theoretical impossibility of this scene. Flaubert must be either deflating, with consummate irony, the illusions of the characters and revealing their supposed love as false posturing or he must be defending, in a deeply touching scene, the ideal nature of this transcending love.[121]

Such are the expected alternatives, but in this case they are false. It would be a strange reader indeed who failed to find the episode moving or who, when he reflected on it, failed to note the romantic clichés, the explicit insincerity, the

occasional ridiculous detail. Madame Arnoux begins with a
'C'est lui! C'est donc lui!' (II, 160): not 'It's you, Frédéric'
but 'It's he, the character in my romance.' And she offers set-
piece speeches: 'Cependant, elle lui dit: "Quelquefois, vos
paroles me reviennent comme un écho lointain, comme le son
d'une cloche apporté par le vent; et il me semble que vous
êtes là, quand je lis des passages d'amour dans les livres"'
(II, 160).[122] Frédéric, on his part, not only lies about the
portrait of Rosanette; he is shocked when he sees her white
hair and 'pour lui cacher cette déception, il se posa par
terre à ses genoux, et, prenant ses mains, se mit à lui
dire des tendresses.' There follows a catalogue of extravagant
and clichéd praise — in the past tense — and eventually,
Frédéric, 'se grisant par ses paroles, arrivait à croire ce qu'il
disait.' So much so that, when he catches sight of the toe of her
boot 'il lui dit, presque défaillant: "La vue de votre pied me
trouble"', which sends Madame Arnoux into predictable
ecstasies: 'Aucune n'a jamais été aimée comme moi!' (II,
161).[123] He is more sincere when, suspecting that she has come
to offer herself to him, he feels both lust and repulsion: 'Une
autre crainte l'arrêta, celle d'en avoir dégoût plus tard.
D'ailleurs, quel embarras ce serait! — et tout à la fois par
prudence et pour ne pas dégrader son idéal, il tourna sur ses
talons et se mit à faire une cigarette.'[124] She, on her part, tells
him that in Brittany she goes from time to time to the top of a
hill to sit on a bench, 'which I have called "Frédéric bench"'
(le banc Frédéric) and, at the last moment, after kissing him
chastely on the forehead: 'But she seemed to be looking for
something, and asked him for scissors', with which she cuts him
a large lock of white hair.

One cannot repress all that; but one must not repress either,
in a hasty reaching for conclusions, the fact that it is a moving
scene. Flaubert appears to have transcended the opposition
between the ideal and its hopelessly inferior manifestations.
Their love is both beautiful and very false; beautiful, not
despite its falsity but because of the falsity inherent in it. There
is a very strong sense of artifice in the passage; they are taking
their cues from one another, reproducing a romantic dialogue.

   . . . elle voulut savoir s'il se marierait.
    Il jura que non.
   — Bien sûr? Pourquoi?

— A cause de vous, dit Frédéric en la serrant dans ses bras (II, 161).[125]

That they should dare do this, that they should speak thus rather than anticipate the replies and remain silent, indicates an enviable lack of self-consciousness, a will to give love reality at the linguistic level. 'Ils se racontèrent leurs anciens jours', putting them into language, casting their lives into the moulds of all those clichés a sentimental literature affords them. They deliberately, as Peter Cortland says, utter phrases that they know the other person will treasure in years of solitude; 'they want to tell each other that they still respect the conventions of their generation, and will unto death play the parts of the faithful lover and the noble much-beset wife-of-another-man.'[126]

They offer fictions and by the excessive conventionality of their offerings pay homage to love as something to be preserved in language. 'Le banc Frédéric' may be ridiculous, but the very arbitrariness of it, the belief that by naming objects in this way one can produce value, confers a certain dignity on this activity. It has so many hurdles to get over, one might say, the potential ironies which threaten it are so obvious, that to proceed thus bespeaks an innocence which one cannot but respect. There is a sublimity in the hope that life will be reorganized and made meaningful by that kind of naming. And similarly, in Madame Arnoux's decision to leave at a quarter past eleven, which structures their encounter in a wholly arbitrary way, one gains a sense of the efficacy of deliberate fictions. We are very close here to Flaubert's concept of the sacred, an arbitrary conferral of meaning so difficult to distinguish from the purely sentimental.

They sacralize their relationship by negating the present in a little drama of delicate touch. Madame Arnoux, 'après un long silence: "N'importe, nous nous serons bien aimés."' Future anterior, 'we will have loved each other well', structuring their lives from a point in the future when all will be past and this can be said of them. 'Sans nous appartenir, pourtant!' replies Frédéric with an untensed verb which might, as Madame Arnoux thinks, hold suggestions for the present and the future. Love must not be tarnished in that way, and she replies, 'Cela vaut peut-être mieux': it is better this way. But Frédéric, it appears, was thinking in the same way as she;

his untensed verb was meant to refer only to the past and not to trouble the present which must be projected intact onto a future. 'Non! non!' he replies, 'Quel bonheur nous aurions eu.' Past conditional: 'if we had belonged to one another in the past' not, 'if we were to possess one another now or in the future'; and that allows her to agree. Their lives must be organized as fiction by these statements. Since Flaubert will not oblige they must attempt for themselves to organize their lives as a nineteenth-century novel told from the point of view of order.

But if we accept this reading of the penultimate scene we find we have made nonsense of our earlier perceptions and indeed of the explicit contrasts in terms of which the rest of the book appears to be constructed. The opposition between Mme Arnoux and Rosanette, between an ideal love and the tawdry manifestations of love, comes to seem an epiphenomenon. This penultimate scene, which overcomes oppositions and produces a fragile romantic triumph, seems to step outside the line of development adumbrated by earlier scenes. It is not, that is to say, the logical culmination of an experience, which enables us to see what Frédéric learned about love; it is rather an affirmation that while life must be lived and while this will entail disappointment and failure, nevertheless one can, if one proceeds with care, create a purified fiction which remains disconnected from one's experience. Instead of conferring meaning on earlier episodes and pointing to their lesson, it seems to empty the sentimental education, which is the ostensible subject of the book, of the content which it appeared to have. L'Education sentimentale is not only a Bildungsroman without Bildung but one which sets aside its preoccupations as false problems and moves outside of the character's empirical history for the values proposed in its culminating scene.

In many of the juvenilia Flaubert's pursuit of a theme led him to neglect the empirical history of individual protagonists and to cite their activities only as exempla which would reinforce his theme. Drawing back, in later years, from the commitment of such a procedure, he discovered a new source of freedom in his mature solution to the problem of narrative structure: create a story on whose empirical character one insists; present symbolic and thematic elaborations as uncertain and illusory excrescences; allow a history to take place

155

and refuse to structure it according to the apparent demands of its explicit theme. Empty history, that is to say, of any teleology except the very abstract one of a general fatalism in which all things run unsteadily to their dissolution. Retain in the novels all the effects of temporal succession but confront the reader with obstacles which will teach him how very difficult and problematic it is to transform time into history by giving it a meaning or a goal.

This use of time in such a way that it refuses to compose itself into history is no doubt what Lukács perceived in *L'Education sentimentale* when in his early work on the novel he maintained that it was the greatest novel of disillusionment. It alone, he argued, attains the true objectivity of the epic, and time is the instrument of that victory. In most novels meaning is created by characters and destroyed by time, but in *L'Education sentimentale* bits of reality are simply juxtaposed in all their hardness, incoherence, and isolation, and it is time that becomes the 'unifying principle of homogeneity, which grinds down and polishes all the heterogeneous fragments and brings them together in a relationship which is doubtless irrational and inexpressible'[127] but which nonetheless provides, as he goes on to say, the appearance of an organic reality burgeoning on its own.

But time is a very poor substitute for meaning; to make it the unifying factor indicates a strong desire for unity, and to claim, as Lukács does, that time, in the sense of process and development, becomes a source of value seems a case of special pleading. The homogeneity that time produces is the result of levelling, of undermining the reader's attempt to make the history intelligible by giving it a goal that would structure it, and thereby of making, under this formal and all-encompassing aegis, everything equivalent.

> Ecco tutto è simile, e discoprendo,
> Solo il nulla s'accresce.

Nothingness is the result of attempting to read the written world.

# 3
# Values

Mit der Dummheit kämpfen Götter selbst vergebens.

SCHILLER

BÊTISE ET POÉSIE. Il y a des relations subtiles entre ces deux ordres. L'ordre de la bêtise et celui de la poésie.

VALERY[1]

## A. *Stupidity*

At the age of nine, in a letter that one is pleased to regard as prophetic, Gustave discovered his first literary project: 'comme il y a une dame qui vient chez papa et qui nous contes toujours de bêtises je les écrirait' (i, 1).[2] And write them he did, for the rest of his life. His final compilation, the *Dictionnaire des idées reçues*, was not published until after his death, but he began collecting specimens for it early on and in 1850 he already speaks of it as well under way. But even when not working specifically on this project he spent much of his time wading through stupidity in his research for other novels: *Madame Bovary* — 'Je suis dans les *rêves de jeune fille* jusqu'au cou' (ii, 372); *Saint Antoine* — 'Actuellement, je fais parler tous les dieux à l'état d'agonie. Le sous-titre de mon bouquin pourra être: "le Comble de l'insanité"' (vi, 276); *L'Education sentimentale* — 'Rien n'est épuisant comme de creuser la bêtise humaine!' (v, 317); and *Bouvard et Pécuchet* — 'La bêtise de mes deux bonshommes m'envahit' (vii, 189).[3] Writing was always an immersion in stupidity, partly, as he explained, because he wished to attempt 'le comique d'idées' (viii, 26).

But such an explanation barely touches the surface. Stupidity, both as a category of his own thought and as a component of his literary practice, is very much at the centre of Flaubert's world. Chapter 2 has explored the ways in which narrative strategies display varieties of stupidity: descriptions which serve no apparent purpose, devices for isolation and decomposition, characters who are themselves stupid in their perceptions and responses, episodes which refuse to range themselves under ostensible themes. The reader of Flaubert's novels might well agree with his statement that 'We suffer from only one thing, la Bêtise, but it is formidable and universal' (vi, 307). Yet stupidity, though the 'unique objet de son ressentiment', was also very nearly the unique object of his joy. To find a perfect example was, as Henry James said, 'his nearest approach to natural bliss'.[4] What was this ubiquitous stupidity? Why should it be so important? To provide some kind of answer seems incumbent upon anyone pretending to an understanding of his work.

The *Dictionnaire des idées reçues*, the most obvious guide to stupidity, is prefaced by an epigraph from Chamfort which suggests one approach to the problem: 'Il y a à parier que toute idée publique, toute convention reçue est une sottise, car elle a convenu au plus grand nombre' (II, 303).[5] Received ideas are stupid because, in their ignorance, the majority will accept ideas that are untrue and, in their intellectual laxness, will distort and oversimplify any true ideas that happen to come their way. The elite know better and because of their superior knowledge can recognize 'sottises' of this kind. Some of the entries in the *Dictionnaire* are stupid in that we can formulate the 'correct' alternative. *Omega*: second letter of the Greek alphabet, because one says 'the Alpha and the Omega'.[6] *Gulf-stream*: famous town in Norway, newly discovered. *Rousseau*: Jean-Jacques and Jean-Baptiste are brothers, like the two Corneilles.

Merging into this category are the facile generalizations which illustrate a willingness to content oneself with the most rudimentary knowledge without pursuing the topic further. *Architectes*: all fools; always forget the stairways in houses. *Estomac*: all illnesses come from the stomach. *Koran*: Book by Mohammed which talks only of women. *Serpents*: all poisonous. *Peru*: country where everything is made of gold. That such ideas are stupid there can be little doubt, but they seem weak stuff indeed for a book that was to be Flaubert's revenge on his age and the repository, as he said, of all his hatred.

It is possible, however, that these entries had a specific role to play in the book. The original plan was to include a preface which would explain that the work was designed to promote respect for order, tradition, and convention, in a word 'right thinking'; this was to be done in such a way 'que le lecteur ne sache pas si l'on se fout de lui, oui on non' (ii, 238). When the bourgeois reader found palpable stupidities alongside his own thoughts and beliefs he would be disconcerted and uncertain how to respond. The more egregious cases would help to point to the *bêtise* of those entries reflecting a bourgeois view of the world. True stupidity, we might suppose, was the bourgeois ideology.

Some entries clearly fit this hypothesis. *Hugo*: was wrong to get himself mixed up in politics. Who speaks here? The semi-cultured partisans of order and the Second Empire who will pay lip-service to culture but are pleased that Napoleon III had reestablished business as usual. *Magistrature*: splendid career for a young man. That, as Flaubert's own case shows, was very much the idea of the professional middle-classes. *Police*: bastions of society. After the great divide of 1848 it is clear who says that. *Drapeau (national)*: the very sight of it is moving. Not to the left-wing, but perhaps to both the moderate republicans and the reactionaries who say the French must be governed by the sword (*Sabre*). But neither of these is the royalist who still hopes for the *Fusion des branches royales*. *Idéal*: completely useless. *Ingénieur*: best career for a young man. These come from the new technocratic and positivistic stratum of the middle-class, who neither find *Ruins* romantic nor say that *Music* makes you dream. How do they relate to those for whom *Spiritualism* is the best philosophical system? The man who rails against the age (*Epoque*) and complains that it is not poetic is not the same as he for whom wealth is all-important (*Richesse*) and business takes precedence (*Affaires*). As one collects more evidence the problems increase. One must say, at the very least, that if all these ideas be bourgeois, the bourgeoisie is a class with a highly confused ideology. But Sartre's conclusion seems more apt: 'more than a thousand entries and who feels that he is the target? No one.'[7]

Sartre goes on to argue that Flaubert himself, as much as anyone else, is the target. Many of the ideas are undoubtedly his, but this only strengthens one's growing conviction that the identification of stupidity does not depend on one's ability to formulate the "correct" alternative view. Stupid opinions are not those of the bourgeoisie as opposed to other, preferable opinions. And hence the entries of the *Dictionnaire* neither represent a coherent view of the world, nor are they rendered stupid by being set against another coherent ideology.

Flaubert's enterprise, in fact, seems very much that of the mythologist, as Roland Barthes has since defined it. To analyse the contemporary myths of bourgeois culture is not to claim that they are necessarily false but only that their historical and conventional character has been obscured by a society which attempts to transform its particular culture into a universal nature.[8] A Rolls-Royce has a great many properties which, given the qualities that are sought in motor-cars, make it a prize specimen, but the Rolls-Royce is still a mythical object: the symbol of excellence and status. It bears an objective relation to wealth in that only the wealthy can afford one, but when we pass from that relation to one of connotation and make it 'signify' wealth, we have entered the realm of myth. The mythologist attacks a kind of fetishism which takes various associations, however sound their factual basis, and makes them the 'natural' meanings of or responses to an object or concept.

In this perspective Flaubert's choice of a dictionary format becomes thoroughly appropriate. One looks something up in order to discover its social meaning. *Chapeaux*: 'protester contre la forme des.' The *action* of complaining about the form of a hat is not necessarily stupid. What is stupid is to make this an automatic and socially-coded response; to make it what one should think whenever hats are mentioned. *Basques*: are the best runners. This may be true, but to make it, as it were, the meaning of *basques*, the socially-required response, is to limit freedom and curiosity in ways which cannot but seem stupid.

The majority of Flaubert's entries are of this sort: stupid, not because the facts on which they rely are false but because the particular meanings offered do not exhaust an object or concept and because they place it in a self-enclosed system of social discourse which comes to serve as reality for those who allow themselves to be caught up in it. This social text allows contradictory meanings so that discussion may take place. *Imprimerie*: one may say either that it is a marvellous discovery or, if someone else has got his word in first, maintain that it has done more harm than good. *Prêtres*: sleep with their maids and have children whom they call their nephews — 'C'est égal, il y en a de bons, tout de même' is the proper response. The novels, of course, are full of this sort of thing. Discussions consist of a ritualistic exchange of clichés in which the world is no longer of any moment, replaced as it is by a limited set of phrases.

There are, therefore, many items which merit their entry in the dictionary only when they are considered not as responses in a particular situation but as possible responses which society has, in its semiotic wisdom, elevated to the status of natural meanings. *Palmier*: gives local color. The object has disappeared, taken up in a social language which suppresses all but one of its possible qualities. *Catholicisme*: has had a very favourable influence on the arts; which is true, but stupid if that is all one can find to say about it. The tangential association or consequence, made a natural response, loses its redeeming features as response. For example, *Diamant*: 'and to think that it is really just coal!' As a spontaneous response to a scientific fact, as wonder that the black and the opaque can become, through a natural agency bordering on the magical, the sparkling and the translucent, this is wholly admirable. It translates a certain attachment to the evidence of the senses and the logic of every day objects and a willingness to explore the unusual. But as a socially-determined association it is of no interest. It is, in fact, no more than a sentence.

If stupidity were ignorance, one might take one's stand on the side of knowledge; if stupidity were bourgeois, one might range oneself with the aristocracy or with the people; but if stupity is cultural language made nature, where can one stand to combat it? How does one gain purchase against clichés which are grounded in truth but have been made the constituents of a world? Flaubert's first attempts to define a posture in which he could rail against stupidity was his invention, with various schoolfellows, of that enigmatic giant, le Garçon.

Our evidence about him is pitifully slight. Some twenty letters make brief reference to him as common property and the Goncourts provide an uncomprehending account of what Flaubert told them; but such as it is the evidence at least indicates that the Garçon was both subject and object. To play the Garçon was to perceive the world in a particular way and laugh at the stupidity of others, but it was also, simultaneously, to make oneself a stupid and grotesque object.

The Garçon's parentage is Flaubert out of Rabelais — or at least out of Rabelais as interpreted in one of Gustave's youthful essays: the vicious satirist who has undertaken destructive mockery. Everything that had been respected he demolished. All human conditions 'pass before the colossal sarcasm of Rabelais, which whips and brands them, and they all emerge bloody and mutilated from beneath his pen' (I, 183). But he was object as well as subject. His laughter, which was so terrible, 'c'est la statue du grotesque' (I, 180). While mocking others he made himself so disgusting that the eighteenth century might judge his works 'a mass of the most obscene garbage that a drunken monk could vomit up'. It had to be thus, writes Flaubert. Setting himself up against the world, Rabelais reveals the stupidity of others by their reactions to his books.

Similarly, Rabelais' giants are both instruments and objects of ridicule; they both exemplify the human qualities which we see magnified in them and set themselves against the ordinary run of men, whom they present to us as pitiful creatures indeed. The Garçon was designed as a modern Pantagruel, who would himself be obscene, stupid, ridiculous, but who would also and simultaneously destroy, by his colossal laughter, the world on which he looked.

The Garçon is not therefore, as some have suggested, the archetypal bourgeois, Homais grown giant. He utters *idées reçues* on the appropriate occasions but with such conceit and bellowing that interlocutors who are not in on the joke become annoyed. And he can take up any other position sufficiently gross and ridiculous for him to make a spectacle of himself. The Goncourts tell a story of Flaubert, at one of Princesse Mathilde's soirées, challenging the sculptor Jacquemart who had told a story concerning Egypt and fleas. Determined to prove that he himself had had more fleas, Flaubert succeeded in engaging Jacquemart in violent argument, to the annoyance and discomfiture of everyone.[9] And such annoyance, it is important to note, would be directed not simply at Flaubert but also at themselves for failing to preserve a detached and amused calm. Making himself ridiculous, the Garçon brings others to see themselves as ridiculous: 'By his shouts and paradoxes he makes emerge the bourgeois who lurk beneath the skin of these aristocrats and artists. Only those bourgeois do not like to be shown their true nature.'[10]

When one plays the Garçon, one makes oneself object voluntarily so as to make others become objects involuntarily. A letter of 1850, written from Cairo, reveals the basic mechanism. Bouilhet, who had out of friendship been visiting Flaubert's mother regularly, is thanked profusely and most tenderly. But don't think yourself obliged to give up all your Sundays, Flaubert continues, or to go to so much trouble. My mother, I know, appreciates your visits so much she'd gladly pay a hundred francs a time. That phrase sets him off on another course:

Il serait gars de lui en faire la proposition. Vois-tu le mémoire que fourbirait le Garçon en cette occasion: 'Tant pour la société d'un homme comme moi. Frais extraordinaires: avoir dit un mot spirituel . . . avoir été charmant et plein de bon ton. Etc.' (ii, 217).[11]

If one were playing the Garçon one could display self-satisfaction and unmask one's relations with others. Bouilhet's visits are presumably undertaken out of duty rather than pleasure, so that to present a bill would be to reveal the true state of affairs which is ordinarily masked by polite formulae. But the Garçon, we are told, would not simply present a bill; that would put him into the situation of professional men whose time we buy but with whom we expect to entertain human relations during that period that is ours. The Garçon details his fees, like a doctor charging extra for each reassuring word, adding a supplement for delicacy. Every moment of his behaviour is an object to be weighted and paid for. He is making, quite literally, a spectacle of himself, not merely revealing the sordid truth of a human relationship but exacerbating it. Like Rameau's nephew, he attains a version of freedom in and through alienation: making himself object in his every moment, he laughs in his Gargantuan way at both himself and his interlocutor. The latter, outraged, finds the tormentor invulnerable in his laughter and cannot avoid being discomfited, for the useless anger has been provoked and controlled by the Garçon. Playing a reprehensible role, he pulls the strings which make others puppets.

Laughter is the Garçon's mode of existence, and the man who laughs is strong among the strong, especially if his laughter be outrageous. 'Je me récrie, je ris, je bois, je chante ah ah ah, et je fais entendu le rire du Gârcon, je tape sur la table, je m'arrache les cheveux, je me roule par terre' (i, 24-5).[12] One must either join in the laughter, which makes one feel self-conscious and foolish, so excessive is it, or one must allow bourgeois indignation to mount and become a spectacle oneself. Either way, the Garçon disconcerts; he pulls the strings. And if one would experience this paradoxical duality one might try, as experiment, what Flaubert often did to avoid boredom: look at oneself in the mirror and laugh one's most outrageous laugh. One is both subject and object of ridicule and can experience in one of its purest forms the stupidity of the human species.

'Comment épingler la bêtise sans se déclarer intelligent?' asks Barthes.[13] How can one prick stupidity without claiming supreme intelligence? One solution, which the Garçon out-lines, is to 'se déclarer bête' and display one's stupidity with a blatant and provocative self-confidence. The Garçon has no positive position; in him, as Sartre observes, materialism makes fun of romanticism and vice versa. Everything is grist to his mill, or at least any position that takes itself seriously. The stupidity of the Garçon is both a mode of comprehension and a property of all that he comprehends.

But the Garçon was an attempt at a lived rather than written solution; it is noteworthy that he appears in none of Flaubert's books — though Yuk, the God of the grotesque in *Smarh* is obviously a relative — for he is a Homeric figure whose epic stature would sort ill with the modes of stupidity that Flaubert's novels express. The structure of the Garçon, however, can be traced in the conception of *Bouvard et Pécuchet*. It was to be, Du Camp reports, an encyclopaedia of human stupidity, and when he asked for an explanation Flaubert replied, 'Je veux produire une telle impression de lassitude et d'ennui, qu'en lisant ce livre on puisse croire qu'il a été fait par un crétin' (I, 35).[14] The book is not to present intelligence mocking stupidity but stupidity both as object and as mode of comprehension. To write the book is itself stupid, as Flaubert felt only too clearly. Representation of the world in sentences is a particularly pointless and gratuitous activity.

Indeed, one might say that as an incarnation of stupidity the Garçon leaves out of account one crucial factor: the stupidity of language. The *Dictionnaire des idées reçues* implies, as I have already suggested, that stupidity is a mode of language, or rather that social language is itself stupid: it is not the instrument or vehicle of a spontaneous response to the world, it is not something lived but something given, a set of codified responses. We do not understand the world or even come to grips with it. We talk about it in phrases which interact with one another in a self-enclosed system. Language, in short, is part of the practico-inert: a set of objects with which man plays but which do not speak to him.

The alphabetical listing of the Dictionnaire makes this point quite nicely. The order is purely arbitrary or linguistic only, unlike those medieval and renaissance compendiums which attempted to reproduce in their arrangement the order of the world. Sentences are simply juxtaposed, as isolated bits of linguistic matter. We can glimpse here Flaubert's basic attitude towards language: one does not speak, one does not construct sentences to express one's relation to the world and to others; one is spoken. Social discourse is always there already and when addressed one need only pick out the response which the system of discourse provides. Whether or not Sartre is right in attributing this attitude to childhood traumas and difficulties in learning to read, it is well documented from the novels themselves, which offer a sense of 'the grotesque stupidity of things said, whatever they may be.'[15] Anything one says is a linguistic object placed on display, and if one looks at it long enough, just as when one repeats a word until it becomes meaningless, its stupidity will become apparent. Cutting speech off from its origins in practical life, Flaubert treats it as a set of phrases rather than the accomplishment of human intentions. 'It's going to rain', says Emma to Léon, who is taking his leave. 'I have a raincoat,' he replies. 'Ah!' (I, 614). Nothing is said. Sentences stand, empty and detached.

To say anything is to take up a banal social discourse. Hence the self-conscious, citational mode of Flaubert's own letters. The sentences he writes are not his, and by distancing himself from them, supplying possible sources — "comme dirait M. Prudhomme', 'comme dit l'épicier' — he protects himself from the stupidity which contaminates any speech. The hope that after reading the Dictionnaire des idées reçues 'no one would dare speak, for fear of saying one of the phrases which were to be found in it' (iii, 67) was simply a desire for revenge and the hope that the despair of language which he had so long experienced might be visited on others.

A melancholy reflection in *Par les champs et par les grèves* provides a nice summary of man's relationship to language. Something rather ordinary surprised me and made me laugh, Flaubert says. It was a telegraph box on a tower in Nantes with a ladder leading up to it.

> Quelle drôle de vie que celle d'un homme qui reste là, dans cette petite cabane à faire mouvoir ces deux perches et à tirer sur ces ficelles; rouage inintelligent d'une machine muette pour lui, il peut mourir sans connaître un seul des événements qu'il a appris, un seul mot de tous ceux qu'il aura dits. Le but? le but? le sens? qui le sait? . . . Un peu plus, un peu moins, ne sommes-nous pas tous comme ce brave homme, parlant des mots qu'on nous a appris et que nous apprenons sans les comprendre (II, 484).[16]

Language lifted away from the world becomes a self-contained system of empty phrases which we exchange and transmit but which we neither invent nor investigate.

This should not imply, however, that for Flaubert man has a rich inner and outer life prior to language, a treasure so particular that no social discourse can capture it. There is, indeed, much evidence to the contrary. Emma's desires are created by a language of romance and she finds nothing in her life to fulfil the promise of those words, 'félicité', 'passion', and 'ivresse', which had seemed so splendid in books (I, 586). Frédéric *admires* passion (estimait par-dessus tout la passion) (II, 13) and hopes to reproduce in his own life the love whose image a culture offers him. Bouvard and Pécuchet spend a fortnight attempting introspection after lunch: 'they searched in their consciousness, at random, hoping to make great discoveries there, and made none, which surprised them greatly' (II, 271). The emptiness of language is paralleled by an inner emptiness.

Indeed, it is as though, having lifted language away from human praxis and intentionality in order to make it stupid, Flaubert, in a crucial but rather devious move, had re-established connections between language and thought on the one hand and language and the world on the other, in order to render thought and world as stupid as language. Whereas stupidity seemed at first the result of a gap between language and the world, the property of a language that was substituted for the world, now, by contamination, it becomes a property of active attempts to manipulate language in what is called 'thought' and also a property of a world of objects which refuses to be composed by language.

Before exploring the links between these varieties of stupidity and considering the possibilities of synthesis we must try to define, in turn, the stupidity of thought and the stupidity of objects.

'Oui, la bêtise consiste à vouloir conclure', wrote Flaubert in a famous letter. 'Stupidity is wanting to conclude. We are a thread and want to know the pattern' (ii, 239). The attempts of intelligence to master the world, to seek out causes and offer explanations, are a form of stupidity. Homais, after all, is stupid *because* he is intelligent, because he attempts to keep up with contemporary science and make his own contribution to it, to display his awareness of knowledge and help others towards the benefits of it. But the stupidity of thought is even more apparent in *Bouvard et Pécuchet*, where Flaubert lists and explores the theories of the best authorities in a wide range of fields, all of which pretend to some kind of explanatory validity and all of which prove contradictory and inept. 'Stupidity is not on one side and intelligence on the other' (iv, 83); such an opposition seems impossible. Those who still believe in sorcerers and divining rods may be stupid, but where does one stand to combat such an opinion; is there a correct opposing view?

As for combating it, why not combat the contrary, which is quite as stupid as it is? There are a whole crowd of such topics which annoy me just as much whatever way they are approached . . . Thus Voltaire, mesmerism, Napoleon, the French Revolution, Catholicism, etc. Whether one speak good or ill of them I am equally irritated. Most of the time conclusions seem to me acts of stupidity (iii, 153–4).

That irritation is the law that governs *Bouvard et Pécuchet*. One opinion is set against another with no attempt to adjudicate between them. What should be done in the garden? 'Puvis recommends marl, Roret manual opposes it . . . Tull exalts tillage at the expense of fertilizer, but Major Beetson suppresses fertilizer in favour of tillage' (II, 211). All theories

167

are rendered equivalent by their failure. That these failures may be due sometimes to want of understanding, at other times to the general perverseness of a recalcitrant Nature, and at still others to the incompetence of the authorities themselves, does not materially affect the case. Oppositions between the theories are effectively neutralized as they take their place with one another in paradigms of stupidity.

Some critics, struck no doubt by the ineptness of the two protagonists and by the subtitle, 'Du défaut de méthode dans les sciences', have assumed that human knowledge is not itself under attack; but that subtitle is highly ironic, since method is perhaps the only thing Bouvard and Pécuchet do not lack. When tackling a new discipline they send off for the best authorities, read and compare them, and attempt to test their conclusions. What probably influences critics on this point is the fact that so much of what is reported seems pseudo-science and so much of what we respect as science is absent, but this is scarcely Flaubert's fault. He would joyfully have included an account of nuclear physics and sub-atomic particles in his list of theories of matter, and one can imagine Bouvard and Pécuchet riding around the district in trains trying to test the theory of relativity. Stupidity is not a property of incorrect theories but rather the inevitable coefficient of the whole attempt to master nature through knowledge.

Indeed, Flaubert's remarks on science in other contexts make it clear that what he admires is an attempt to establish facts. He is attracted to Positivism precisely insofar as it appears to have abandoned a search for causes and contented itself with exhaustive taxonomic descriptions. Explanation, in his view, lies outside the province of science and any attempt to attain it is a step into the abyss of stupidity. 'Note that the sciences began to make progress only when they set aside the notion of cause' (iv, 357). 'Try to hold firm to science, to pure science: love facts for themselves' (iv, 399). The only kind of knowledge worthy of respect is that which presents and classifies facts and, offering no conclusions or explanations, cannot be translated into action. Attempts to relate knowledge and activity are instances of presumptuous stupidity. Hence medicine for Flaubert, as Sartre notes, is not an attempt to master disease and cure the sick (which makes one wonder what sort of example Flaubert's father presented) but only dissection and naming of parts, analysis without synthesis. The notion that the search for causes is anti-scientific (v, 148) and deplorable is related, of course, to Flaubert's rejection of practical life, but it cannot avoid affecting the artistic life he has adopted. As a general denigration of synthesis, it is particularly inimical to the pursuit, in novels, of thematic conclusions. Nor does it promote a desire for organization.

This seems apparent in Flaubert's ambiguous attachment to binarism. His predilection for pairs has been noted by most critics, though as I have suggested above, many of his oppositions are factitious and unproductive. Binary opposition — 'cette logique élémentaire qui est comme le plus petit commun dénominateur de toute pensée'[17] — is a metaphor for all thought in its ability to bring order into any disorder. It is not surprising that for Flaubert it should be linked with *bêtise* since any application of it presumes to isolate crucial features in simple antitheses and hence to move towards conclusions with a minimum of intellectual effort. One remembers the passage in the first *Education sentimentale* where Henry, the provincial newly-arrived in Paris, watches the faces of passengers in the omnibus, 'establishing between them similarities and antitheses' (I, 279). That is stupid both as an attempt to grasp and comprehend the world and as an intellectual construction which takes place in a language lifted away from the world which does not allow itself to be organized so easily.

Yet Flaubert himself is very much wedded to the binary principle, especially when drawing up plans. The project for a novel on 'Un ménage parisien sous Napoléon III' is rigidly symmetrical: 'Madame catches Monsieur deceiving her; then Monsieur catches Madame deceiving him — jealousy. She wishes she had married a true lover who had become a great man; he wishes he had married a tart who had become very rich.' And opposed to them, 'in the background his sister and her husband, a respectable and perfectly egotistical household.'[18] The task of writing such a novel would thus become one of struggling with the stupidity of his symmetrical plan.

The problem of binarism may serve as a useful pivot on which to turn from the stupidity of intellect to the stupidity of the world, for precisely because of his dislike of facile antitheses and his tendency to make oppositions unproductive, Flaubert can in descriptions use binarism as a device of anti-synthesis: doubling objects without allowing this to produce meaning. He is at irritatingly great pains, Claude Duchet writes,

> to note objects in pairs, so that they thereby take on connotations of penetrating stupidity and repetitive monotony: 'she remained leaning on the edge, between two pots of geraniums', 'she rested her elbow alongside her plate, between the two smoking candles'; or even connotations of satisfied plenitude, as if the bourgeois thought in pairs.[19]

Citing numerous examples, he concludes that we are dealing with both a stylistic tic and a vision of the world.

> One could even say that one of the reasons for Flaubert's hatred of boots is that they call for double notation . . . Passing from clothes to person, the figure two decomposes bodies, as it were, into fascinating objects of flesh. Here is Charles by the fireside, 'his two hands on his stomach, his two feet on the andirons'. Here are the country-folk at the fair in their Sunday-best, like bourgeois in stiff collars and white cravats: 'et l'on appuyait ses deux mains sur ses deux cuisses.'[20]

The unnecessary numerical specifications add an element of gratuitous facticity and produce, as Duchet suggests, somewhat grotesque but fascinating objects. They are stupid because of their particularity.

It might seem that Flaubert displays here a sense of stupidity closely related to Valéry's:

> La 'bêtise' de tout se fait sentir. Bêtise, c'est-à-dire particularité opposée à la généralité. 'Plus petit que' devient le signe terrible de l'esprit. Le Démon des possibles ordonnés.[21]

*Bêtise* is what escapes the ordering intellect, whatever makes itself felt as a particularity which falls outside the concept and is simply there. Yet with 'smaller than', one of those many demons of logical possibility which are at the mind's beck and call, one can order any pair and thereby denature the objects in question. Stupidity would seem to be opposed to organization, but Valéry at least recognizes that such an opposition is at best ambiguous: 'Démon' and 'terrible' indicate reservations about the value of easy organization. But he would not go so far as to bring these operations under the aegis of stupidity, and it is here that Flaubert shows a much deeper understanding of the constraints on and requirements of a sophisticated literary theory of *bêtise*.

He understands, that is to say, that in literature there is never a question of objects which escape the organizing powers of language and mind. Stupidity cannot be an absence of organization. If it is to be a literary category one must reflect on the ways in which absence of organization may be signified and therefore one cannot think of stupidity as a residue which, by definition, does not makes its way onto the page. Stupidity is already a type of organization. The use of pairs, 'his two arms on his two thighs' or whatever, offers a rudimentary disposition which holds out no possibilities for development and comes thereby to signify the purely factual and fatuous. The stupidity of objects is itself a mode of organization, and one might say that for Flaubert, as opposed to Valéry, 'le Démon des possibles ordonnés" is *bêtise* itself.

Viewed in this way, Flaubert's binary predilections become wholly comprehensible — or at least insofar as the attractions of stupidity are ever fully comprehensible. The stupidity of objects is dependent on a sense of possible order, of which doubling is the most elementary index, and a failure to fulfill the expectations such possibilities arouse. The stupidity of the world, in Flaubert, is always the coefficient of a rudimentary order, whether that of the syntax which pretends to compose items into a coherent proposition, or that of the more elaborate objects described at some length.

Emma's wedding cake and the elaborate toy which was destined for the Homais children but did not find its way into the final text due to the insistence of Bouilhet, are excellent instances of stupidity as a coefficient of organization.[22] The former, of course, is ridiculous in its mixture of styles and in the contrast between its elements and what they represent: 'a castle-keep in Savoy cake, surrounded by tiny fortifications in angelica, almonds, raisins, and orange quarters; . . . jam lakes and nutshell boats' (I, 584). It was 'une pièce montée qui fit pousser des cris', a deliberate spectacle which is doubly alienated and fetishistic: first, because its form is so divorced from its practical purposes (it will, after all, be eaten), and secondly, because its ingredients are made to serve functions which are not their own. The toy, however, is an even purer example of stupidity and its attractions: a scale model of a town and all the activities taking place within it, it is also non-functional and purely representational. 'Both the height of gratuitousness and highly essential', as Thibaudet says,[23] such an object holds attractions which anyone who has been fascinated by an architectural scale model or an elaborate electric train set can understand. One takes pleasure in discovering the accuracy of representation and the means by which it has been achieved. Perfectly useless, such objects with their high degree of organization, are directly and un-abashedly mimetic, presenting us with a whole and allowing us to explore its parts. Lévi-Strauss even argues that the 'modèle réduit' is the very type of the work of art, whose intrinsic virtue is to compensate for the reduction of spatial dimensions by the addition of new dimensions of intelligibility.[24]

That is, of course, the traditional defence of mimetic art, but Flaubert's objects illustrate the stupidity of this kind of intelligibility. Blocking the discourse of the text — that is why Bouilhet insisted on the excision of the long description of the toy — they offer a high degree of organization which leads nowhere. Closed, autonomous, absolute, 'these objects are *there*: the observer, flustered and fascinated, cannot question these monuments to the genius of stupidity, these complacent and flowering arabesques.'[25] They figure the absurdity of representational art itself; language divorced from its human origins and goals but retaining a high degree of organization as it accedes to the condition of the practico-inert.

It should be clear that for Flaubert the attractions of such objects lie in their stupidity; one stands fascinated before them, *béant* or *ébahi*, because they have no function, prove nothing. The mind is released from any commitment to prac-tical life and can simply explore.

Stupidity of this kind is a property of aesthetic objects also: 'Masterpieces are stupid; they present a tranquil face, like the very productions of nature, like large animals or mountains' (ii, 451). The masterpiece does not display intelligence or reach towards conclusions but offers itself with no ostensible purpose. The *bêtise* of novels is, however, more than a version of negative capability; they command attention, as a mountain does when it rises before one, and are not subsumed by any human project. Their tranquil appearance, a kind of bovine placidity, does not actively invite interpretation, as would a surface complexity that bespoke figured secrets. They are *de trop*; one may play around them but does not exhaust them.

Inexhaustibility is, for Flaubert, a compelling property of both art and stupidity.

> What seems to me the highest thing in art (and the most difficult), is not to evoke laughter, or tears, or lust, or anger, but to work as nature does: that is to say, to *induce reverie*. And the most beautiful works have in fact this quality. They are of serene aspect and incomprehensible. As for their technique, they are immobile like cliffs, stormy like the ocean, full of foliage, greenery, and murmurs like woods, sad like the desert, blue like the sky. Homer, Rabelais, Michelangelo, Shakespeare, Goethe seem to me *inexorable*. Such works are unfathomable, infinite, multifarious. Through little gaps one glimpses precipices; there is darkness below, dizziness (iii, 322–3).

This passage brings about, under the aegis of stupidity, a combination of terms which requires some elucidation. Why choose natural metaphors to discuss the workings of masterpieces? What is the relationship between reverie, incomprehension, and profundity? An answer would enable us to attack that enigmatic account of the temptations of stupidity which obsessed Flaubert for most of his life: *La Tentation de Saint Antoine*.

First of all, incomprehension was for Flaubert the road to reverie. Henry in the first *Education sentimentale* 'sat for a whole hour reading the same line of a newspaper' (I, 279), and that this should be called 'reading' rather than, say, 'staring', is quite significant. 'I reread this week the first act of *King Lear*', Flaubert reports. Shakespeare 'stupifies and exalts me'; 'je n'y vois qu'une immensité où mon regard se perd avec des éblouissements' (iv, 46). This 'vastness where the gaze loses itself in dizziness' is the experience of reading that Flaubert desires. Reading is an act of passing through the text ('through little gaps one glimpses precipices'), not synthesizing it, but either looking for stupid phrases which command admiration (that is research) or seeking between the lines for something which, as Sartre says, lends itself to his 'directed reverie'.[26] He claims to have been completely flattened for three days after reading Act III, scene i of *Lear*, but his comments make clear that he is discussing another scene and that he has not only misinterpreted it but failed to grasp elementary facts about the plot (iv, 18).

The image of Flaubert sitting before these texts in an inspired and devouring reverie recalls the one picture of serious intellectual effort that he offers us in his works: the German mathematician in the first *Education sentimentale*. 'Shahutsnischbach ... was always working at mathematics, mathematics were consuming his life, he understood nothing about them. Never had M. Renaud had a more studious or stupid young man' (I, 293). Again the choice of words is revealing. The student is not involved in one of those intellectual tasks which would be possible without understanding, nor is it simply that he has great difficulty and must therefore work harder to keep up. 'Il n'y comprenait rien' and yet 'il travaillait toujours au mathématiques.' One thinks of the hours the young Flaubert spent staring at his law books, taking nothing in, understanding nothing, because he was merely reading sentences, contemplating them, and finding them stupid.[27] Or of the considerable periods he spent 'studying' Greek but never attacking the verbs, because, as Sartre says, he did not want to understand and cherished the opacity of texts which provoked reverie the more readily because they were incomprehensible.[28]

If the highest goal of art is to *faire rêver* then it is quite appropriate that masterpieces should be incomprehensible and that Flaubert should have sought in his own writing to set obstacles in the way of synthesis. Whether incomprehension results from the stupidity of the subject or of the object is perhaps a minor matter, since the goal is a mental activity that is self-directing. The subject is to find no instructions in the object. Understanding is a participatory movement which grasps the object either as the result of human intentions or as a form with a teleological intentionality of its own. Either way, one organizes it with respect to a purpose or function. Reverie, then, is the result of contemplating the object under another aspect, denying or failing to reach the purpose which would integrate it. Treating potentially purposive objects as mere material stimuli, reverie rejects understanding and seeks stupidity.

Whence Flaubert's predilection for natural metaphors. One cannot understand a stone or a mountain. One can understand facts about them or problems that are posed when a human project or discourse operates on them, providing a focus, asking a question. 'Why is the stone this colour?' But natural objects have no such focus in themselves, and hence the task of science, as Flaubert sees it, is merely to note and describe, not to understand. 'That's the beauty of the natural sciences: they do not wish to prove anything. Consequently, what breadth of facts and immense space for thought? One ought to treat men like mastodons or crocodiles' (iii, 154). To treat men in this way is to deny the relevance of that immense fund of knowledge one has by virtue of being a man oneself. Refusing to understand them, one transforms them into curiosities available for contemplation and reverie. This is Flaubert's habitual procedure. He is annoyed when people whose lives impinge on his own talk or behave stupidly, but as soon as he can achieve sufficient distance and take the sentences or behaviour as natural specimens which need not be understood, they can be cause for joy and reverie. The stupidity which transforms the human into the non-human neutralizes annoying qualities and produces an opacity which is a source of value.

Inexorable and 'impitoyables', masterpieces offer the mind none of the consolations of easy recuperation. They do not address it, and so any message to be drawn from them must be constructed by the mind in self-conscious fashion. Like the reading of rocks or clouds, interpretation is an activity always threatened by its possible gratuitousness, and the placidity of great works only heightens the threat. The ending of *Candide*, Flaubert remarks, 'that tranquil conclusion, stupid like life itself' is for me the striking proof of Voltaire's genius. Neither melodrama nor synthesis, neither tragedy nor success, the ending is calm and even mediocre. Tailing off, explicitly rejecting reflections on the final state of affairs, it asserts its own reality and stops there, 'stupid like life itself' (ii, 398).

But for Flaubert it is also profound, no doubt because of Candide's own refusal to think. Thought itself, the adventures of a mind attaching itself to a particular problem and working towards some end, is not profound. Depth, for Flaubert, is not a determinate space; it is not, for example, the attribute of a thought which, difficult to grasp, holds itself back from the mind, inviting it to traverse a space in order to accede to it. Depth is rather the result of superficiality; one breaks through a thin and brittle surface and finds that there is no bottom below: 'such works are unfathomable . . . there is darkness below, dizziness.' Indeed, it is when one regards something as stupid, when one severs it from a human context which might serve as a bottom beyond which one need not explore, when one thus makes it a pure surface phenomenon, that it becomes properly profound. What could be more stupid, after all, than the 'bêtise sublime' of carving one's name in huge letters on Pompey's column? The name itself, 'Thompson', is quite meaningless, yet it stares one imperiously in the face, looms before one as a surface which one does not know how to deal with. 'It can be read a quarter of a league away. There is no way to see the column without seeing the name 'Thompson' and consequently without thinking of Thompson.' There is in Flaubert's reaction a hint of jealousy: 'This idiot has become part of the monument and perpetuates himself with it', but it is due above all to his admiration for the profundity of this stupidity. 'Not only that, he overwhelms it by the magnificence of his gigantic letters.' These letters testify for him to the 'serenity' of stupidity, and he concludes that 'Stupidity is something unshakeable. Nothing attacks it without breaking itself against it. It is of the nature of granite, hard and resistant' (ii, 243).

Sartre has written some brilliant pages on Flaubert's response to Thompson: Flaubert finds confirmation of his sense of writing as 'l'acte pur de bêtise' and of its triumph as a correlate of its stupidity. But Sartre is wont to stress the gesture of Thompson the man, who instead of admiring a work of art used it to his own ends, stole the glory that rightfully belonged to another, and succeeded both because matter itself, the stone of the column, lent him permanence and because 'la matière du dedans, celle que s'est coulée dans les coeurs, lui confère l'immortalité'.[29] But to treat it in this way is already to make it less stupid, or rather to make oneself more stupid; for Thompson did not, after all, achieve anything. All that is immortalized is a name borne by many others, and it is precisely that absence of efficacy which gives his inscription its profound stupidity. It stands before the viewer as a surface, a *signifiant* with an absent *signifié*. To treat the inscription as a calculated act designed to achieve a particular goal is to supply a meaning, to understand it, and thereby to negate the gratuitous stupidity which makes it fascinating.

This aspect of stupidity's attraction is borne out by a letter to George Sand in which, while discussing beauty as the goal of art, he gives a most curious illustration.

I remember once how moved I was and what violent pleasure I felt when looking at a wall of the Acropolis, a completely bare wall. Well, I wonder whether a book, quite apart from what it says, could not produce the same effect. In the precision with which parts are fitted together, the rarity of its elements, the high polish of the surface, the harmony of the whole, is there not an intrinsic virtue, a kind of divine force, someting eternal like a principle? (I speak as a Platonist.) (vii, 294).

It would, of course, be his *livre sur rien*, placid and tranquil, which did not address man; just a blank wall, which is one of our models of stupidity. It would be profound because it would be only a surface that provoked reverie in the spectator, 'écrasé sans savoir pourquoi' (iii, 62). One can catch glimpses of a divine order, but if one tried to express that order one would fall back into the mode of *bêtise*.

If one attempts to bring together the various manifestations of this ubiquitous concept one discovers that it cannot be defined in terms of a few common properties which all its instances share. It is not, for Flaubert, a positively defined concept which he can simply apply. Were that the case it would not occupy the role in his mental and artistic life that it does. It is a concept which, as the French allows us to say, 'le travaille et qu'il travaille'. It works or exercises him and he must, in turn, work it, as one works metal or stone. Indeed, the concept seems to contain within itself the whole structure of Flaubert's intellectual adventure. The best way to grasp this complex structure is perhaps to show how it differs from irony as Kierkegaard defines it.

It might seem, Kierkegaard writes, that as 'infinite absolute negativity' irony were identical with doubt. But 'doubt is a conceptual determination while irony is the being-for-itself of subjectivity.'[30] As a youth Flaubert was given to doubt: 'how many long and monotonous hours have I spent in thinking, in doubting' (I, 230). Doubt applies to a proposition or attitude that men have adopted and questions it in the name of something else; it implies at least the possibility of an alternative positive statement. With doubt the subject feels oppressed because he must attempt to penetrate the phenomena in question and offer a mode of discourse of his own, committing himself in some way, if only to justify his refusal to go beyond doubt. Irony, however, at least in Kierkegaard's sense, implies no positive alternative. The subject feels free. He 'is always seeking to get outside the object, and this he attains by becoming conscious at every moment that the object has no reality.' Whereas doubt leads one to do battle, 'with irony the subject constantly retires from the field and proceeds to talk every phenomenon out of its reality in order to save himself, that is, in order to preserve himself in his negative independence of everything.'[31]

Irony is purely an attitude of mind which, though it may talk phenomena out of their reality, does not predicate other qualities of its objects because that would already imply a positive determination of some sort. Flaubert's stupidity, on the other hand, is both a mode of perception and a quality of objects, an attempt to free oneself from the world coupled with an oppressive consciousness of the reality of that world. More complex and in a sense more realistic than irony, it incorporates some residue of doubt and involves, one might say, three stages.

The first stage corresponds roughly to the initial perception of both the doubter and the ironist: the recognition that the being of society lies in its discourse. Clichés, propositions, theories, assumptions, are all attempts to organize the world through language, to master it, to humanize it, and to give it a meaning. One might react by doubting the truth of propositions and values, but that would require explanation. One might quote them ironically, but that gives one little purchase against them. After all, according to Kierkegaard, Socrates had to die because he became so totally identified with irony that there was no way left for him to live. If one wishes to give some substantial realization to one's sense of the incompleteness and partiality of society as constituted by its modes of discourse, if one wishes to show the foolishness of its attempts to create natural signs, one must develop another strategy.

That strategy is the second stage of stupidity. Stupidity is a mode of perception which makes things stupid. Take anything, a sentence, an activity, and isolate it, cut it off from the human intentions and goals that might give it a meaning, treat it, in short, as an object, and it will become stupid by virtue of the very stupidity and failure of understanding with which one regards it. Shaving, perfectly comprehensible in terms of human physiology and social conventions, becomes ridiculous when considered in and of itself. Phrases set down in the dictionary, taken out of social contexts where they might translate a response which was not wholly reprehensible, become mythical objects. The Garçon, by his own stupidity, provokes responses in others which make them pure automata and also displays the stupidity of those whom he imitates. Stupidity as a mode of perception is not simply the free attitude of irony, which makes little contact with its objects; it produces, rather, a correspondence between mind and its objects so that both come to partake of the same quality. The world is ordered but, seen *sub specie inanitatis*, that order is without point.

The movement of this second stage, which by stupidly dehumanizing and fragmenting the world permits one to see it as stupid without delineating positive alternatives, enables one to accede to the third stage, at which stupidity becomes a positive quality. It is as though by characterizing the world as stupid Flaubert has saved it for himself. The operation which reduces it to a surface and makes it a series of signs without meaning leaves the subject free before it. It remains the world and therefore carries the presumption of importance and order, but once that is shown to be, precisely, an empty presumption, the subject is free to fill it in the activity of reverie. He can glimpse a 'divine' order beneath a surface whose 'bottom' has been destroyed by stupidity in its second phase. The attempts to create natural signs have been undermined, and the subject can now prize innocent placidity, blankness, tranquillity, a simple being-there: versions of stupidity which serve as *signifiants* to empty *signifiés* which he can explore without naming: 'cela est sans fond, infini, multiple.'

Viewed in this way, Flaubert's sense of stupidity helps to bring together a good many diverse pronouncements and attitudes: the desire to write 'un livre sur rien', the comparison between masterpieces and natural objects, the practice of realism and the hatred of ordinary life, the ambiguous attitude towards clichés and absurd statements, his view of himself as analyst despite his failure to undertake analysis. This complex structure permits one to understand that stupidity oppresses because it locates the observer in the human and imposes on him the task of disengaging himself, distancing himself, making stupidity a mode of perception, in order to break free. But it also exhilarates because that task can be accomplished and leaves one, at least momentarily, with a feeling of freedom.

I should like to think that Flaubert's obsession with *Saint Antoine*, an obsession which he himself clearly did not understand, was due to the fact that it was to be a synthesis of his attitudes towards stupidity. But whether or not such an hypothesis has any bearing on the psychology of the author, it is crucial, I would maintain, to the psychology of the reader. For *La Tentation de Saint Antoine* is so blatantly stupid a work, especially when the three texts are placed side by side, that unless one attempts to read it as symptom, and as symptom of the ways in which the problems of stupidity may work themselves out in literature, it is difficult to summon up the stamina to proceed.

If the example of *Bouvard et Pécuchet* is anything to go by, one might postulate that the *Tentation* too was designed to be exasperating and incomprehensible, 'un livre sur rien' in that all these phantoms and temptations amount, finally, to nothing. As a monstrous excrescence the work poses in rather too imperious a fashion the question of what is stupid, how stupidity relates to temptation, and whether it is a desire for knowledge or stupidity that makes one tempted by the monstrous. For the reader who follows the title and attempts to use it to structure the book the problems of reading are acute. We know something of temptations because we presume to a knowledge of human psychology, but the traditional lures of sex, wealth, and power are represented by pasteboard figures who are easily summoned and quickly dismissed, and the remaining temptations seem notable primarily for their grotesqueness and stupidity. The question which the reader is forced to ask himself is whether he is wrong in thinking these figures stupid and in discounting for that reason their power as temptations, or whether he is right in thinking them stupid but wrong in assuming that this makes them less effective as temptations.

We might expect to find an answer in the psychology of the Saint himself, for it is he, after all, who is being tempted, and we ought to be able to discover in his response an attitude towards the figures that pass before him, which, if it does not satisfy as an attitude which we might ourselves adopt, would at least provide some point of departure that would permit us to make our way through the pages with greater conceptual ease. But in fact the Saint has no psychology. We cannot tell whether he is stupid or intelligent, whether he is particularly credulous, for the simple reason that he is not adequately situated. A contemplative, outside the world of action, supposed already to hold the world for nought, outside of time in his freedom of vision, he escapes any standard of *vraisemblance* one might wish to apply to him. At the one point, for example, when he seems to enter the human condition by finding Apollonius boring, it then appears, just as we begin to think that his modes of thought are ours, that he was seriously tempted after all. Fortunately our theory of stupidity can come to the rescue and provide the much-needed guidance.

Like *Bouvard et Pécuchet*, the *Tentation* is a citational work. Jean Seznec has identified many of its sources and Michel Foucault has stressed the importance in the work of a multi-layered dialectic of text and vision.[32] The word made flesh passes before Saint Antoine just as sentences pass before Bouvard and Pécuchet. The characters attempt to assimilate the word in different ways: Bouvard and Pécuchet, in the mode of *faire*, move through the word to practical activity, whereas Saint Antoine, in the mode of *être*, seeks a condition, a belief that will inform his existence. But in both cases the text juxtaposes its citations in paradigms of non-functional contradictions which make all views seem stupid. And whereas for Bouvard and Pécuchet this is cause for despair and annoyance, since they do not know what to do and whatever they do seems to fail, for Saint Antoine, who is approaching the citations in a different mode, the problem seems more acute and at the same time more foolish. Since he has no practical goal like grafting fruit trees or making radishes grow he could simply turn away from these juxtaposed visions. Why does he not do so?

The answer, at least in part, might be a purely empirical one: he is alone and bored and has nothing better to do. But as the temptations progress and the narration continues at the second level of stupidity, isolating and juxtaposing them, making them objects, Saint Antoine begins to accede to the third level of stupidity and find them attractive *because* rather than in spite of their foolishness. If one attempts to trace this movement one finds that one proceeds through most of the versions of stupidity encountered elsewhere in Flaubert.

First of all, for example, we encounter intelligence and theory as manifestations of *bêtise*. Hilarion, who replaces in the final version the eighth mortal sin of 'logic' that appeared in earlier versions, overwhelms Antoine in argument by citing scripture, bringing out contradictions in it and in the Christian tradition. He then brings before Antoine a babble of heretics all shouting contradictory precepts and doctrines:

> Marcion: le Créateur n'est pas le vrai Dieu!
> Saint Clément d'Alexandrie: La matière est éternelle!
> Bardesanes: Elle a été formée par Sept Esprits planétaires.
> Les Herniens: Les anges ont fait les âmes!
> Les Priscillianiens: C'est le Diable qui a fait le monde! (I, 536)[33]

When Antoine asks, 'Who was Jesus?' he receives thirteen different replies. And when he calls them liars they reply in chorus:

> Nous avons des martyrs plus martyrs que les tiens, des prières plus difficiles, des élans d'amour supérieurs, des extases aussi longues.
> Antoine: Mais pas de révélation! pas de preuves!
> Alors tous brandissent dans l'air des rouleaux de papyrus, des tablettes de bois, des morceaux de cuir, des bandes d'étoffe (I, 540).[34]

We are clearly confronted here with a distancing and reductive mode of perception which reduces theories to ridiculous objects.

Then we encounter the comical pride and boring self-satisfaction of Apollonius, who speaks at such great length of his life, works and virtues (echoed by his foolish acolyte, Damis), that even Antoine becomes bored: 'What are they getting at?' 'They babble on as if they were drunk'; 'Excuse me, strangers, it is late'; 'Stop it'; 'Enough' (I, 548–9). But when he is gone Antoine admits,

> Celui-là vaut tout l'enfer! Nabuchodonosor ne m'avait pas tant ébloui. La Reine de Saba ne m'a pas si profondément charmé. Sa manière de parler des dieux inspire l'envie de les connaître (I, 551).[35]

It is perhaps here that he begins to feel the attractions of stupidity, for immediately afterwards, as all the images that men have worshipped pass before him and Hilarion, they enjoy themselves tremendously, holding their sides with laughter. But his development is by no means complete, for as the images come nearer to human forms 'they irritate Antoine more' and he finally recoils in horror from a huge iron statue, like that in *Salammbô*, whose innards contain a furnace for the sacrifice of children.

Next we have *bêtise* as solidified language in the person of the Buddha. 'I too have done astounding things', he begins, an old man recounting his youth. 'I used to eat only one grain of rice per day — *and* the grains of rice in those days weren't as big as they are today.' Or, 'I remained immobile for six years'. All this is recounted in rather a comic mode: 'Having defeated the Devil, I spent twelve years living exclusively on perfumes'; then, since I had acquired the five virtues, the eighteen substances, etc., I became the Buddha. 'All the gods bow; those with several heads bow them all simultaneously.'

The Buddha is followed by other Gods, who first interest and then tire Antoine; but at the end, after Jehovah, comes the Devil who, bearing him off to the heavens, offers knowledge. His lesson is that the world has no goal and God is 'la seule substance', matter itself. And this, once Antoine is back on earth, seems the last necessary step in his education in stupidity. All matter is finally divine, but it does not have immediate meaning, for the forms it takes are epiphenomena. Hence there is no reason to try to understand them; one may regard them simply as matter, as objects in which or through which reverie may glimpse the transcendental *signifié* of the divine. And so, as the monsters pass before him — les Nisnas, les Blemmyes, les Cynocéphales, le Sadhuzag, le Martichoras — he feels a natural horror but also a definite attraction. And when the Catoblépas, a black buffalo with the head of a pig that drags on the ground at the end of a long thin neck, speaks to him, he is sorely tempted: 'Sa stupidité m'attire.' Surrounded by monsters of all kind, animal, vegetable, and mineral, he finds suddenly, like Jules in his terrifying encounter with the dog, that 'il n'a plus peur' and he shouts out his desire to become one with the universe, to take on all the forms he has observed, 'être en tout, . . . être la matière!' (I, 571).

The fact that the sun then rises, bearing on its face the image of Christ, and that Antoine returns to his prayers, renders highly ambiguous the problem of temptation: has God at the last moment saved him from his desire to become matter, or is the sunrise merely an ironic comment on the structure of temptation which will require Antoine to begin his cycle again? The tale of temptation does not conclude, but the moments of Flaubertian stupidity give the work a certain unity. The attitude of mind which makes the vast collection of heresies, theories, images, and objects into instances of stupidity does not dispense with them but makes them more powerful as temptations, since in them the mind can attain the kind of exaltation and freedom which Antoine expresses in his final paragraph. The supreme accomplishment of stupidity as both a property of objects and a mode of vision would be to overcome all alienation by making the actual forms of the world disappear and allowing the mind itself to create the world out of a universal and undifferentiated matter. But to state that proposal would be itself stupid, which is perhaps why the drama cannot conclude.

I write at length of stupidity not because of a strong interest in Flaubert's mental pathology but because the structure of the concept seems to give an organization to attitudes which determine Flaubert's literary practice. In recognizing the importance of the concept I am not claiming, with Sartre, that Flaubert was always defined for himself as a stupid man, *l'Idiot de la famille*, though in comparison with analytically-minded contemporaries like Kierkegaard and Marx he was, as Valéry said, 'a very tolerable artist but without much grace or profundity of mind'.[36]

What I should want to maintain, though, is that a desire not to understand, not to grasp the purposes that language, behaviour, and objects serve in ordinary practical life, is one of the determining features of Flaubert's writing. Granted, he puts it somewhat differently: 'A force de vouloir tout comprendre, tout me fait rêver' (i, 192). But he recognizes that understanding has been displaced by reverie, though he might prefer to think of reverie as beyond understanding. And he grasps also the connection with stupidity, for he moves immediately to deny it: 'Il me semble, pourtant, que cet ébahissement-là n'est pas la bêtise.' He is right in that it is not mere foolishness but complex stupidity as a mode of perception and source of value, which transforms 'le bourgeois', as he says, into 'quelque chose d'infini'. Stupidity, as a refusal to understand, negates ordinary meaning to replace it with an open and exploratory reverie. To see how this was done in the novels one must consider the style which was to make the world stupid while remaining itself an object of admiration. To comprehend the world without understanding it, to treat men, for example, as mastodons or butterflies and to fix them sprawling on a pin, was the task of Flaubertian irony.

## B. Irony

> What Gods will be able to rescue us from all these ironies?
> SCHLEGEL

> In earthly art Irony has this meaning: conduct similar to God's.
> SOLGER

Irony has always had a good press, since those who write of it are by profession intelligent and since more than any other form it supports the elitism of intelligence. Kierkegaard maintains that the true ironist does not wish to be understood, and though such exemplars be rare specimens we can at least say that irony always involves the possibility of misunderstanding and thus offers the critic or analyst the opportunity to display his own perspicacity. He will be quick to point out the possibilities of irony lest his failure of recognition allow others to assign bounds to his intelligence and to accuse him of lack of subtlety. For the reader and critic irony is both an opportunity and a threat, an occasion for the exercise of intelligence but an occasion on which others may get outside and comprehend him in turn.

To sketch the demands which irony makes on the reader is already to reveal something of its structure, and in particular of the dizzying dialectic which it establishes. 'La vorace ironie' forces one to move through stages of self-consciousness, stepping back continually to judge one's prior judgments without ever finding firm ground on which to take one's stand and halt the process. The ironical self is divorced from the empirical self which it scrutinizes, and though the operation of scrutiny result in the projection of a new and newly-enlightened empirical self, a new ironical self must arise to judge it in turn. Irony is the desire of the subject never to let itself be defined as object by others but always to undertake a protective self-transcendence, which, however, exposes more than it protects.

Flaubert is, of course, aware of irony's vicious spiral, the sapping of confidence which it brings, the inability to act, except in roles, which it promotes. But this is a less powerful source of anxiety for him than it is for Baudelaire, who as a lyric poet is led by the conventions of verse to adopt narrative postures that are vulnerable to ironic scrutiny. Flaubert secretes few empirical selves in his works, and he is more exposed in private life, which, since it is both more ephemeral and less demandingly judged by others, is a less fertile terrain for this particular kind of anxiety. If, as he says, 'irony seems to me to dominate life' (ii, 407), that is partly because he has chosen inactivity; if irony and fear of the resulting view of himself kept him from vice (iv, 170), that is not wholly to be deplored. It may also have kept him from love — 'the idea of how I would look at that moment made me laugh so much that all my will melted in the flames of an inner irony' (i, 236) — but only, he tells Louise Colet, in the case of other women. For the most part irony is a highly desirable posture: 'the ironic acceptance of life and its complete formal recasting in art' is the most worthy of attitudes (iv, 15), and he urges his friend Ernest Chevalier, who has become a lawyer, not to take himself seriously, to conserve always a philosophic irony, 'pour l'amour de moi' (i, 183).

All of which is to say that when considering Henry James's question — whether he was 'absolutely and exclusively condemned to irony' or whether 'he might not after all have fought out his case a little more on the spot?'[37] — there seems no need to offer a biographical or pathological defence and to attempt to justify the irony of the works by appeal to an existence racked by irony. One must consider, rather, the functions of irony within the works themselves and the validity of claims that such irony is in itself a positive value.

The most basic feature of irony is perhaps its dual structure: it presupposes two orders which are in contrast with one another and in whose contrast lies whatever value the form can generate. Since our most pervasive dualism, or at least that which is thought most worthy of attention and productive of meaning, is one of appearance and reality, we tend to cast suspected ironies into that mould. An ironic statement has a literal meaning, but that meaning is only semblance and the true proposition is hidden and must be reconstructed. Indeed, it is the incongruity of the literal meaning, the perception of it as semblance, which leads us to identify a possible irony and seek the hidden reality. Situational irony, as opposed to verbal irony, relies even more obviously on this particular structure: pride goeth before a fall; the order postulated by the proud protagonist is revealed as mere semblance when he falls into the contrary order of poetic justice. The proleptic assertion of one order is undermined by consequences which we feel are 'appropriate' in that they derive from another, though not necessarily preferable, order.

Situational or dramatic irony is thus a device of cohesion, which knits together incidents and gives them a meaning by relating them to a law of the world. The irony of Charles encouraging Emma's relationships with Rodolphe and Léon gives more shape to the plot of *Madame Bovary* than it might otherwise have had, and the irony of the Blind Man's appearance at three crucial moments in Emma's life and the implicit commentary provided by his songs and actions gives a metaphorical neatness to her fate. But generally such gross dramatic ironies play only a minor role in Flaubert's novels, and in *L'Education sentimentale* and *Bouvard et Pécuchet* the order which situational irony proposes — the irony of dreams or projects failing in appropriate ways — seems little more than that of a general negative fate: human projects are doomed to systematic failure.

It is not difficult to understand why this should be so. Situational irony cuts rather too neat a figure and implies, even if its message be discouraging, a fundamentally predictable and orderly world. It is a mode of existential recuperation frequently used in daily life to temper disappointment: 'that's just what would happen', we say when it begins to rain just as we start a picnic lunch, suggesting that nature is not wholly indifferent to us but acts in accordance with an order which might be grasped. And thus when Balzac has Grandet expire from the effort of attempting to seize the priest's gold cross, or Valérie Marneffe die 'bien punie par où elle a péché', the world is rendered more orderly and intelligible by these dramatic ironies than if they had been struck down in some irrelevant and haphazard way. Such coherence is not one of Flaubert's goals, and he shows a consequent preference for verbal rather than situational irony.

What makes verbal irony an especially fascinating problem for anyone concerned with the strategies of reading is that no sentence is ironic *per se*. Sarcasm may contain internal inconsistencies which make its purport quite obvious, but for a sentence to be properly ironic it must be possible to imagine some group of readers taking it quite literally, otherwise there is no contrast between apparent and assumed meaning and no space of ironic play. The perception of irony thus depends upon a set of expectations which enable the reader to sense the incongruity or *invraisemblance* of literal or apparent meanings and to construct an alternative ironic meaning which accords with the *vraisemblance* which he has established for the text. In ordinary conversation these expectations are drawn from shared knowledge of external circumstances: knowing both George and Harry one can decide that what George has just said about Harry does not accord with the text of justifiable attitudes towards Harry and that therefore it must be taken ironically; but in the case of literature one's expectations depend on an even more complex sum of cultural and literary experience.

When Flaubert writes that during her illness Emma had a vision of heavenly bliss and purity to which she resolved to aspire, his language does not itself offer decisive indications of irony:

> Elle voulut devenir une sainte. Elle acheta des chapelets, elle porta des amulettes; elle souhaitait avoir dans sa chambre, au chevet de sa couche, un reliquaire enchâssé d'émeraudes, pour le baiser tous les soirs (I, 647).[38]

Our perception of irony depends on a series of cultural norms which we assume we share with the narrator. One does not simply decide to become a saint, as one might decide to become a nurse or to take up the piano; and if saintliness were the proper object of a decision, the way to become a saint would not be to purchase the equipment. Moreover, our model of sainthood presumably clashes with the concrete form that Emma's desire takes: emeralds on a relic box do not ensure the progress of the soul, nor does the self-indulgence of the desire to have it at the head of one's bed in order to kiss it from time to time.

Thus irony seems to depend, in the first instance, on the referentiality of the text: we must assume that it refers to a world with which we are familiar; if it were fantasy or fairy-tale, or if it concerned a primitive tribe in Borneo, we would have no standards by which to judge actions as foolish and self-indulgent unless the text itself proposed these judgments. It is no doubt for this reason that the novel has been thought the form most propitious to irony. Referring us constantly to a known world, it makes relevant our models of behaviour and enables us to detect the foolishness of apparent meanings.

But even at this initial stage there is a dialectic between text and world, for our sense of irony in this passage is strengthened, perhaps even provoked, by the fact that we expect Emma to be a foolish and self-indulgent woman. Were this not the case we should probably pass easily over the passage in question; but in fact we can link it up with other reports on her thought and conduct. When she finds that despite her prayers 'aucune délectation ne descendait des cieux' she draws from that failure and her continued sacrifice an image of herself:

> Emma se comparait à ces grandes dames d'autrefois, dont elle avait rêvé la gloire sur un portrait de La Vallière, et qui, traînant avec tant de majesté la queue chamarrée de leurs longues robes, se retiraient en des solitudes pour y répandre aux pieds du Christ toutes les larmes d'un coeur que l'existence blessait (I, 647).[39]

Her vision dwells not on the piety and self-sacrifice of a convent life but on the embroidered train of the long gown in which she might majestically move along corridors. Such analogues help to confirm our perception of irony.

Yet clearly our knowledge of the world and our knowledge of the world of the novel do not in themselves suffice to account for the discovery of irony. Those factors might remain constant, but if the text itself undertook to formulate disparagement of Emma's desires, then there would be no discrepancy between apparent and assumed meaning. We might still detect a situational irony in the neatness with which sexual ambitions become religious, but there would be no verbal irony. While we need not actually find in the verbal surface an assertion which runs counter to what our empirical knowledge would lead us to assert, we must at least detect, in the apparent disinterestedness of the text, a failure to assert what we take to be the appropriate judgment.

Moreover, and this is the final factor in the perception of irony, we must in our reading have formed impressions of a kind of narrative *vraisemblance*, of the way in which the text habitually operates, so that we can determine whether the text is actually being ironic or whether, on the contrary, it is describing without irony projects on which we, in our superior wisdom, can pass ironic judgment. In the latter case, we would say that it is ironic that Emma should be described in this way but not that the text itself was ironic.

It would seem, then, that the perception of irony depends on four different factors which are rather too easily grouped together under the ambiguous heading of 'context': our models of human behaviour which provoke judgments of what the text presents, our expectations about the world of the novel which suggest how details concerning actions or characters are to be interpreted and thus help give us something to judge, the apparent assertions which the sentences in question make and which provide material that we find incongruous and recuperate as irony, and finally our sense of the habitual procedures of the text which provides a justification for ironic reading and reassures us that we are only participating in that play to which the text invites us. The nature of these various determinants of irony indicates only too clearly the freedom and anxiety we make ours when we call a text ironic, for at the very moment when we propose that a text means something other than what it appears to say we introduce, as hermeneutic devices that will lead us to the truth of the text, models which are primarily to be defined as our expectations about the text and the world. Irony, the cynic might say, is the ultimate form of recuperation, whereby we ensure that the text says only what we desire to hear; but one might also turn that definition around and, focusing on its less cynical face, say that in calling a text ironic we indicate our desire to avoid premature foreclosure, to allow the text to work on us as fully as it can, to grant it the status of sacred words which are presumed to contain at some level, however deep, the answers which we might seek. In other words, it is precisely because the procedures for identifying and reading irony require the active participation of the reader that the ironic text displays that negative capability which is reputedly the feature of the greatest works.

One can see, then, that while irony as an attitude of mind involves a relatively simple dialectic of freedom and anxiety — the subject trying to secure his freedom by becoming a new subject that judges himself as object — the irony of a text offers a more complex dialectic: the mind does not simply judge itself and judge itself judging itself; it must judge the text against expectations which result from judging the text and must judge itself judging the text against those expectations. The intervention of the work itself as both subject and object is what adds new complications to the ironic process; for what W. H. Auden says of all 'real books' applies especially to the ironic text: it reads us, forcing us as we explore those hidden depths which we have decided exist to wonder whether our searchlights are in fact projectors and what it is in us that might enable us to make such a distinction. Irony, we might say, frees the writer, but, insofar as it gives his work the character of a sacred and written text, it frees the reader only by chaining him to the problems of his own subjectivity.

A single trivial but typical example will illustrate the involuted and anxious nature of ironic reading. Having failed his first medical exam, Charles set to work, learned all the questions by heart, and passed on the second attempt with a reasonable mark. 'Quel beau jour pour sa mère! On donna un grand dîner' (I, 578). That full stop ends the paragraph; the next passes on to Charles' future.

The irony of the first sentence is easily identified: our cultural models enable us to understand a mother's pride but still make it ironic for the mother rather than the son to be pleased; and we are prepared for such a reading by the stress the text has laid on her role in organizing his life. Moreover, the exclamation mark calls the sentence to our attention as potentially ironic. It is rather the second sentence which enables one to experience the antinomies of irony.

Suppose that one does wish to take it as an ironic comment on the festivities, suggesting, by its brevity and flatness, that they were indeed mediocre or at least provoked by a mediocre occasion. How does one attain and justify such a reading? Our models of human behaviour are not of much use, as they tell us that dinners are appropriate responses to such events, though they may also tell us something of the awkwardness that so often attends celebrations. We must rely, rather, on our expectations about the world of the novel and try to imagine 'un grand diner' involving these characters. The family, after all, is not a happy one, and festivities involving the braggart father, the shrewish and over-protective mother, and the lumpish son might have left much to be desired. But, alternatively, we might stress the presumed elaborateness of the festivities in contrast with Charles' mediocre success and try to find irony there. And the existence of those alternatives indicates what shaky ground we stand on: is the dinner itself mediocre or is it an excessive response to a mediocre occasion? Some such hypothesis, some imaginative filling-in of the scene, is required for the perception of irony, but it seems strangely unimportant which scene one constructs. If this be true, and I think that it is, then our response appears to be governed not by the empirical content of our expectations — not, that is to say by a firm and detailed sense of how these characters would behave — but by a formal expectation, derived, shall we say, from our sense of the function of earlier descriptions of Charles; that mediocrity and foolishness are to be the ultimate *signifiés* of any sequence concerning Charles and his family. Such a view, if openly stated, appears highly problematic, but it would seem to underlie and make possible the perception of irony.

Having gone that far, there seem two obvious questions that one must ask. First of all, from what perspective, on what grounds, can one pass ironic judgment on a dinner held to celebrate success in an examination? What values is one proposing in so doing, and are these values not so eccentric that one ought to hesitate before attributing them to the text? This question finds no easy or adequate reply, and the very difficulty of stating in clear and acceptable terms the grounds of one's judgment must intensify a self-conscious uneasiness. Secondly, is this imaginative filling-in an appropriate response to a text which deliberately remains silent, telling us no more about the dinner than that it was 'grand'? Our sense that 'How many children had Lady Macbeth?' is an illegitimate question should make us doubtful of the propriety of guessing what the dinner was like. Awareness of the danger of substituting a world for the text makes the process of ironic reading even more self-conscious and problematic.

And yet, and yet, the brevity and silence of the sentence looms before us, demanding, especially now that we have dwelt on it, some kind of response, some naming of its effect. Moving from world to text we might try to justify a perception of irony with the thought that the phonetic ugliness of the line must bear some meaning. The assonance of vowels which are similar enough to echo one another but different enough to avoid harmony — 'on donna' and 'donna un grand' — and the awkward juncture between 'donna' and 'un' can be read as a grunting commentary.[40] Such a sentence must have a deflating effect. But if we look on that argument with a critical eye we can immediately see that it depends either on an assumption about the function of sound patterns in novels which we would be hard put to defend in general terms, or, if we wish to make no claims about novels in general, on notions of Flaubert's craftsmanship and its relation to his intentions: Flaubert would not have made this line phonetically ugly unless he wished it to be ironic. Whatever encouragement we might draw from such an hypothesis, it does not provide very firm ground on which to base a reading.

Indeed, the determining consideration might seem to be that once we have raised the question of irony we cannot easily abandon it without making the sentence utterly devoid of interest and denying the existence of that detachment which we have been so anxiously and, in this case, so verbosely exercising. Or, to approach the problem from a different angle, one might say that the only convincing arguments against the irony of a particular sentence are those which show that such irony would not be consonant with the world of the novel and the habitual procedures of the text; and hence, when we rely on our expectations about the text and its world in order to produce a presumed irony, we have nothing against which to judge that presumption except our own annoyance at the in-determinacy and shakiness of our own interpretive procedures. And since these procedures, the moves by which we distance ourselves from the language of the text and try to see it in a new light across that distance, are what constitute irony, we have in effect made the sentence ironic and experienced the freedom and alienation which irony produces. To dismiss the sentence and our own critical labours as futile and uninteresting does not deny irony because a sentence which so exercises us without yielding positive results is still, and precisely for that reason, highly ironic.

Beyond a certain stage one has no defence against the thought of irony; it invades one, as the expectation that the text will be ironic becomes the dominant consideration and produces that mode of detached questioning which is both exhilarating and demoralizing. But this is the end rather than the beginning of experience; one is led to it by more substantial and tangible ironies which are made obvious by a modicum of cultural knowledge. One should look briefly at some of these ironies which can be named and defended before considering once again the vertiginous uncertainties into which one is lured by expectations of irony.

The clearest ironies in Flaubert are perhaps those which deflate the pretensions of characters, either by signal departures from our models of human conduct or else by the description of illusions which contrast with realities announced by the text. Coming back in an exalted mood from his first dinner with the Arnoux, Frédéric, in a moment of epiphany on the Pont-Neuf, feels awakening powers and asks himself whether he should become a great painter or a great poet: 'il se décida pour la peinture, car les exigences de ce métier le rapprocheraient de Mme Arnoux. Il avait donc trouvé sa vocation! Le but de son existence était clair maintenant, et l'avenir infaillible' (II, 26). Even without knowledge of Frédéric one can identify that irony which undermines a thought-process notable for its lack of rigour by presenting it in logical terms. Slightly different cultural models make Léon's opinion about the best name for Emma's child an object of irony: 'M. Léon . . . is surprised that you don't choose Madeleine, which is exceedingly fashionable just now' (I, 604). And our notions of human behaviour enable us to identify irony when Frédéric 'wished for a serious illness, hoping in that way to interest her' (II, 33). Somewhat more interesting are ironies which rely on our sense of the incongruity of certain juxtapositions. 'On discutait sur l'immortalité de l'âme, on faisait des parallèles entre les professeurs' (II, 28), or 'Ce qui l'inquiétait principalement, c'était la frontière du Rhin. Il prétendait se connaître en artillerie, et se faisait habiller par le tailleur de l'Ecole polytechnique' (II, 29). Such examples could be multiplied almost indefinitely: Emma 'avait envie de faire des voyages ou de retourner vivre à son couvent. Elle souhaitait à la fois mourir et habiter Paris' (I, 594).[41] Sentences which juxtapose and pretend to knit together items which our notions of appropriate human responses and behaviour render incongruous are perhaps the most frequent devices of Flaubert's irony.

Often, however, the contrast on which the irony is based comes less from our own knowledge of the world than from inconsistencies in the text itself which presents both a reality and an illusion. When Frédéric accompanies Mme Arnoux on an errand,

'le temps était froid, et un lourd brouillard, estompant la façade des maisons, puait dans l'air. Frédéric le humait avec délices . . . A cause du pavé glissant ils oscillaient un peu; il lui semblait qu'ils étaient tous les deux comme bercés par le vent, au milieu d'un nuage' (II, 32–3).[42]

In other cases the contrasting items may be separated by larger stretches of text, but the scrupulous and attentive reader will have little difficulty in noting, shall we say, Frédéric's changing perceptions of Rosanette and Emma's of Charles.[43] However, the ironies he discovers, at least in the more interesting cases, may depend less on explicit contrasts which enable him to distinguish unequivocally between an appearance and a reality than on a general contrast between modes of discourse. Our experience of the novels gives us a sense of the various codes in which thoughts and events may be rendered, and we quickly come to identify the appearance of one of these codes with irony. As soon as we feel confident of our ability to recognize and categorize a particular type of discourse, that discourse comes to be read as if it were being quoted or displayed by the text with a modicum of distance; and as we accept that distance in sighing 'oh, more of that sort of thing', we undertake an ironic reading.

*Madame Bovary* is exceptional in that an early chapter devoted to Emma's convent education and its extracurricular accompaniments sketches for us the main features of the principal code. Attracted to the concrete expressions of a vague sentimentality, Emma accepts religion insofar as its metaphors are sexual or pathetic and peoples her mind with particularized novelistic images of amorous adventure:

Ce n'étaient qu'amours, amants, amantes, dames persécutées s'évanouissant dans des pavillons solitaires, postillons qu'on tue à tous les relais, chevaux qu'on crève à toutes les pages, forêts sombres, troubles du coeur, serments, sanglots, larmes et baisers, nacelles au clair de lune, rossignols dans les bosquets, *messieurs* braves comme des lions, doux comme des agneaux, vertueux comme on ne l'est pas, toujours bien mis, et qui pleurent comme des urnes (I, 586).[44]

Naturally enough, these images mingle with historical melodrama, the cult of Mary Queen of Scots and other noble and unfortunate ladies. The experience of which this code speaks is either socially exotic — noble ladies reclining on sofas or in carriages, contemplating the moon, a flower, or a plumed rider — or culturally exotic — mountains, waterfalls, ruins, palm trees. And the most striking feature of this romantic code is not that it speaks of an ideal which puts to shame the reality of the world but that it does so in terms which by their very concreteness become unrealizable. To aspire to be a chatelaine who, beneath gothic arches passes her days, chin in her hand, 'watching a plumed horseman on a black horse galloping towards her through the countryside' (I, 586) is to condemn oneself to disappointment. Flaubert satirizes the misplaced concreteness of this code in a splendidly anti-climatic passage about engravings representing:

paysages blafards des contrées dithyrambiques, qui souvent nous montrent à la fois des palmiers, des sapins, des tigres à droite, un lion à gauche, des minarets tartares à l'horizon, au premier plan des ruines romaines, puis des chameaux accroupis; — le tout encadré d'une forêt vierge bien nettoyée, et avec un grand rayon de soleil perpendiculaire tremblotant dans l'eau, où se détachent en écorchures blanches, sur un fond d'acier gris, de loin en loin, des cygnes qui nagent (I, 587).[45]

The nicely deferred ending compensates for the obviousness of the preceding ironies and indicates that it is not simply because of its impossible juxtapositions that one should distance oneself from this code.

When we recognize later passages as instances of this code, we thereby enter the domain of irony. Emma's own exotic reveries of countries with sonorous names, where one travels in a post-chaise over mountain roads to the sounds of cow-bells, waterfalls, and songs, stopping at night beside a gulf beneath lemon trees, not only are distant from possible experience but dwell on concrete and surface details which would not satisfy if they were experienced:

> Que ne pouvait-elle s'accouder sur le balcon des chalets suisses ou enfermer sa tristesse dans un cottage écossais, avec un mari vêtu d'un habit de velours noir à longues basques, et qui porte des bottes molles, un chapeau pointu et des manchettes! (I, 588).[46]

Gérard Genette notes quite correctly that whereas visions, such as Emma's mystical experience during her illness, are accompanied by distancing verbs (elle croyait voir, croyait entendre) and vague details, reveries in Flaubert surprise us by the clarity and precision of details and thereby resist our attempt to take them as inner musings which are less real than narrated events.[47] But of course we do take them in this way, and their resistance, their substantiality, has the effect of strengthening the irony by making them stand forth clearly in the text and call attention to themselves.

It is largely our acquaintence with this code which confirms our ironic view of Emma's own behaviour, for her affairs with Rodolphe and Léon are presented as attempts to produce in her own life events which might serve as referents for the language of this code. 'J'ai un amant! un amant!' she repeats to herself, delighted that this language should finally have become applicable and that she should have entered 'la légion lyrique des femmes adultères' (I, 629). And for Léon she does indeed participate in the language of romance:

> Elle était l'amoureuse de tous les romans, l'héroïne de tous les drames, le vague *elle* de tous les volumes de vers. Il retrouvait sur ses épaules la couleur ambrée de l'*odalisque au bain*; elle avait le corsage long des châtelaines féodales; elle ressemblait aussi à *la femme pâle de Barcelone*, mais elle était par-dessus tout Ange! (I, 664).[48]

Moreover, it is precisely a language of sentimental clichés that Emma and Léon exchange in their early conversations, which Rodolphe proffers at the Comices agricoles and in the letter with which he breaks off the affair, which Emma uses in her letters to Léon even after she has begun to grow tired of him (I, 669), and which guides Emma in her responses to particular situations. Hearing a step in the passage during one of her trysts with Rodolph, she asks:

As tu tes pistolets?
Pourquoi?
Mais . . . pour te défendre, reprit Emma.

She would have preferred him to be more properly dramatic (I, 631). Or again, she would dress Léon in black and have him grow a pointed beard 'in order to resemble portraits of Louis XIII' (I, 668). And though she does at one point, when watching *Lucia di Lammermoor*, distance herself from this code — 'now she knew the triviality of passions which art exaggerated' (I, 650) — she immediately constructs a novel around the singer Lagardy. She cannot escape from the code or its irony.

There are, of course, other codes in *Madame Bovary*, other types of discourse which the text cites: the pompous official oratory of the Comices agricoles, pseudo-science and -culture of Homais, the bourgeois discourse of the citizens of Yonville. Presented either in direct quotation or in a *style indirect libre* which reduces and deadens by omitting the effective and spontaneous engagement of characters in speech, these linguistic specimens are read with a certain detachment and judged as ironic comments on their various sources. Much the same is true of *L'Education sentimentale*, where there is an interplay of a greater variety of codes: the romantic discourse which Frédéric adopts early in the book and which serves to structure his thoughts of Madame Arnoux; the code of the rational *arriviste*, which Deslauriers identifies in referring to Rastignac as a model and which treats society as an intelligible organism or machine that must be mastered; the artistic discourse of Pellerin, which imposes a particular view of the world; the code of revolutionary oratory; the social and political commonplaces encounterred in the Dambreuse salon and elsewhere. It is not so much that our models of human behaviour and of cultural appropriateness reveal any one of these codes as foolishly distorting; rather the co-existence of so many different codes produces an indeterminacy in which we can never be sure when the author is responsible for his language, when he may be citing sources which we happen not to identify but which represent a limited position like any other; and consequently the general sense of potential irony, a sense of the possibility of distancing ourselves from any of the sentences which the text sets before us, comes to hover over the book as a whole.

Irony of this sort is, of course, a polemical device. Directed for the most part against particular characters and their view of the world, it suggests that the implied author of the text holds other views, even if we cannot precisely define them; and it was no doubt this absence of positive values due to the choice of an ironic mode of expression that James had in mind when he wished that Flaubert might have fought out his case a little more on the spot. But it could certainly be argued that the function of these ironies is not primarily to convey to the reader a particular view of the world or to make out a definable case but rather to set in motion the negative operations of irony so that they may be constantly present as possible modes of processing other sentences in the text. If we are once accustomed to undertaking ironic readings of sentences which refer explicitly to the thoughts and behaviour of characters, on the assumption that alternative positions may always be constructed, then we will at least be attuned to treating in like manner sentences where polemical intent would be difficult to locate but where detachment still seems the safest posture.

In favour of such a view one could argue, first of all, that there is no surer way for a writer to make readers attend to his style than to force them to pore over his sentences, searching for subtle marks of irony. But secondly, at a slightly different level, one might maintain that the ambition to write 'un livre sur rien' can be realized only if readers can be cajoled into sucking the apparent content out of the sentences and leaving only that empty form which asks to be filled but makes one chary of actually filling it. Kierkegaard speaks of the ironic method, as practised by Socrates, as asking a question 'not in the interest of obtaining an answer, but to suck out the apparent content with a question and leave only an emptiness'.[49] But that account is not entirely just, certainly not if applied to Flaubert, for such unmitigated sucking would become entirely tedious. It is, indeed, only half of the process, which might be best described in terms of Schiller's *Spieltrieb*, the drive towards play which is the basis of the aesthetic attitude. Pure appearance, which is the object of this drive, is highly ambiguous, foiling in turn the *Stofftrieb* and the *Formtrieb* by becoming form when one seeks matter and matter when one seeks form.[50]

The play of potential irony in Flaubert seems to work in precisely this way; the sentence becomes a surface which escapes the determinations that one tries to give it. The simplest examples are perhaps the one-sentence paragraphs with which Flaubert sprinkles his works. After a long paragraph recounting Frédéric's regular and pointless wanderings up and down the Champs-Elysées, the next paragraph declares: 'Il allait dîner, moyennant quarante-trois sols le cachet, dans un restaurant, rue de la Harpe' (He went to dine, at a cost of 43 sous, in a restaurant, rue de la Harpe) (II, 16). There is no polemical irony here, no view of the world which can be pilloried by a 'correct' attitude. And if we try to dwell on the form which calls the sentence to our attention — its isolation, its off-setting of the phrase 'dans un restaurant' — we find little joy and must yield to the feeling that it simply asserts a fact, namely that he went to dine in a particular restaurant. Yet if we dwell upon that assertion, the sentence comes to seem increasingly pointless; we cannot do much with the cost of his meal or the location of the restaurant, and therefore we find ourselves drawn back to the form which, by its foregrounding of the sentence, by its trailing of phrases in a sought-for awkwardness, seems to undermine not this particular proposition — there is little there to undermine — but novelistic discourse in general.

The most cursory examination of *Bouvard et Pécuchet* and *Trois Contes* will reveal the extent to which the single-sentence paragraph becomes the staple of Flaubert's ironic style. 'Elle avait eu, comme une autre, son histoire d'amour'; 'Théodore, la semaine suivant, en obtint des rendez-vous'; 'Le moment arrivé, elle courut vers l'amoureux'; 'A sa place, elle trouva un de ses amis'; 'Quand le temps était clair, on s'en allait de bonne heure à la ferme de Geffosses' — these are a few paragraphs of 'Un Coeur simple'. And in *Bouvard et Pécuchet* the procedure is even more frequent: 'Comme il faisait une chaleur de 33 degrés, le boulevard Bourdon se trouvait absolument désert' is the first paragraph, 'Deux hommes parurent' the fourth, and 'Quand ils furent arrivés au milieu du boulevard, ils s'assirent, à la même minute, sur le même banc' the sixth. The desire to isolate, to increase the blanks and halts in the text, has obviously become one of the major determinants of Flaubert's style. Instead of placing a fact in a paragraph which would link it with causes, consequences and reactions, he now sets them apart, like impassive and enigmatic monuments. We can, if we like, read in the spacing a metaphor for a world of discrete particulars, a world viewed by science, as Flaubert seems to have conceived it; but such a move leaves out of consideration the fact that such isolated sentences are interspersed with longer paragraphs and so figure in a textual rhythm which foregrounds them and exposes them to the ironic attention that other elements of the text have aroused.

Such sentences are magnets for ironic attention for the simple reason that irony is always most at home in brief, aphoristic, and enigmatic forms, where an intention has less space to manifest itself and the reader more leisure for self-conscious exploration. But once the ironic consciousness is attracted to these forms, it finds that it can no longer, as it could in other cases, judge propositions against an empirical context — knowledge of the world or expectations about the world of the novel. It cannot summon up from these funds of experience attitudes to set against the sentences. It must rather shift into a higher key and precipitate meta-ironies. The context is now the novel as form rather than particularities of its or our world. The sentence, thrust before one as a sentence in a novel which seems to be doing little else than being a sentence in a novel, cries out, 'I am literature, I am organizing the world for you, transmuting it into fiction, representing it'. And when one attends to its factitiousness, its cumbersome foolishness as it lies stranded in isolation on the white page, one feels that if this is its function then it is a poor function indeed, nor is it performed gracefully or effectively. There is a dislocation, not between linguistic *signifiant* and linguistic *signifié*, but between the sequence of linguistic signs and their significance in the novel. It is not that they no longer function. 'Deux hommes parurent' is a necessary antecedent to the next paragraph; but other sentences could have served that function equally well, if indeed that function need be served at all. The foregrounding of the sentence puts on display the connection between linguistic signs and novelistic function and calls attention to the artificiality and even arbitrariness of that connection. Valéry, it seems, had so strong and persistent a sense of this arbitrariness that he was unable to take novels seriously: 'la manie perverse des substitutions possibles me saisit'.[51] But for most of us such reactions must be specially provoked.

We seem to be faced, then, with a version of what is often

called Romantic irony: the posture of a work which contains within itself an awareness of the fact that while pretending to give a true account of reality it is in fact fiction and that one must view with an ironic smile the act of writing a novel in the first place. Nowhere is this more apparent than in *Bouvard et Pécuchet*, where the pointlessness of the characters' activities is matched only by that of the novelist in inventing and recording them and where, as Hugh Kenner says, Flaubert undertook to produce, with supreme artistry, the effects of gross artistic incompetence.[52] But if one simply labels such procedures as 'Romantic irony' one is using the term very much as a 'sense for the negative',[53] a name with which one can arrest the process and make it an object of admiration rather than a source of disquiet. Admiration should be rather harder to earn, and to give Flaubert a chance to earn it one should look at the procedures by which his style — 'une manière absolue de voir les choses' (ii, 346) — becomes the instrument of 'infinite absolute negativity'.

The irony which interests us here is not a limited negativity, which negates this or that particular in the name of an alternative; it is rather a sense that the author is distanced from his language, which is proffered as if by citation, but that one does not know where he stands. Flaubert, Barthes writes,

en maniant une ironie frappée d'incertitude, opère un malaise salutaire de l'écriture: il n'arrête pas le jeu des codes (ou l'arrête mal), en sorte que (c'est là sans doute la *preuve* de l'écriture) on ne sait jamais s'il est responsable de ce qu'il écrit (s'il y a un sujet *derrière* son langage); car l'être de l'écriture (le sens du travail qui la constitue) est d'empêcher de jamais répondre à cette question: *Qui parle?*[54]

And thus many of the techniques described in Chapter 2 as devices which undermine the attribution of meaning, the identification of a narrative posture, and the use of characters as reflectors, become the vehicles of this uncertain irony. The text throws up sentences which the reader finds it difficult to process and recuperate, and the assumption that this is the result of deliberate artistry opens a space of potential irony. The sentences, separated from a responsible source, take on a certain monumentality. Like the isolated single-sentence paragraphs or like Thompson's inscription on Pompey's column, they have a flatness or blankness which results from the fact that their significance in the novel seems inadequate to the stress their foregrounded situation gives them. The magnificence of Thompson's letters contrasts with the triviality of their meaning. The use of a complete paragraph to tell us that Frédéric went to dine in a restaurant in the rue de la Harpe creates the presumption of a significance greater than any we succeed in giving that fact.

This disparity between novelistic *signifiant* and *signifié* is one of the major factors that creates the impression of language being cited. In *Bouvard et Pécuchet* and *Trois Contes* the compositional clumsiness which had always marked Flaubert's style becomes so pervasive that one can no longer doubt its role as a deliberate distancing device. Calling attention to sentences as sentences but without providing any supplementary meaning to compensate that attention, awkwardness becomes a feeble sign of the written.

Its forms are varied. Proust noted that adverbs and adverbial phrases are placed in the 'ugliest, most unexpected and heaviest way' and that Flaubert did not fear the heaviness of certain verbs, constantly using 'avoir' where other writers would seek nuance and diversity: 'Les maisons avaient des jardins en pente.' 'Les quatre tours avaient des toits pointus.'[55] Flaubert's *c'était* is another case in point. Used in the juvenilia for a rudimentary dramatic value — an identification following a description — it becomes in the later works the instrument of flatness and banality. 'C'était l'époque des vacances.' 'C'était l'époque où le père Rouault envoyait *son* dinde, en souvenir de sa jambe remise.' 'C'était par un beau matin d'été.' *C'était* is a device of isolation and fragmentation, since the alternative would invariably be to attach the predicate of the sentence to another sentence as dependent clause. 'A cet époque, quand les vacances avaient commencé . . .' Or, after 'Rodolphe . . . l'entraînait sans parler jusqu'au fond du jardin,' one could have omitted the jump to a new paragraph and the introductory 'C'était' and continued straight on: 'sous la tonnelle, sur ce même banc de bâtons pourris où autrefois Léon la regardait si amoureusement . . .' (I, 631). The introduction of *c'était* is generally a way of isolating a fact, presenting it shorn of its potential links with thought and activity.

As for the placing of adverbs, Flaubert's idiosyncrasies here are well known. Thibaudet, in what, alas, is still the best discussion of his style, cites some phrases of a splendid clumsiness: 'Je commence à terriblement me repentir de m'être chargé de ta personne.'[56] But for the most part the effects depend not on grammatical errors of this sort but on the simple isolation of adverbs, either tacked on following a comma at the end of the sentence, or left in their proper place but offset by grammatically unnecessary commas: 'les petits glands rouges de la bordure tremblait à la brise, perpétuellement' (II, 11), or 'c'était pour lui un grand bonheur que de ramasser, quelquefois, ses ciseaux' (II, 60). Indeed, the deployment of adverbs seems only a particular instance of Flaubert's general tendency to fragment his sentences by placing items so that, interrupting the flow, they require commas or by setting off phrases by commas when there is no need to do so. Thibaudet quotes an example which might serve as parody: 'Car, je t'aime.'[57] Others, less noticeable, merely carry faint suggestions of randomness and discontinuity: 'et il s'en alla au hasard, par les rues' (II, 111); 'Plus loin, il remarqua trois pavés, au milieu de la voie, le commencement d'une barricade, sans doute' (II, 112); 'et on attaquait maintenant le poste du Château d'Eau, pour délivrer cinquante prisonniers, qui n'y étaient pas' (II, 112).

It is difficult to assign precise semantic value to these commas and pauses, and that is what produces potential irony: one's sense of an elaborate artifact whose meaning cannot be pinned down. Often the principal effect of sentence structure seems that of rhythmical postponement and anti-climax. At the races, 'une cloche, suspendue à un poteau couvert de chiffres, tinta.' When the flag is dropped, 'Alors, tous les cinq, se penchant sur les crinières, partirent' (II, 82). Alternatively, one may read it as a correlate of a dissociating impressionism which produces fragments that the sentence must try to fit together, as in the splendidly typical view of the women spectators:

> Les femmes, vêtues de couleurs brillantes, portaient des robes à taille longue, et, assises sur les gradins des estrades, elles faisaient comme de grands massifs de fleurs, tachetés de noir, çà et là, par les sombres costumes des hommes (II, 82).[58]

The irony in sentences like these, if irony there be, comes from a certain elephantine grace, a formal perfection which bears the marks not of easy fluencey but of laborious assembly and excessive determination. Given the context, that is to say, one might expect the function of such a sentence to be that of telling us what Frédéric saw, but it clearly does more than that, even if we cannot say exactly what; and by going beyond that novelistic function, by giving us a sense that it is determined by other, formal considerations, it makes that simple representative function something of an epiphenomenon which it partly negates. The chilly perfection of the form distances itself from apparent content and becomes a mode of ironic negation.

This is no doubt the effect Sartre has in mind in describing the work of the Flaubertian sentence:

> His sentence aims at the object, seizes it, immobilizes it and breaks its back, closes around it, turns itself to stone and petrifies the object as well. It is blind and deaf, bloodless, without a breath of life. A deep silence separates it from the sentence that follows. It falls into the void, eternally, and drags its prey along in this infinite fall. Any reality, once described, can be stricken from the inventory.[59]

But it is important to realize that the sentence does not carry out an active vendetta against the object; the effects Sartre describes so vividly are the result of the passivity of the sentence which, showing its artful face, suggests to us an unconcern with the objects which it goes beyond and leaves behind it as the jetsam of this formal quest.

Proust, as one might expect, was more perceptive when he noted that the attraction and effectiveness of Flaubert's style depended on a certain awkwardness;

> When Flaubert writes: 'Une telle confusion d'images l'étourdissait, bien qu'il y trouvât du charme, *pourtant*'; when Frédéric Moreau, whether he be with la Maréchale or Mme Arnoux, 'se met à leur dire des tendresses', we cannot think that this 'pourtant' is graceful, nor that this 'se mettre à dire des tendresses' is particularly distinguished. But we are fond of them, these heavy blocks of matter that Flaubert's sentence raises and lets fall with the irregular noise of an excavating machine.[60]

Indeed, the sentences charm us precisely because they do not destroy, as Sartre suggests, with active and definable irony but go their ponderous way in what Proust called the 'trottoir roulant' of Flaubert's style.

The style changes, of course; *Bouvard et Pécuchet* and *Trois Contes* have few of the long trailing periods that characterize *Madame Bovary*, *L'Education sentimentale*, and especially *Salammbô*. They display their compositional artifice rather more self-consciously in short, flat phrases. Of Julien we are told, 'Il affranchit des peuples. Il délivra des reines enfermées dans des tours' (II, 182). Or, 'Le temps n'apaisa pas sa souffrance. Elle devenait intolérable. Il résolut de mourir' (II, 186). Rising to no heights, proceeding with synoptic unconcern, the sentences seem to say 'this is the story, which I am, simply, relating'. Transitions between paragraphs, for example, can be made in the most obvious and artificial ways: 'C'est que, peut-être, nous ne savons pas la chimie!' New paragraph. 'Pour savoir la chimie ... (II, 219). Or 'Et elle refermait la porte.' Paragraph. 'Elle l'ouvrait avec plaisir devant M. Bourais ...' (II, 168). When links are so patently displayed the effect is one of dissociation: a language refusing to rise to any occasion, lifeless, like a series of quotations taken from an unknown text. 'Toutes ses expériences ratèrent. Il était chaque fois fort étonné (II, 211). Or, 'Les cantaloups mûrirent. Au premier, Bouvard fit la grimace. Le second ne fut pas meilleur, le troisième non plus ... Alors Pécuchet se tourna vera les fleurs' (II, 211). Such flatness is itself a kind of distance, negating the reality to which the sentences are presumed to refer but without offering any definable alternative view, any value in the name of which one might take another view of the world.

Discontinuity, fragmentation, awkwardness, flatness, are modes of ironic distancing which produce a space of uncertainty without filling that space with alternatives. Calling attention to themselves as language, the sentences produce a discrepancy between novelistic signs and novelistic function which we can recuperate only by giving it the formal name of irony; but we bother with such recuperation only if we are impressed and attracted by the style. Otherwise, we might slide quickly past. It is quite understandable, then, that those who praise Flaubert as a stylist should find themselves in the awkward and indeed paradoxical position of praising what they feel at times to be clumsy writing. As Flaubert himself knew, we delight in what we find difficult to recuperate, in the surface which, thrust before us, promises depths that we find difficult to explore.

'Les chefs-d'oeuvre sont bêtes' with their placid faces. 'Mais nous les aimons ces lourds matériaux . . .'

The relationship between this kind of irony and stupidity is not difficult to discern. The flatness and banality of 'Le docteur se déclara pour le progrès' contains precisely those depths which attracted Flaubert to stupidity.

> Sometimes the most banal word grips me in a strange attitude of admiration. There are gestures or tones of voice over which I'm lost in astonishment and imbecilities which I find dizzying. Have you ever listened carefully to people speaking a foreign language that you don't understand. That's the sort of state I'm in (i, 192).

The foreign language provides an appropriate metaphor: an impenetrable surface that implies concealed depths and to which reverie is the appropriate response. When Frédéric and Cisy are preparing for their abortive duel we are told that 'Le ciel était bleu, et on entendait, par moments, des lapins bondir' (II, 91). This is indeed 'une niaiserie qui donne le vertige', a splendidly idiotic sentence whose referential function seems so hopelessly inadequate that one can only stand back and contemplate it. This is a very special kind of irony, not directed against persons, nor even against any view of the world, but only, perhaps, a moment of the novel's own self-consciousness. It is, at any rate, an instance of 'le plus haut dans l'art', the ability to produce contemplative reverie. And indeed, one might argue that such ironies, though they partake of the negative in producing an absence which the reader essays to fill up, are in themselves a positive value, that such ironies might be able to lead one beyond irony to a point where one can find the positive in the negative. To explore this possibility we must look more closely at *Trois Contes* and the problematic *Salammbô*.

## C. *The Sentimental and the Sacred*

> Everything spiritual and valuable has a gross and revolting parody, very similar to it, with the same name. Only unremitting judgment can distinguish between them.
>
> EMPSON

The preference of the ironist for unstated and perhaps un-statable meanings has its analogue at the level of character:

since anyone capable of stating a position is vulnerable to ironic treatment, those characters are treated best who are least committed to language. Given the close identification of language and stupidity for Flaubert, this should scarcely surprise us. If language itself is inadequate, those who entrust themselves to it will be the first victims of the inexorable social forces that lead to the cliché. Emma, a character in search of a novel, becomes a victim of both the text's ironies and the irony of adultery because of her adoption of and response to the language of romance. To Rodolphe, who plays with her by taking up this language, she sounds like all mistresses, since, as we are told, passion always expresses itself in the same forms and he could not distinguish the difference in sentiments behind them. But, as the text assures us in a rare direct judgment, the deepest feelings often produce the most trite and empty metaphors, and 'la parole humaine est comme un chaudron fêlé où nous battons des mélodies à faire danser les ours, quand on voudrait attendrir les étoiles' (I, 639).[61] The anxiety which Flaubert hoped the *Dictionnaire* would instill, making people afraid to speak for fear of uttering one of the entries, might well have proved salutary. If Emma had not given expression to her feelings, if she had not so thoroughly committed herself to language, she would have been much less vulnerable, both to events and to ironic judgment.

Those who make no claims for their language fare better. The innocent Dussardier of *L'Education sentimentale* utters clichés not his own which do not detract from his simplicity; Saint Julien is seldom made to speak, lest he disqualify himself for sainthood; the swiftness with which Bouvard and Pécuchet move from one mode of discourse to another gives them a kind of independence and credulous simplicity; and of course Félicité of 'Un Coeur simple' finds greatest fulfilment in meaningless babble with her parrot. They have no language which they could claim captures their existence, and this is what protects them, for as soon as the critic speaks of them he begins muttering clichés about the purity of simple folk, the joys of unalienated consciousness.

Félicité, the perfect feudal serf, does have a sense of the order of her life, finding it inappropriate that her mistress should die before she does, happy to die of the same ailment herself. But she is silent for the most part, alienated from language, 'une

femme en bois fonctionnant d'une manière automatique'
(II, 166), like a wooden robot; and when she grows deaf and
speaks so loudly that her confession must be heard in the
sacristy, that is more a revelation of her condition than a change
in it. She converses with her parrot, who repeats his three set
phrases — 'Charmant garçon', 'Serviteur Monsieur', 'Je vous
salue, Marie' — while she replies 'by words without sequence,
but into which her heart overflowed' (II, 175). Arbitrary signs,
which make no pretence of accurately conveying human
feelings, seem to be, for that very reason, the forms which
contain the greatest depths.

When she does speak to others the very banality of her discourse, its blatant exposure to irony, works to save it from any
effective irony. Or rather, since the text seems ready to exploit
satiric possibilities the reader takes her defence. Asking Bourais
where Havana is, whether her nephew could return by land,
she is baffled by the map and begs the sniggering Bourais to
show her the house where Victor was staying. He is convulsed
with laughter but she understands nothing, 'elle qui s'attendait
peut-être à voir jusqu'au portrait de son neveu, tant son intelligence était bornée!' (II, 171).[62] We are amused, no doubt, but
do not want to class ourselves with Bourais by joining in his
amusement. We prefer to be won over by her innocence and
unpretentiousness, valuing the sense of our own broadminded-
ness that comes from protecting or defending one so charmingly
vulnerable.

Another ironic opening is, of course, her conflation of her
parrot and the Holy Ghost. When she buys a portrait representing the latter with purple wings and emerald body and hangs
it next to the stuffed parrot,

Ils s'associèrent dans sa pensée, le perroquet se trouvant sanctifié
par ce rapport avec le Saint-Esprit, qui devenait plus vivant à
ses yeux et intelligible. Le Père, pour s'énoncer, n'avait pu choisir
une colombe, puisque ces bêtes-là n'ont pas de voix, mais plutôt
un des ancêtres de Loulou. Et Félicité priait en regardant l'image,
mais de temps à autre se tournait un peu vers l'oiseau (II, 176).[63]

She creates a sign, offering a reason for the connection between
Holy Ghost and parrot, but a reason which by its misplaced
concreteness becomes a simple act of faith. The text makes
clear the insubstantiality of the connection, and when in the

last sentence of the tale it tells us that 'elle crut voir, dans les cieux entr'ouverts, un perroquet gigantesque, planant au-dessus de sa tête' (II, 177), it does so with the appropriate scepticism and narrative distancing of 'crut voir'. But as Flaubert himself observed, the ending is 'not at all ironic, but on the contrary very serious and very sad' (vii, 307). Why should this be?

In the first place, her lack of pretension prevents there being anything to deflate. Her vision is sufficiently arbitrary for us to be distanced from it, and so when the text offers the implicit criticism of 'crut voir' (rather than simply 'voyait') that does not fulfill any need on the reader's part but acts, rather, as a distancing which challenges his sympathy to overcome this coldness and estrangement. It is as though the text were engaged in probing and testing, trying on ironies to see if there is anything to be deflated, attempting to ensure the sloughing off of the purely sentimental by subjecting it to a cold and detached treatment, but doing so only in order that the purity of whatever successfully resists this treatment might be guaranteed. The mechanism here is closely analogous to what Empson calls 'pseudo-parody to disarm criticism'[64]: by implying 'she only thought she saw a parrot, of course, being stupid and deluded', the text prevents the reader from having to entertain such disagreeable sentiments, offers a kind of guarantee of its own readiness to detect and quash pretence or sentimentality. Saying something that needed saying, it prevents us from having to say it ourselves and allows us to accept the other view, now that it has been appropriately tested.

But secondly, and this is perhaps the most striking accomplishment of the story, we can take the ending as finally transcending irony only if we have come to postulate a kind of order which makes the identification of the parrot and the Holy Ghost worthy and appropriate. And no doubt the reason why we have been led to postulate, however unconsciously, an order of this kind is our desire to give some sort of meaning to Félicité's life and hence to the tale itself. For it is patently clear that Félicité does not herself succeed in organizing and interpreting her experience. She is written, as it were, by a social context: 'Elle avait eu, *comme une autre*, son histoire d'amour,' which confers on her no distinctiveness. Her life is composed of habitual actions — 'every Thursday', etc. — and can be narrated primarily in the imperfect. It has none of the unity of an individual project. And so, if we are to produce such unity and give the tale a teleological determination we must assume some kind of sacred order which her life fulfills. Thorlby writes that 'the resolution of such suffering and love as Félicité's is made in heaven', but that 'across the very threshold Flaubert draws his most daring line'.[65] That is exactly right: to state explicitly her saintliness and the sacred character of her suffering and vision would be to expose oneself to multiple and inescapable ironies; but to draw the line across the very threshold, while presenting her in as testing a way as one can, is to leave an uncompleted structure which the reader must complete if he is to feel satisfied. We allow the arbitrary connection between the parrot and the Holy Ghost and permit the potentially sentimental to pass over into the sacred.

But this is only a single case. If we can extract some positive value from an irony that tests itself, we as yet have little understanding of the relation between the sacred and the sentimental and the conditions which permit or compel a passage from one to another. *Salammbô* offers a much more problematic case, and if we examine the operations of irony there we shall be better equipped to return to *Trois Contes* and to the general problem of sacred and sentimental objects.

Irony both undercuts and promotes the activity of interpretation. On the one hand, its most frequent targets are views of a situation which it suggests are foolish, deficient, or otherwise at odds with the 'facts', and it thus strikes indirectly at the general process of organizing the world in relation to oneself so as to make sense of it. If irony as a mode carries any single warning it is that concluding is dangerous. But on the other hand, as I have already suggested, many of the delights come from the call to interpretation that it issues. An ironic sentence, by definition, requires the interpreter to prove his own ingenuity in supplying an absent meaning; and it is thus a form of language which defers and tantalizes, which confers importance on the process of interpretation, while simultaneously bearing implicit warning of its dangers. How can the reader enter the space of irony and confidently join in the interpretive play when he is simultaneously being asked to smile at the interpretations of others — as often as not simply on the grounds that they are interpretations?

This is one of the basic problems confronting the reader of Flaubert: how is he to make sense of novels which thematize the difficulties of making sense and especially ridicule attempts to read life as if it were a novel, in accordance with those very operations which the reader is engaged in performing? In works like *Madame Bovary* and *L'Education sentimentale* our knowledge of the world provides some guidance, assuring us that Emma and Frédéric are foolish and that we may therefore feel safe. But in *Salammbô* the problem is especially acute because the characters, who do not seem to be mediocre or foolish, are engaged in a desperate attempt to understand their relation to their situation, and our lack of knowledge of the setting, not even Greece or Rome but Carthage, deprives us of any external standards which might permit confident judgment of their interpretations. Here, more than in any other of Flaubert's works, the reader finds in the activity and bewilderment of the characters a metaphor for his own process of reading.[66] The characters, that is to say, are trying to understand themselves and their world just as the reader is; they are not committed to language but are trying to find a language, and the rebuffs they encounter or solutions they discover offer an explicit thematization of the problems of reading.

That the book defies comprehension has become a critical commonplace. Sainte-Beuve wondered what was the point and why it had been undertaken. Jean Rousset finds it 'an enigmatic book'; Denis Porter sees it as 'un livre sur rien', without meaning except as a manifesto of aestheticism.[67] Lukács asks 'what can a world thus re-awakened mean to us?', finds a 'lack of relation between the human tragedy . . . and the political action', and speaks of a plot that is 'lifeless, not only because it is cluttered up with the descriptions of inessential objects, but because it has no discernible connection with any concrete form of popular life that we may experience.'[68] Thibaudet, calling it a novel 'so unusual in appearance and so detached from life', comes closer than the others to defining its mysterious attraction:

> Flaubert wanted to write a gratuitous work which would support itself purely by the force of its style, and which, instead of bringing history towards us, would drag it violently away, to the edge of a desert, so as to make this portion of humanity into a block of pure past, a dead star like the moon, under whose influence *Salammbô*

comes. And it is precisely this hallucinatory effect of a dead thing which has helped to give *Salammbô* its symbolic hold on the imagination.'[69]

Distanced from us, as the gratuitous reconstruction of a world not our own nor even part of our past, the work seems deliberately to aspire towards what Lukács calls the 'psuedomonumentality' of objects alienated from the inner life of characters and readers. The world of the novel, like the novel itself, is strange and monstrous, cruel and immobile, suffused, as Brombert says, with a 'combination of violence and tedium'.[70]

The readers, consequently, have the same problem as the characters: how are they to organize and relate to this strange world? what sort of connection can be made between the inner and outer, between the psychological drama and the historical and political circumstances?

The characters certainly feel this strangeness and estrangement: they stand, gaping and bewildered, *ébahis* and *béants*, looking at one another and at the scenes before them. The Mercenaries watch the Carthaginians sacrificing their own children, 'béants d'horreur', trying to fathom the meaning of this barbarous behaviour. When Mâtho steals the sacred veil of Carthage and brings it to Salammbô's room, the two of them — enemy leader and daughter of the Carthaginian general — 'restèrent béants à se regarder', wondering what each represents to the other and what their encounter means. Vision involves a recognition of strangeness and a desire to find ways of overcoming it.[71]

The opening scene of the novel is an elegantly proleptic dramatization both of the problem of understanding and of the principal modes of response which the novel will develop. The spectacle of the Mercenaries feasting in Hamilcar's gardens is an orgy of gluttony, drunkenness, and general destructiveness which affords little meaning until two interpreters appear. The first, Spendius, a slave whom the soldiers have freed, immediately grasps the possible political significance of the events and offers a reading of it: reminding them of their strength, he suggests that they should be drinking from the cups of the Sacred Legion and thus brings to the fore the underlying political tension between a wealthy and snobbish Carthage and the Mercenaries who have been hired to do their fighting but are as yet unpaid. This mode of interpretation continues when he accompanies Mâtho on a tour of the grounds: 'I can show you a room where there is a gold bar beneath each tile', there for the taking. And after Mâtho's rejection of this suggestion he assumes that his goal was rather the pillage of Carthage, but he has to take the uncomprehending Mâtho by the arm and point out the wealthy city, defenceless before them, and the band of Mercenaries whose hatred was now aroused. 'Do you understand me, soldier?' he continues to a mute Mâtho. 'We shall walk draped in purple, bathe in perfume surrounded by slaves.' Remember the hardships you have undergone in the service of Carthage. Think of the wealth and happiness that can be yours. We are strong; they are weak and divided. Command and you will be obeyed. Carthage is ours for the taking (I, 699).

Spendius' interpretive discourse is based on an understanding of the realities of power and an assumption of their over-riding importance. His speech is related to action and is a mode of duplicity and intrigue, but he acquires a certain ascendency by virtue of his 'understanding' of the world.

The other interpreter, and indeed the cause of Mâtho's in-attention to Spendius' reasoning, is of course Salammbô, who appears on the steps of the palace, high above the feasting soldiers, as a mysterious and unknown power — 'Personne encore ne la connaissait'. Coming down the steps towards them, she stops: 'Immobile et la tête basse, elle regardait les soldats.' When she descends among them they draw back, sensing 'quelque chose des Dieux' which envelops her, and she herself, seeking understanding, seems to 'regarder tout au loin au delà des espaces terrestres'. When she first speaks it is not to the soldiers but invoking the sacred fish which they have killed. They do not understand, of course, but

Ils s'ébahissaient de sa parure; mais elle promena sur eux tous un long regard épouvanté, puis s'enfonçant la tête dans les épaules en écartant les bras, elle répéta plusieurs fois: 'Qu'avez-vous fait! qu'avez-vous fait' (I, 697).[72]

The Mercenaries do not know, for their relationship to the sacred is as confused as is the readers'. What does killing and eating the sacred fish *mean*? By way of an answer Salammbô invokes a religious hierarchy and begins to chant sacred tales.

The Mercenaries, of course, do not understand, but they sense something of the potency of the sacred, and open-mouthed, held by her, 'ils tâchaient de saisir ces vagues histoires qui se balançaient devant leur imagination, à travers l'obscurité des théogonies, comme des fantômes dans des nuages' (I, 698).[73]

These are the two principal modes of ordering that the book offers: a language of politics which accepts religion as a persuasive device but denies it any status as an interpretive system, and a language of ritual and religious symbols whose relation to action is more problematic but which seems to the major characters, Salammbô and Mâtho, a way of coming to understand their experience. Mâtho, trying to explain what has happened to him in his encounter with Salammbô, wondering what force has overtaken him and come to govern his activities, reads himself as cursed and takes Salammbô as the embodiment of the Goddess. Salammbô, whose life has so far been ordered by her role as servant of the Goddess, participates in a similar sacramental reading of experience and casts Mâtho in the appropriate sacred role.

The terms in which these characters come to see one another can be adopted, almost without alteration, as a critical reading of the novel, which confirms the close relationship between the characters and the readers as interpreters. Jean Rousset, for example, stressing that 'the book should be read on the plane of myth', writes:

> Salammbô, the human star, has sworn herself to Tanit, the moon, whom she worships at night on the upper terrace, while Mâtho, siderial god, diurnal hero, is associated with Moloch, the god of the sun. This symbolism determines their behaviour: . . . they attract and repel one another, linked each to each by a blind will which they obey without understanding . . . Set above and apart from the groups that they dominate, they live alone between heaven and earth.[74]

But the reader accustomed to Flaubertian irony may well wonder whether he should be so quick to accept the language in which characters choose to view themselves. If we do not allow Emma Bovary with impunity to identify herself with novelistic heroines, should we not be a little more sceptical of the language which characters use to identify themselves with heavenly bodies or gods? Certainly there is much which suggests the necessity of an ironic view of religious discourse: when the Carthaginians crucify captured Mercenaries we are told, 'the sanction of the gods was not lacking, for on all sides crows swooped down from the heavens' (I, 747). The conjunction, as so often in Flaubert, seems to turn irony against individual or communal attempts at thinking, and we are inclined to discover irony here because of our reluctance to admit such savagery as something sacred. Similarly, when the Carthaginians are slaughtering their own children and we are told that 'the God's appetite, however, was not sated. He wanted more' (I, 781), we are likely to want to distance ourselves from that language.

Even in the opening scene the attempts at a sacramental reading are put to the test of irony by a narrative voice which implies the possibility of a purely sexual interpretation. After speaking to the Mercenaries, Salammbô drops her lyre and is silent,

> et, pressant son coeur à deux mains, elle resta quelques minutes les paupières closes à savourer l'agitation de tous ces hommes.
> Mâtho le Libyen se penchait vers elle. Involontairement elle s'en approcha, et, poussée par la reconnaissance de son orgueil, elle lui versa dans une coupe d'or un long jet de vin pour se reconcilier avec l'armée (I, 698).[75]

A soldier provides the interpretation: 'in our country when a woman gives a soldier a drink she is inviting him to share her bed.' And with that a fight breaks out, provoked by a Numidian chief's sexual jealousy.

Indeed, one common critical approach assumes the priority of the sexual adventure and reads all else as illusion to be ironically deflated. Lukács speaks of Salammbô herself as 'a heightened image, a decorative symbol, of the hysterical longings and torments of middle-class girls in large cities', and finds the historical and mythical elements 'no more than a pictorial frame within which a purely modern story is unfolded'.[76] Salammbô's language is pure delusion; her problem is one of romantic longing and sexual frustration. Sherrington, taking this position to its extreme, argues that there is nothing in the novel 'to suggest that Salammbô and her contemporaries were any less likely than Emma to be mistaken about their role in life simply because they lived in more exotic surroundings.'[77]

The critic's task in interpreting the book is to find 'the reality under the illusion', and he has no doubt about what that reality is: Salammbô's desires are 'clearly sexually based, and exacerbated by surrounding physical conditions, such as strong perfumes, fasting, and other religious rites.'[78] In our superior knowledge and freedom from superstition we can see that 'every "supernatural" event . . . has an ordinary physiological or psychological explanation', and Flaubert's narrative strategies, as vehicles of his most profound intention, are devoted to showing 'people confused because they are unwilling or unable to look at facts'.[79]

Such a simplistic purpose would do Flaubert little credit, and one might well wonder why he should have bothered to resuscitate Carthage if it was only to show that Carthaginians were prey to religious delusion and refused to face facts. If the novel is read in this reductive way it becomes fundamentally uninteresting, and nothing illustrates the novel's complexity better than the two-faced role which Sherrington is forced to adopt in order to discuss it intelligently. With respect to the characters he plays Gradgrind — 'in this life we want nothing but Facts, sir; nothing but Facts!' — and sneers at their attempts to order their lives in symbolic terms, but he is quite willing to use precisely these terms in his own symbolic reading of the novel. Thus, while the characters are deluded when they identify themselves or one another with the solar and lunar deities, the critic can write that 'the sunrise passage is, indeed, quite remarkable in its symbolism', that 'the sun sets on Mâtho's death, as it is now rising on his strength and vigour . . . in a long series of parallels between Mâtho and Moloch', that the Mercenary army leaves Carthage 'marching by moonlight (i.e. Tanit — gentleness, in contrast with the last scene)'.[80] Mâtho is deluded in identifying Salammbô with Tanit,[81] but the critic may see Salammbô's pallor as 'a symbol of the moral leprosy of Carthage'.[82] The mythical terms into which Salammbô and Mâtho translate the mystery they sense in each other's presence is but an 'elaborate superstructure', but the critic is allowed to discover, in a scene which 'at bottom' represents 'an enflamed male paying an illicit nocturnal visit to a lady's bedroom', an elaborate symbolic pattern: 'the blue net, the bed suspended from the roof, the white clothing, all place an almost embarrassing emphasis on the Salammbô-

Tanit parallel', and Mâtho's appearance in a flash of fire and mention of the sunrise give 'more than adequate prominence to the other half of the symbolism'.[83]

In order to make sense of the novel Sherrington must use the language and imagery which he treats as illusion when the characters use it, and this illustrates not merely the blindness of a critical discourse which fails to reflect on the implications of its own interpretive methods, but the dangers of trying to simplify Flaubert's irony. For if the novel is to have any value, the judgments one passes on characters' attempts to make sense of things will come to apply also to one's own attempts to make sense of the book. Critical discourse cannot therefore allow itself to remain blind to the relationship between its own interpretive procedures and those displayed or exercised within the novel itself. As Sherrington implicitly recognizes, the novel does present us with all the material for mythic and symbolic reading, and we cannot sneer at the characters' attempts to interpret their lives in these terms without sneering at ourselves by implication. 'If such attempts are regarded by the reader as metaphors for his own activity they cannot be treated entirely ironically',[84] for he too, as critics' remarks on the enigmatic character of the book show, possesses no certain principles of intelligibility. The novel subjects religious discourse to multiple ironies, but we cannot reject that discourse entirely without leaving too much in the novel unexplained:

> The reader is in no better position than the characters to discover the 'reality' behind their situations. Or rather, he is only quantitatively better off, in that he has access to all situations and all points of view; but this does not provide him with an overall principle for making the situations intelligible. The only reality behind the chaotic appearances of the novel is the reality of the activity of reading it. Hence the pattern which takes most account of the resemblance between the situation of the reader and that of the characters seems the nearest approach to what is really happening in the novel.[85]

If one attempts to create a pattern which takes account of the resemblance one will find that all modes of understanding have their limitations but that some are more limited than others in their failure to deal successfully with the more important aspects of characters' experience. Spendius, who is a surrogate for the critic determined to view religious and symbolic discourse with irony and to get behind it to the political and psychological reality, does not succeed in understanding the extraordinary power of Mâtho and Salammbô or the nature of their relationship. When Mâtho is suffering in his tent, convinced that a curse has been laid upon him and unable to escape the dominating thought of Salammbô ('Her eyes burn me, she envelopes me, she pierces me'), Spendius tries to find cures in his modes of understanding: 'Come on, you're weeping like a coward! Aren't you ashamed to let a woman make you suffer so!' But he is clearly wrong to compare Mâtho, as he does, to the young men who anxiously sought his help in the days when he was a pimp. Don't be silly, comes the reply. 'Do you think I'm a child?' I've had hundreds of women, 'but this one . . .' (I, 703–4). Spendius again misinterprets, thinking in the language of politics and taking Salammbô's position as daughter of the enemy general to be the 'reality': 'If she weren't the daughter of Hamilcar . . .' 'No!' cries Mâtho, 'she is not like the other daughters of men'; when she appeared the torches waned; there emanated from her whole being something sweeter than wine and more terrible than death. 'Elle marchait cependant, et puis elle s'est arrêtée.' If we accept Spendius's mode of understanding we are unable to read any of the wonder of this last sentence, nor are we able later to account for Mâtho's power and effectiveness as a leader when 'the power of Moloch flowed through him'. Whatever plots Spendius may form on the basis of his fallen understanding, he cannot act without Mâtho, and the mysterious power which his speech cannot explain determines, in fact, the 'reality' of Spendius's position.

Another reductive reading which, like Sherrington's, identifies Salammbô's desire as purely sexual, is offered by old Giscon who, as a prisoner in the Mercenary camp, heard the scene in Mâtho's tent when Salammbô recovered the sacred veil: 'I heard you gasping with love like a harlot'; I wish I could cry out to your father, 'Come see your daughter in the Barbarian's arms! To please him she has put on the garment of the Goddess, and in yielding her body to him she has abandoned, along with the glory of your name, the honour of the Gods, the vengeance of the nation, and the very safety of Carthage!' (I, 761). We know this to be an imperfect understanding: whatever her sexual motives Salammbô has come to recover the veil and without that sacred errand would have had neither the will nor the courage to venture into the Mercenary camp.

Indeed, one must remember that Salammbô's expedition to the tent was part of a plan conceived by the priest Schahabarim and which he hoped would save both his country and his faith (I, 753). The most learned man in Carthage, he approaches the sacred in much the same way as the reader, with a kind of curious detachment born of scepticism and a desire for secure belief which would make things intelligible: 'the more he doubted Tanit the more he wished to believe in her.' And though he does, in presenting the plan to Salammbô, translate into sacred terms what he expects will be a sexual adventure, hesitating and seeking circumlocutions when Salammbô asks how exactly she is to get Mâtho to give her the veil, the success of the venture is ironic proof of the efficacy of the sacred. Schahabarim's 'tu seras humble et soumise à son désir qui est l'ordre du ciel', and 'the Gods will dispose' are meant as ironic statements concealing a sexual bargain; but in fact the encounter does take place at a mythic level, though myth be severely tested by the habitual techniques of Flaubert's irony.

This scene in Mâtho's tent is the central episode of the book in that for a moment the political and psychological dramas are fused; it is crucial also to our determination of the status of religious symbols and hence of the relationship between the sexual and the sacred. The setting itself — an enemy camp on the eve of a battle — contributes something to the dramatic intensity, which here reaches a level that Flaubert rarely allowed himself to achieve, but more is due to the protagonists' sense of wonder and power. When Salammbô rips off her veil and allows Mâtho to recognize her,

> Il se recula, les coudes en arrière, béant, presque terrifié.
> Elle se sentait comme appuyée sur la force des Dieux; et, le regardant face à face, elle lui demanda le Zaïmph; elle le réclamait en paroles abondantes et superbes.
> Mâtho n'entendait pas; il la contemplait, et les vêtements, pour lui, se confondaient avec le corps (I, 758).[86]

There follows a sacramental description fusing garment and body which ends with her ear-rings made of hollowed pearls and from which, through a small hole in the bottom, from time to time, a drop of perfume falls onto her bare shoulder. 'Mâtho la regardait tomber.' The fascination, the absorption is heightened by a wondrous sentence in which Flaubert's mastery of deferment brings irony into the service of delicacy:

> Une curiosité indomptable l'entraîna; et, comme un enfant qui porte la main sur un fruit inconnu, tout en tremblant, du bout de son doigt, il la toucha légèrement sur le haut de sa poitrine; la chair un peu froide céda avec une résistance élastique (I, 758).[87]

The nature of the spell soon changes, however, and the scene moves from adoration through anger and pride and back to unbounded adoration in which he takes her for the Goddess herself. But such intensity is fragile, and Flaubert does not hesitate to test it by offering possible ironies. 'Ils ne parlaient plus. Le tonnerre au loin roulait. Des moutons bêlaient, effrayés par l'orage' (I, 759). Here we have a hint of the *Comices agricoles*, or a suggestion that we test our attitude towards Salammbô by juxtaposing her with sheep. We find also the suggestions that the experience might be purely sexual: 'Salammbô, accustomed to eunuchs, yielded to her astonishment at this man's power' (I, 759). The way is thus open for an ironic reading of the sentence which reports her submission: 'Salammbô était envahie par une mollesse où elle perdait toute conscience d'elle-même. Quelque chose à la fois d'intime et de supérieur, un ordre des Dieux la forçait à s'y abandonner.'[88]

Ironic possibilities are offered, as if a non-ironic reading were of no value unless it had successfully passed through the crucible of irony. It is no doubt because the text continually threatens to treat Salammbô as an antique Emma Bovary that we are forced to make distinctions, forced to recognize that Salammbô and Mâtho succeed in living their myths to an extent that Emma never does and that they do so partly because their world, unlike Emma's, is unintelligible unless structured by these myths. To say, with Sherrington, that Salammbô is 'mistaken about her role' seems silly, since we, like the character herself, are engaged in trying to discover what that role is. If the role cannot be named except by metaphors, that is precisely because it is successfully presented as 'quelque chose à la fois d'intime et de supérieur', a momentary fusion of the personal and the transcendental, of the sexual and the sacred.

The synthesis which the scene momentarily enacts cannot, of course, last. The self-consciousness that follows threatens the identification of the sexual and the sacred. Mâtho sheds the mantle of the sun-god and becomes a sentimental lover, and Salammbô wonders, 'So this is the man who makes all Carthage tremble?' When she secures the sacred veil she is, in best Bovaresque fashion, 'surprise de ne pas avoir ce bonheur qu'elle s'imaginait autrefois. Elle restait mélancolique dans son rêve accompli' (I, 760).[89] But whereas in *Madame Bovary* and *L'Education sentimentale* such phrases indicate the futility of particular desires and the relative inadequacy of experience, here we find an irony which tests but does not undermine the reality and power of what has happened; and the final scene of the novel, when Mâtho, who is being whipped through the streets of Carthage, encounters Salammbô again, is ample testimony to the power of the symbolic bond between them:

> Mâtho regarda autour de lui, et ses yeux recontrèrent Salammbô.
> Dès le premier pas qu'il avait fait, elle s'était levée; puis, involontairement, à mesure qu'il se rapprochait, elle s'était avancée peu à peu jusqu'au bord de la terrasse; et bientôt, toutes les choses extérieures s'effaçant, elle n'avait aperçu que Mâtho. Un silence s'était fait dans son âme, un de ces abîmes où le monde entier disparaît sous la pression d'une pensée unique, d'un souvenir, d'un regard. Cet homme, qui marchait vers elle, l'attirait (I, 796).[90]

The pluperfect provides a modicum of distance — holding the scene off and testing it, but the non-restrictive relative clause of the last sentence restores some of the intensity, granting it the rights it has earned. The power of Salammbô's experience, as it acts upon her, cannot be doubted, and in order to read the scene properly we must grant the validity of the sacred metaphors as a mode of understanding. Otherwise the silence and the abyss would be novelistic impertinences. Indeed, the primacy of this unlivable symbolic order is confirmed in the only way it can be in Flaubert: by a death resulting from no external cause. The difference between Salammbô and Emma, one might say, is that Emma had to take poison in order to die whereas Salammbô, like Charles and like the youthful narrator of *Novembre*, dies by a mental negation of life, thus asserting the priority of her ordering of experience over any which the world itself or the body might attempt to impose.

Such a death may, as the ending of *Novembre* suggests, seem strange to those who have suffered but must be accepted in a novel, 'par amour du merveilleux'. And now, perhaps, we know how to read that ending. Such a death must be accepted as the affirmation of a sacred order, and the sacred is a formal concept which permits an ordering of experience and confers value on it but which lacks a precise content which would make it a satisfactory determinant of practical affairs. Like the Zaïmph itself, transparent gauze which offers only a bluish tint to the sight, the sacred is pure form, a device of order, and Salammbô, as the concluding sentence tells us, dies because she had touched the Goddess's veil. She has tried to fill up the empty form of the sacred, to become herself a Goddess, and though she may in one sense have succeeded, such success is clearly not for this world.

'Ainsi mourut la fille d'Hamilcar pour avoir touché au manteau de Tanit' could, of course, be the ironic report of a collective superstition, but Flaubert's ironies cut both ways and we cannot take that position with any confidence because 'we do not know what it *means* to have touched the veil of the goddess. The Zaïmph remains a symbol for a possible narrative integration which the text denies us. To this extent the reader shares the characters' awe in the face of sacred power.'[91] The notion of the sacred becomes a formal requirement of the novel, an image of coherence and completion which the reader holds before him in the hope that he may be able to attain it.

Whether or not he actually attains it is uncertain. One might say that sacred order can be neither stated nor acted and that therein lies the ultimate correspondence between the situation of the characters and of the reader. Statements or fulfilments of the sacred tend, especially in a positivistic age, to become the merely sentimental. Or, to put it another way, the sacred as a mode of discourse is always in danger of being undermined by our empirical assumptions about reality as soon as it is connected with reality.

That problem is adumbrated in Salammbô's quest for knowledge of the sacred within the novel. She learns all the names of the Goddess and would very much like to see the veil, 'for the idea of a god cannot be clearly separated from its representation' (I, 709); and when the priest speaks of the various 'gates' for souls in the heavens, she 'strove to perceive them, for she took these conceptions for realities; she accepted as true in themselves pure symbols or even turns of phrase, a distinction which was not always quite clear to the priest either' (I, 753).

Can such a distinction ever be made clear? Can we ever reach a point where we would be able to judge just how much truth symbols carry or just how much distance separates language from experience? The symbol, which since the Romantic movement has been taken as the privileged mode and crowning achievement of literary activity, is supposed to display the fusion of language and experience, the transmutation of individual experience into general truth, the identity of life and form, and therein lies its attractions for both characters and readers. But the symbol is a fragile construct, especially in the novel, whose temporal structure leads it almost invariably to undermine the atemporal synthesis, in which all time is eternally present, to which the symbol aspires. The lyric can stop on a moment of epiphany; the novel leads up to it and beyond, making time its principle of continuity and thus providing, by its very structure, a threat to intimations of order and transcendence. The fate of the sacred in the novel is to be profaned; but it may be that our ability to understand profanation as such becomes the source of our sense of the sacred. Salammbô's and Mâtho's metaphors are made more valid by the fact that after having lived them for a moment they cannot go on and that the reader is aware of that difference. Frédéric's last scene with Mme Arnoux is the more sacred because it is threatened at every moment with profanation. The sacred is perceived only through its vulnerability.

If this is so then one might say that in Flaubert the value of symbols depends on their place in an allegory of interpretation. The sacred character of the Zaïmph comes not from its 'connection' with the goddess, which is easily deflated by irony, but from the fact that it figures in the book as a representation of that aspiration towards unity and meaning which governs both the reader's and the characters' behaviour. As a symbol it is fragile, but that fragility gives it a solid and worthy place in the temporal drama of the quest for fusion which takes place both at the level of action and at the level of interpretation.

In order to prevent this suggestion from remaining wholly abstract, we should turn back to symbolic objects in other novels, especially those which sit uncomfortably on the line dividing the sentimental from the sacred. The object foolishly venerated is one of the easiest targets for the analyst, but Flaubert understood very clearly its value as an objective correlative for emotions which are not the less worthy for their application to trivial objects: 'one feels profoundly the *melancholy of matter*, which is but that of our souls projected onto objects' (iv, 313). The marriage bouquet and cigar case in *Madame Bovary*, Mme Arnoux's box or her lock of hair in *L'Education sentimentale*, Félicité's parrot, are all sacred to the protagonists. As objects deprived of their original function and made emblematic, they are gazed on with that kind of stupidity which seeks stimuli for reverie. The objects of *Madame Bovary* are treated with more irony than the others, primarily because the reverie expresses itself more precisely and in that way bears a closer relationship to action. But all are highly vulnerable and come thereby to represent the strength of the characters' aspiration towards some kind of sacramental fulfilment which would confer meaning on their lives.

Indeed, it is noteworthy that those which seem the most sacred are those which as signs are the most arbitrary: the parrot, whose association with the Holy Ghost is purely contingent, and the Zaïmph, which the religious code has simply decreed to be sacred. Emma's elaborate suppositions about the cigar case, her desire to reconstruct its history, are attempts to make it a motivated sign which in fact reduce its sacred character — though not, of course, for her. Frédéric's worship of the flat in which he thinks Mme Arnoux lives is highly motivated, and it depends so much on that motivation that it becomes ridiculous when he discovers that she does not live there after all; whereas, for example, a picture of the Holy Ghost which did not look in the least like a parrot would not be a decisive blow against the parrot, since it is an arbitrary sign. The more arbitrary the sign, the purer the faith, since it does not rely on external justifications. In *Salammbô* we are told that the Mercenaries have become very confused about religion

F.-P

because of the diversity of beliefs and practices to which they have been exposed, and that their floating anxiety and sense of veneration has come to fasten itself upon chance objects: 'une amulette inconnue, trouvée par hasard dans un péril, devenait une divinité; ou bien c'était un nom, rien qu'un nom, et que l'on répétait sans même chercher à comprendre ce qu'il pouvait dire' (I, 725).[92]

That sort of faith avoids the stupidity of attempts to motivate signs, which is a mark both of the symbolic and the sentimental. One avoids it either by the supreme innocence of Félicité or by the self-consciousness and awareness of fragility that we find in the penultimate chapter of *L'Education sentimentale*, when Frédéric and Mme Arnoux succeed in severing their romantic discourse from the world of experience and so give the clichés, which are sullied by any attempt to live them, a sacramental purity. That their procedure is fundamentally allegorical should by now be sufficiently clear: allegory is that mode which recognizes the impossibility of fusing the empirical and the eternal and thus demystifies the symbolic relation by stressing the separateness of the two levels, the impossibility of their remaining linked in time, and the importance of protecting each level and the link between them by making it arbitrary. The corrosive irony applied to sentimentality, which shows that attempts at fusion can always be viewed differently and thus be made to fail, contributes to the allegorical mode by evoking, as the positive face that its negative procedure implies, the desire for connection which only allegory can make in a self-conscious and demystified way.

The sacred, one might say, is the sentimental purified by irony, emptied of its content, so that it may come to represent in the allegory of interpretation the formal desire for connection and meaning which governs the activity of readers and characters. In that sense, some notion of the sacred, however ill-defined, hovers over the novels as the teleological force which enables them to be read as warnings against the tawdry and premature ways of investing things with meaning. One of the functions of *Salammbô* and *Trois Contes* is to give us the sacred in more tangible form, so that its role may become clearer; but it is noteworthy that to do that Flaubert had to leave his contemporary environment for the quasi-feudal world of 'Un Coeur simple' or the more exotic worlds of 'Hérodias', 'La

Légende de Saint Julien Hospitalier', and *Salammbô*. The sacred emerges in *Salammbô* as the necessary correlate of our desire to unify and make sense of the book; in 'Hérodias' our fore-knowledge of the Christian tradition enables us to read Herod's ill-defined awe of John the Baptist as perfectly proper, thus protecting him from possible ironies and, by the same token, committing us to the sacred as a functional concept; and finally, in 'Saint Julien' the result announced by the title and the distancing performed by the claim that the text recounts the story as represented in a stained-glass window allow us to structure the story as progress towards sainthood, although Julien does not effectively and empirically *become* a saint — the attribution of sainthood is not, in that sense, motivated — for that would require an interiority and psychological investigation which Flaubert deliberately eschews. Indeed, this last tale is perhaps the best example of the need to make the sacred something arbitrary, established by fiat. But in all three cases, as in 'Un Coeur simple,' the notion of a sacred order emerges as the necessary correlate of our desire to order experience in ways that escape delusion and destructive irony.

In the modern world, however, the sacred has become practically submerged by the sentimental. The operative codes by which things are given meaning have none of the arbitrariness and redeeming distance of religions; they are either novelistic modes which promise fulfilment that they cannot deliver or else purely practical codes which reflect all the limitations and active engagement of life in a particular and contingent society. Precisely because of their motivated relationship to ordinary life, the ways of reading experience which such codes promote are highly vulnerable to a vision which can regard them with sufficient distance to expose their pretensions to 'natural' meaning. The stupidity which refuses to comprehend objects in accordance with received modes of understanding but prefers to seek freedom and enrichment in reverie, the irony which explores alternative views both as polemical activity and as a way of enlarging horizons, are both attempts to enact, in the novels, the allegory of mind striving to avoid the limitations of particular social modes of understanding and to win through to something of the purity and inviolacy of the sacred, which one may define as arbitrary meanings guaranteed not by man but by God.

Anthropologists tell us that the sacred is not a class of special things but a special class of things, and therein lies, perhaps, the fundamental difference between the sentimental and the sacred. The former, attempting to make their 'specialness' an intrinsic and motivated quality, are exposed by this pretension, whereas the latter, defined arbitrarily by some version of the absolute, are invulnerable. Flaubert's novels make some such notion of the sacred a necessary fiction: the positive which enables all his negatives to have a meaning. If he was tempted to call his version of the absolute 'style' — 'une manière absolue de voir les choses' — which would test, negate, and occasionally purify whatever it touched, we can answer that to destroy is always to destroy in the name of something and can apply the formal name of 'the sacred' to what is finally, insofar as we succeed in reading the novels as allegories of the adventures of meaning, our aspiration towards a secure and fully self-conscious understanding.

# Afterword

The most important fact about Flaubert's novels is that they are novels, and if one sets out to investigate how they work, what effect they have, or even what they mean, one must start from the fact that they are read as novels. The operations which this involves, the ways in which one moves from pages covered with sentences to one's response to a literary artifact, are thus the primary facts which any properly critical reading must take into account. Though there may be considerable difficulty in establishing these facts — and the preceding chapters no doubt illustrate this difficulty more than they overcome it — any critical evaluation or interpretation is, in the end, based on assumptions about their nature.

That in itself would suffice to justify attending to the process of reading: the desire to understand what one is doing would be hard to fault. But reading deserves attention for a more important reason: if to be a novel is to be a text that is read in particular ways, then the distinguishing characteristics of a given novel will come from the nature of its interaction with the procedures of reading. Where does it accord with and where resist the operations that one expects to be able to perform on it? When faced with a text one attempts to organize and understand it, and the distinctive qualities of the text will result from the ways in which it conditions, facilitates, and undermines this activity. The reader feels this interaction, of course, even when not thinking about reading, and knows whether he finds the text obscure or problematic; but if he wants to comment more precisely on the nature of the text and its activity, then he must try to make explicit the interpretive procedures he is attempting to apply, so as to see where the text fails or eludes him.

The novel is writing, not a world. To explain what sort of writing it is one must show how it relates to one's reading: what light does it shed on my habitual modes of synthesizing and understanding, what obstacles does it make me overcome, what new interpretive experience does it induce? And if the novel is viewed as writing, then the answer to the question, 'what kind of writing is it?', will be an important component of what we generally call theme. For whatever else the text may offer, it offers an experience of reading which becomes the principal reality against which the text is tested. In *Salammbô*, for example, our decisions about what is real and what illusion depend directly on our attempt to make sense of the text. And through this mode of operation the text becomes, among other things, an allegory of interpretation and understanding. Though this may be true of all novelists in some way, it is particularly true of Flaubert, whose major techniques are developed to set at a distance and undermine conventional modes of discourse and understanding and whose characters, caught up in this process, do little other than attempt to give meaning to their experience. As the characters are engaged with a refractory world, the reader is engaged with a refractory style whose devices, when they play little role in the integration of plot, character, and theme, create the adventures of reading.

When I have challenged the interpretations of other critics I have done so on one of two grounds, both of which assume the importance of attending to reading. First, if one tries to read Flaubert in the way one reads Balzac, one may produce results but does so at the cost of ignoring the ways in which the text resists this kind of reading and hence of neglecting its most distinctive features. My suggestion has been that one should explicitly reflect on such resistance and try to incorporate it in one's account of the book rather than seek merely to overcome it in the name of models of intelligibility. Secondly, I have argued that critical discourse must not be blind to its own procedures, must be aware of the implicit assertions they carry, and must relate these assertions to what it claims to find in the text. If one passes ironic judgment on interpretive procedures in the novel one must try to maintain a certain consistency with regard to one's own. Critical discourse which prizes lucidity and self-awareness must not be blind to its own procedures and their implications.

However defensible on their own terms, both these grounds for attacking other critics depend on a sense of what one is reading towards, a particular gesture which commands one's choice of texts and the perspective in which one places them. In the Introduction I spoke of this as a desire to make the text interesting, and I ought now to be in a position to explain how it is that Flaubert becomes interesting.

The preceding chapters seem to concentrate on two levels of response, which one might call that of the project and that of the sentence. The fascination of the first was clear enough to Henry James, who speaking of the novels as 'splendidly and infinitely curious' defined their and his curiosity by a series of questions:

> Why may, why *must* indeed in certain cases, the effort of expression spend itself, and spend itself in success, without completing the circle, without coming round again to the joys of evocation? How can art be so genuine and yet so unconsoled, so unhumorous, so unsociable? . . . How can it be such a curse without being also a blessing? . . . Why in short when the struggle is success should the success not be at last serenity?[1]

Such questions are not biographical. They are about the novels as projects and the adequacy of their goals. What answer do the novels contain to the basic question, 'why write a novel?' What fulfilment can author and reader derive from a style whose preferred mode is the negative? The preceding chapters have, I hope, indicated something of the interest the novels hold when considered in the light of such questions and have also sketched an answer by reading them as challenges to the easy construction of meaning.

But at a slightly different level one may attach oneself to the problem of how the text itself, the text in its detail rather than as 'organic whole', operates. Flaubert spoke of his desire to write a novel where one would have only to construct sentences, and the texts show such a desire to have been well-founded. Valuing not the completed structure but the fragment (which gains in power from its isolation), one may open Flaubert at random and discover sentences which by their construction become little monuments, like the blank wall of the Acropolis which Flaubert so much admired, and draw the reader into the intricacies of Flaubertian irony and the exhilaration of Flaubertian stupidity. Calling attention to themselves as language, exceeding plausible representational functions, implying meanings which they defer and postpone, they become the instruments of that realism which, as Barthes says 'explores as deeply as possible that *unreal reality* of language'[2]: the excess of the sign which, more than and other than its own referent, imperiously insists on its own primacy.

Such sources of interest lead one to devalue a particular mimetic conception of the novel and to maintain that insofar as a novel succeeds, as Lawrence says, in presenting us 'with new, really new feelings, a whole line of new emotion',[3] it does so by inducing us to bring to bear on the text modes of ordering which then become available as techniques for reading our own experience. The link between the novel and other forms of experience becomes the process of constructing meanings, and the novel becomes valuable by the quality of critical attention which it brings to bear on this process: the complexity and intricacy of the experiential imagination that is engaged or provoked in the construction of meaning.

In this respect Flaubert is a particularly fascinating novelist because of the ways in which his works lead to a demystification of the interpretive process, subject it to the severest tests, display its artificiality with a maximum of self-consciousness by promoting an awareness of the novel's deceitfulness as mediator. To read one's life as a novel can be a very questionable activity, and the novels are prompt to question it, showing the flaws in our drive towards unity and intelligibility, making us feel that we are not very much at home in the interpreted world, much as we should like to think that we were. Other novelists, of course, have posed much greater obstacles to understanding, greater challenges to our interpretive operations. But Flaubert is perhaps more insidious and for that reason the more effective. His realism provides firm links with an empirical world and draws the reader into a process which appears very familiar, only to expose him to the drama of the sentence and to the demystification of his role in making sense of the text.

# Notes

*Introduction*

1. *Selected Literary Criticism*, ed. M. Shapira (Penguin, Harmondsworth, 1968), pp. 281 and 254.
2. *The Letters of Ezra Pound*, ed. D. O. Page (Faber, London, 1951), p. 140. *Hugh Selwyn Mauberly*, in *Selected Poems* (Faber, London, 1959), p. 173.
3. Roman Jakobson, 'Linguistics and Poetics', in *Style in Language*, ed. T. Sebeok (MIT, Cambridge, 1960), p. 353.
4. See, for example, B. Eichenbaum, 'Comment est fait *Le Manteau* de Gogol', in *Théorie de la littérature*, ed. T. Todorov (Seuil, Paris, 1965), pp. 212–33.
5. Preface to *What Maisie Knew*, in *The Art of the Novel*, ed. R. P. Blackmur (Scribner's, New York, 1934), p. 145.
6. Preface to *The Golden Bowl*, *ibid.*, p. 329.
7. For further discussion see my *Structuralist Poetics* (Routledge, London, 1974).
8. *Critique et vérité* (Seuil, Paris, 1966), p. 65.
9. I quote from what in other respects might be taken as two polar extremities in criticism: Russian formalism, with its concept of 'defamiliarization' — see V. Shlovsky, 'L'Art comme procédé' in *Théorie de la littérature*, ed. Todorov (Seuil, Paris, 1965), pp. 76–97 — and F. R. Leavis, *The Great Tradition* (Penguin, Harmondsworth, 1962), p. 10.
10. It is an *instance* of 'a haphazard arrangement of leaves', but it does not *signify* that of which it is an instance; whereas a cultural object signifies any category under which it can be brought.
11. Cf. Fredric Jameson, 'Metacommentary', *PMLA* 86:1 (Jan. 1971).

*1. The Rites of Youth*

1. 'I am bored. I wish I were dead or drunk, or God so I could play tricks.' Flaubert, *Oeuvres complètes* (Seuil, Paris, 1964), I, 158. References to this edition will henceforth be included in the text.

2. 'On the Suffering of the World', in *Essays and Aphorisms*, trans. R. Hollingdale (Penguin, Harmondsworth, 1970), p. 47.

3. *Génie du christianisme*, part II, book III, chapter ix, 'Du vague des passions'.

4. Alfred de Musset, *Confessions d'un enfant du siècle* (Garnier, Paris, 1968), p. 17.

5. *L'Idiot de la famille* (Gallimard, Paris, 1971– ), III, 107–78.

6. 'We have seen stars and waves; we have seen sands as well.'
'What bitter knowledge one gets from travel! Today, yesterday, tomorrow, the world, so small and monotonous, shows us our own image: an oasis of horror in a desert of boredom.' *Les Fleurs du mal*, CXXVI.

7. 'When the low, heavy sky presses down like a lid on the mind, groaning from the tedious anxieties that prey on it . . .' *Les Fleurs du mal*, LXXVIII.

8. For a brief but admirable discussion of this aspect of Baudelaire, see Leo Bersani, *Balzac to Beckett: Center and Circumference in French Fiction* (OUP, New York, 1970), pp. 150–54.

9. 'I am a cemetery abhorred by the moon . . .' *Les Fleurs du mal*, LXXVI.

10. *Selected Literary Criticism*, ed. Shapira, pp. 54–5. Cf. Eliot's claim that Baudelaire confused Evil with its theatrical representations. *Selected Essays* (Faber, London, 1951), p. 427.

11. *L'Idiot de la famille*, III, 160–61. See also Maurice Schroder, *Icarus: The Image of the Artist in French Romanticism* (Harvard, Cambridge, 1961), p. 133ff.

12. 'He dies in what he weeps and hopes for', Musset, 'Lettre à M. de Lamartine', in *Poésies nouvelles* (Garnier, Paris, 1962), p. 65.

13. *L'Idiot de la famille*, I, 186. See also I, 182–216.

14. *L'Idiot de la famille*, I, 144. See also I, 13–179, 283–93, and 768–73.

15. I am indebted to Sartre's brilliant discussion, *L'Idiot de la famille*, II, 1728–2136. I am, however, concerned only with the function of the crisis in the project that the literary works imply, not with the facts of the crisis itself or with the extent to which it was chosen.

16. 'The one who is now alive and is me does nothing but contemplate the other, who is dead. I have had two distinct lives; external events symbolized the end of the first and the beginning of the second; that is mathematically exact. My active, passionate, emotional life,

full of contradictory movements and multiple feelings, ended at age twenty-two. At that point I made great progress all of a sudden, and something else began. Then for my purposes I divided the world and myself in two: on the one hand, things external, which should be colourful, diverse, harmonious, superb, and which I accept only as a spectacle to enjoy; on the other hand, things internal which I compress to make as dense as possible.'

17. 'Ah! Writing! To write is to take hold of the world, with all its prejudices and virtues, and sum it up in a book. You feel your thought take form, grow, live, draw itself up on its pedestal and remain there for ever . . . Now I am exhausted, worn out, and fall from weariness into my chair, without even the strength to thank you for having read me . . .'

18. 'Well now, my readers, brave and esteemed Sir, and you, kind and attentive Madam, what do you think our friend in the coffin would have replied if some tactless fellow had asked his opinion of God's goodness? Would he have replied, "It may be", "Is it so?", "I don't know"? For my part, I think he would have said "I doubt it" or "I deny it".'

19. 'Often, looking at all these men going their ways, pursuing some a name, others a throne, still others some ideal virtue — all things more or less empty and senseless, seeing this vortex, this fiery furnace, this disgusting chaos of pleasure, vice, fact, feeling, matter and passion, I have asked myself: 'where is all this going? on whom will this vile dust fall? and since it will all be gone with the wind where is the absolute Nothingness that can enclose it all?'

20. 'that great idiot which for so many centuries has turned round in space without advancing one jot, which shrieks, dribbles, and tears itself to pieces.'

21. 'if everything is not a mockery and foul joke, if all that's preached in schools and spun out in books, if everything that's seen, experienced, or spoken, if everything that exists . . . I break off, so bitter it is to say. Very well then, if all this is not a piteous illusion, so much smoke, Nothingness itself.'

22. 'You have just been speaking with one of these vile creatures, men without principles for whom virtue is but a word and the world a joke. From there they go on to look at everything in a base way.'

23. 'weak but proud man, miserable ant who can barely crawl about on your grain of sand.'

24. 'Sometimes it seems that I've existed for centuries, that my self holds the rubbish of a thousand past lives. Why should that be? Have I loved or hated? Have I pursued any quest? I still don't know.'

25. 'I was, thus, what you all are: an individual who lives, sleeps, eats, drinks, weeps, laughs, turned in on himself and finding there, wherever he goes, the same debris of hopes no sooner raised than destroyed, the same dust of all that's been crushed, the same paths so oft taken, the same unexplored depths, which are both frightening and boring. Are you not as tired as I am of waking up every morning and seeing the sun? tired of living the same life and suffering the same pains? tired of feeling desire and repulsion? tired of waiting and possessing?'

26. 'and if someone who, to reach this page, has passed through all the metaphors, hyperboles, and other figures which fill up the preceding pages still wants to know the ending, let him continue; we shall provide one.'

27. 'who inclined to distortions and rambling nonsense and greatly abused his adjectives.'

28. 'I am much struck by the chance which made the book stop here, at the very point where it would have become better. The author was about to enter society and would have had much to teach us, but he gradually abandoned himself to an austere solitude from which nothing emerged. He thought it appropriate, that is, to complain no longer — a proof, perhaps, that he had really begun to suffer. Neither his conversation, letters, nor papers, amongst which I found this after his death, offered anything to reveal his state of mind after the time when he stopped writing his confessions.'

29. 'Finally, in December of last year, he died; but slowly, little by little, by the action of thought itself, without any organ of the body being affected, as one dies of grief — which may seem unlikely to those who have suffered much, but which must be accepted in a novel, for love of the fantastic.'

30. *L'Idiot de la famille*, II, 1747–50.

31. '— There it is!
— What?
And Satan replied:
— You see, Hell is the *world*!'

32. 'The earth was sunk in lethargic slumber, its surface entirely still, and only the ocean waves, breaking in

foam on the rocks, could be heard. The screech-owl's cries echoed in the cypress groves, the lizard dragged its slimy body over the tombstones, and the vulture was coming to swoop on the rotting bones which lay on the battlefield.'

33. 'Humanity, which for a moment had raised its face to heaven, had turned it back to earth and taken up again its former life. Empires marched on, with their ruins which fall, disturbing the silence of time, into the calm of nothingness and eternity. Races had contracted a leprosy of the soul, and all was made vile. There was laughter, but it smacked of anguish; men were weak and cruel; the world was mad . . . it drove towards its death.'

34. *L'Idiot de la famille*, II, 1571.

35. *Souvenirs, notes, et pensées intimes* (Chastel, Paris, 1965), pp. 71–2.

36. 'Let it remain in the trembling, evanescent breeze, in the sounds that echo from shore to shore, in the silver-browed star that whitens your surface with its soft light!'

37. 'Everything which sang, flew, trembled, sparkled, the birds in the woods, the leaves quivering in the breeze, the rivers flowing in flower-studded meadows, barren rocks, storms, pounding waves, embalming sands, falling leaves, snowy graves, rays of sun and moonlight, all songs, voices, smells, all these things which form the vast harmony called Nature, poetry, God, echoed in his soul . . .'

38. 'Whoever watches the leaves tremble in the breeze, rivers meander through the fields, life fret and swirl in things, men live, do good and ill, the sea's waves roll on, the heavens unveil their stars, and who asks himself, "Why leaves? Why does water flow? . . . Why storms? Why is heaven so pure and earth so foul?", finds that these questions lead to a darkness that none escapes.'

39. 'She watched the crowd flowing into the theatres and cafés, this world of lackeys and lords, spread out like a parti-coloured coat on a festival day. All that seemed to her a fantastic scene, a vast stage, with its stone palaces, its illuminated shop windows, its elegant costumes, its foolishness, its cardboard crowns and kingdoms of an hour. Here a dancer's coach splatters the populace, there a man dies of starvation while seeing piles of gold behind windows; everywhere laughter and tears, everywhere wealth and poverty, everywhere vice insulting virtue.'

40. 'There I saw young girls in blue dresses and white dresses, pimpled shoulders, jutting shoulder-blades, faces of rabbits, weasels, martens, dogs, cats, and certainly imbeciles — and all that was chattering, jabbering, dancing, and sweating — a pile of people more hollow than the sound of a boot on the pavement surrounded me.' *Souvenirs, notes, et pensées intimes,* p. 79.

41. Roger Huss, *The Early Work of Gustave Flaubert up to and including the first Education sentimentale (1845),* Unpublished PhD thesis, Cambridge University Library, 1972. Chapter III, pp. 118–66.

42. 'whose beautiful architecture he could admire; he saw in the streets manure carts drawn by a horse and an ass, bakers' wagons drawn by hand, milkmaids selling their milk, caretakers sweeping out the gutters.'

43. 'Hands on his thighs, his eyes wide open, he stared stupidly at the brass legs of an old dresser with mahogany veneer which stood there.'

44. 'he gazed at the windows of drapers' shops and print-sellers, he admired the gaslights and posters. In the evening he went out onto the boulevards to see the prostitutes, which amused him very much in the first days, since there was nothing like it back home.'

45. 'He took bus rides from one end of Paris to another and observed all the faces of of those getting on or off, establishing parallels or antitheses between them.'

46. 'Glasses were passed quickly, pell-mell, from hand to hand; the foam spilled on the tablecloth and on fingers; the women laughed. Thus there are unfailing pleasures.' 'M. Renaud obeyed his wife, bowed to everyone, enquired after each one's health, offered everyone chairs, drew up footstools for the ladies and rugs for the men; he was obsequious, quick, he glided, he soared.'

47. 'Madame had her privy purse and secret drawer; Monsieur rarely scolded and had already for some time ceased to share Madame's bed. Madame read late in bed at night; Monsieur dropped off immediately and almost never dreamed, except perhaps when he was slightly drunk, which happened to him from time to time.'

48. 'It was his last day in pathos. Henceforth he abandoned his superstitious fears and was not afraid of encountering mangy dogs in the countryside.'

49. *L'Idiot de la famille*, II, 1929.

50. 'meanwhile he used all the strength of his intellect in trying to understand them, and he begged luck to grant him an unexpected power which would put him in touch with the secrets revealed by this voice and instruct him in its language, which for him was as mute as a closed door. But nothing occurred, nothing happened, though his mind struggled to descend into these depths; the wind blew, the wind murmured, the dog howled.'

51. 'They confronted one another, asking each other the unsaid. Quaking at this mutual contact, they were both terrified by it, they frightened one another; the man trembled under the dog's gaze, in which he thought he saw a soul, and the beast trembled at the man's gaze, where it perhaps saw a god.'

52. 'He was sure however that he had not dreamed, that he had really seen what he had seen, which led him to doubt the reality of life, for in what had transpired between him and the monster, in everything touching this event, there was something so intimate, so profound, and at the same time so clear, that one could not but recognize a reality of another kind, as real as the ordinary reality which it seemed to contradict. Now everything tangible and palpable that existence offers was passing out of his mind, as secondary and futile, an illusion which was only the surface.'

53. 'It had been essential that life enter into him without his entering life and that he be able to meditate on it at leisure so as to tell later the flavours that composed it.'

54. *Beyond Formalism* (Yale University Press, New Haven, 1970), p. 302.

55. *Goethes Werke* (Wegner, Hamburg, 1963), VI, 124.

56. 'The black pall, decorated with white tears, rose from time to time uncovering the bier. The tired bearers slowed down, and it moved forwards in continuous jerks, like a launch pitching over the waves. They arrived. . . . while the priest spoke, the red earth, piled up on the sides, ran down at the corners, continually, silently.'

57. *L'Idiot de la famille*, II, 1617–18: 'steal language from men, divert it from its practical ends, subject its forms to rendering in themselves inarticulable negations and you will have incarnated in your sentences the loadstar of imagination, Beauty or complete Evil, by

making it felt in the case of language itself that the world is created and sustained by a free and malignant power. Style is the silence of discourse, the silence in discourse, the secret and negative goal of written language.'

58. Wallace Stevens, 'The Snow Man', *Collected Poems* (Faber, London, 1955), p. 9.

59. 'Thinking of all these little factitious arrangements men make which five minutes of nature sufficed to upset, I admired the true order reestablished in the false . . . There is there something of an immense farce which worsts us. Is anything so ridiculous as melon covers? Well, those poor melon covers really had a time of it! . . . It is rather too generally believed that the sun exists to make cabbages grow. From time to time God must be put back on his pedestal. And so he undertakes to remind us by sending now and then some plague, epidemic, unexpected upset, or other manifestation of the Rule, that is to say, Contingent Evil, which is not perhaps the Necessary Good, but which is Being nonetheless.'

2. *The Perfect Crime — The Novel*

1. 'The thatched roofs, like fur caps pulled down over the eyes, come down over a third of the low windows, whose bulging panes of old glass are decorated in the middle with a boss, like the bottoms of wine bottles. On the plaster wall, which is diagonally traversed by black beam-joists, a withered peartree sometimes clings, and the ground floors have at their door a little swinging gate to keep out the chicks, which come to pick up, on the threshold, bits of wholemeal bread dipped in cider.'

2. See Roland Barthes' brilliant discussion in 'L'Effet de réel', *Communications* 11 (Paris, 1968), pp. 84–9.

3. Champfleury, 'Lettre à M. Veuillot,' *Figaro* (10 July 1856), quoted by Bouvier, *La Bataille réaliste* (Paris, 1914), p. 305.

4. *The Concept of Irony*, trans. L. M. Capel (Collins, London, 1966), p. 265.

5. 'La Comtesse de Tende', in *Romans et nouvelles*, ed. E. Magne (Garnier, Paris, 1961), p. 410.

6. 'In the middle was a round table . . . enhanced by that white porcelain tea service, decorated with half-worn-away gold filigree, which one sees everywhere these days.' 'The front of the pension gives onto a tiny garden, so that the facade falls at right angles to New Saint Geneviève Street, at the point where you see it suddenly dip.' *Le Père Goriot* (Gallimard, Paris, 1961), pp. 23 and 20.

7. Molière, *Les Précieuses ridicules*, VIII. For further discussion see my article, 'Paradox and the Language of Morals in La Rochefoucauld', *Modern Language Review*, 68: 1 (1973), and Gérard Genette, *Figures* (Seuil, Paris, 1966), pp. 205–21.

8. La Rochefoucauld, Réflexions diverses XVI, in *Maximes*, ed. Truchet (Garnier, Paris, 1961), p. 218.

9. Stendhal, *La Chartreuse de Parme*, ed. Martineau (Garnier, Paris, 1961), chap. xii, p. 196.

10. *The Letters of Ezra Pound*, p. 140.

11. *L'Oeil vivant* (Gallimard, Paris, 1961), p. 232. See an excellent discussion in Bersani, *Balzac to Beckett*, pp. 106–21.

12. 'It smells stuffy, musty, rancid; it chills you, smells damp, penetrates your clothes; it smacks of a room where people have dined; it stinks of scullery, servants' hall, poorhouse.' 'Perhaps it could be described if a procedure were invented for weighing up the nauseous elementary particles contributed by the distinctive catarrhal clouds of each pensioner, young and old.' *Le Père Goriot*, p. 24.

13. *La Cousine Bette* (Garnier, Paris, 1962), pp. 1–2.

14. *Ibid.*, pp. 2–3.

15. See, for example, *Eugénie Grandet* (Garnier, Paris, 1961), p. 112.

16. *Le Père Goriot*, p. 19.

17. 'where one would explain how the work was intended to reestablish the public's links with tradition, order, and social norms, and written in such a way that the reader couldn't tell whether or not one was having him on.'

18. Flaubert, *Le Second Volume de Bouvard et Pécuchet*, ed Bollème (Denoël, Paris, 1966), p. 35.

19. Marie-Jeanne Durry, *Flaubert et ses projets inédits* (Nizet, Paris, 1950), p. 276. Flaubert would have been especially delighted that his editor should take this suggestion at face value and solemnly explain that he wished his particular moral point of view to be understood.

2. *Les Gommes* (10/18. Paris, 1963), p. 161.

21. 'sums up the salon, the dining room, the garden, prefigures the kitchen, and anticipates the residents.' *Le Père Goriot*, pp. 26–7.

22. *La Cousine Bette*, p. 49.

23. 'It was one of those composite caps, where one finds elements of the busby, Lancer cap, bowler, otterskin cap, and cotton nightcap, one of those wretched objects, in short, whose mute

ugliness has the depths of expressiveness of an imbecile's face. Ovoid and swelled out by ribs, it began with three circular bulges; then came, in alternation, divided by a strip of red, lozenges of velvet and rabbit fur; next came a kind of sack which ended in a cardboard polygon, covered with complicated braid embroidery and from which hung, at the end of a long and excessively thin cord, a little sheaf of gold wire, as a kind of tassel. It was new; the peak shone.'

24. Albert Thibaudet, *Gustave Flaubert* (Gallimard, Paris, 1935), p. 96; Victor Brombert, *The Novels of Flaubert* (Princeton, 1966), p. 41.

25. *The Novel in France* (Hamilton, London, 1950), pp. 265–6.

26. *The Novels of Flaubert*, p. 130.

27. 'Rich were the garments, but more rich still were the charms . . .' *La Peau de chagrin* (Garnier, Paris, 1960), p. 66.

28. 'Frédéric was at first dazzled by the lights; he could make out only silk, velvet, bare shoulders, a mass of colours swaying to the sounds of an orchestra hidden behind the greenery, between walls hung with yellow silk, with pastel portraits, here and there, and crystal candelabra in Louis Seize style.'

29. 'Tall lamps, whose frosted globes looked like snowballs, towered over baskets of flowers which were set on small tables, in the corners; — and, opposite, beyond a second and smaller room, one could make out, in a third room, a bed with twisted posts, which had a Venetian mirror at its head.'

30. 'The Parisian, whose beauty lies in an indescribable grace, vain in both mind and dress, armed with an all-powerful helplessness, lithe but hard, a heartless, passionless siren but knowing the arts of counterfeiting passion and the accents of the heart, was not absent from this dangerous gathering.'

31. '. . . numbered about sixty, the women, for the most part, dressed as peasants or countesses, and the men, nearly all middle-aged, in costumes of carters, stevedores, or sailors.'

32. 'An old buck, dressed, like a Venetian Doge, in a long cassock of purple silk, was dancing with Rosanette, who was wearing a green jacket, knitted breeches, and soft boots with gold spurs. The couple opposite consisted of an Albanian, weighed down with Yatagans, and a blue-eyed Swiss girl, as white as milk, as plump as a quail, in shirtsleeves and a red bodice.'

33. 'There was also an angel, a golden sword in her hand, two swan's wings on her back, and who, coming, going, losing her partner — a Louis the fourteenth — at every moment, didn't understand the movements of the dance and kept upsetting the quadrille.'

34. 'This whirling movement, faster and faster in regular rhythm, dizzying, producing a kind of intoxication in his mind, provoked other images, while all the women passed by in a single dazzling spectacle, and each offered a distinctive stimulus according to her type of beauty.'
'The Polish girl, who moved with langorous abandon, made him long to clutch her to his heart while they sped in a sleigh across a snowy plain. A vista of tranquil pleasure, on the shore of a lake, in a chalet, unrolled beneath the feet of the Swiss girl, who waltzed with her body erect and her eyes lowered. Then, suddenly, the Bacchante, leaning back her dark head, made him dream of ravenous caresses in oleander groves, in stormy weather, to the chaotic sound of tabors.'

35. 'A German cuckoo-clock, striking two, provoked countless jokes about the cuckoo. Talk of all sorts followed: puns, anecdotes, boasts, wagers, lies held to be true, improbable assertions, a torrent of words which soon broke up into separate conversations.Wines were passed, one course followed another, the doctor carved. An orange, a cork were thrown across the room. People left their places to chat with someone else.'

36. 'The blue fumes of the punch gave a hellish tint to the faces of those who could still drink.' 'Strewn with the dead and the dying, the boudoir and the small salon presented the image of a battlefield.' *La Peau de chagrin*, p. 75.

37. 'Drunkenness, passion, delirium, oblivion, were inscribed in every heart, on every face, written on the carpet, expressed in the disorder, and they cast over every gaze a light veil which made visible intoxicating vapours in the air.'

38. R. J. Sherrington, *Three Novels by Flaubert* (Clarendon Press, Oxford, 1970), p. 323.

39. *The Novels of Flaubert*, pp. 177–8.

40. *Ibid.*, p. 178.

41. 'The trees became larger, and from time to time the coachman said: "Here are the Siamese twins, the Pharamond, the King's Coppice . . ." omitting none of the famous sites and sometimes even stopping to show them off.'

42. *The Sentimental Adventure* (Mouton, The Hague, 1967), p. 86.

43. 'Some of them, of amazing height, looked like patriarchs or emperors, or, the ends of their branches touching one another, formed triumphal arches with their long trunks; others, which had grown obliquely from the ground, looked like pillars about to fall . . . The diversity of trees offered a changing spectacle.'

44. 'gnarled, huge, which contorted themselves, stretched up from the ground, embraced one another, and, solid on their torso-like trunks, threw out their arms in desperate appeals and furious threats, like a group of Titans frozen in their anger.'

45. 'But the very frenzy of their chaos inspired rather visions of volcanoes, floods, great unknown cataclysms. Frédéric said they had been there since the beginning of the world and would stay there until the end.'

46. Here and there, like promontories on the dry bed of an ocean, rose rocks in vague animal forms: tortoises stretching out their necks, seals that crawled along, hippopotamuses and bears.'

47. 'Frédéric was seized by an inexpressible and retrospective lust. In order to divert this desire, he began to gaze tenderly at Rosanette.'

48. 'One illuminates you with his ardour, the other projects his mourning on you, Nature'. *Les Fleurs du mal*, LXXXI.

49. 'Isn't it a great pity to see this easy-going fellow, this vagabond, this out-of-work actor, this comedian, attempting, because he can play his role "artistically", to implicate eagles, crickets, streams and flowers in his song of misery.' *Les Fleurs du mal*, CXV.

50. 'The sky was charming, the sea was smooth; For me all was dark and bloody henceforth, Alas! My heart was, as in a thick shroud, buried in this allegory. On your island, O Venus, I found nothing standing but a symbolic gibbet on which my image hung.' *Les Fleurs du mal*, CXVI.

51. 'Before leaving they went for a walk along the river bank.
The sky, a soft blue, rounded like a dome, rested at the horizon on the jagged outline of the woods. Facing them, at the other end of the meadow, there was a steeple in a village, and, further on, on the left, the roof of a house formed a red patch on the river, which seemed immobile along the

whole length of its winding course. Reeds were bending, though, and the water shook gently the stakes driven into the bank to hold nets; a wicker eel trap, two or three old launches were there. Near the inn, a girl in a straw hat was drawing buckets from a well — each time one came up Frédéric listened with inexpressible pleasure to the grating of the chain. He did not doubt that he was happy for the rest of his days, so natural did his happiness seem to him, so inseparable from his life and the person of this woman.'

52. *The Sentimental Adventure*, p. 80.

53. *Ibid.*, pp. 80–81.

54. 'Directly ahead were the fields, on the right a barn, and the steeple of a church, and on the left a screen of poplars. Two main paths, in the form of a cross, divided the garden into four parts. The vegetables were arranged in beds, from which rose, here and there, dwarf cypresses and trained fruit-trees. On one side an arbour-way led to a bower; on the other a wall held up espaliers; and a lattice fence, at the back, opened onto the countryside. There was beyond the wall an orchard; behind the bower, a thicket; beyond the lattice fence, a small track.'

55. 'Flaubert et la matière', *Europe* 485–7, 'Flaubert' (Sept–Nov, 1969), pp. 206–7.

56. *Essais critiques* (Seuil, Paris, 1964), p. 232.

57. 'The reader will accede to meaning through the practical labours that he will be invited to undertake and that he will pursue from the beginning to the end of his reading, but which *despite him* will collapse beneath his eyes, displaying its inanity.' *L'Idiot de la famille*, II, 1981.

58. *Qu'est-ce que la littérature?* (Gallimard, Paris, 1972), pp. 173–4.

59. *Flaubert: The Making of the Master* (Weidenfeld, London, 1967), pp. 292–3.

60. *The Novels of Flaubert*, pp. 41–2.

61. *L'Idiot de la famille*, II, 1202.

62. *Commentaire sur 'Madame Bovary'* (La Baconnière, Neuchâtel, 1951), pp. 17–18.

63. *Three Novels by Flaubert*, p. 81.

64. 'Flies, on the table, crawled down the sides of glasses which had been used and buzzed as they drowned themselves at the bottom, in the dregs of cider', 'on her shoulders little drops of perspiration', 'making the soot on the fire-back like velvet, gave a bluish tinge to the cold cinders.'

65. Quoted in Sherrington, p. 197.

66. *Three Novels by Flaubert*, p. 195.

67. 'At first the Suffete strode around with large swift steps; he was breathing noisily, he stamped on the ground with his heel, he passed his hand over his forehead like a man bothered by flies.'

68. 'There were chrysolites broken off mountainsides by means of slings, carbuncles formed from lynxes' urine, glossopetrae which had fallen from the moon, tyanos, diamonds, sandastrum, and beryls, with the three varieties of rubies, the four kinds of sapphire, and the twelve sorts of emerald . . . There were topazes from Mount Zabarca that protect one from terror, opals from Bactriana which prevent miscarriages, and horns of Ammon which are placed beneath beds to encourage dreams.'

69. 'Then talk turned to Delmas, who could, as a mime, have considerable success in the theatre; and there followed a discussion in which Shakespeare, censorship, style, the lower classes, the takings at the Porte-Saint-Martin, Alexandre Dumas, Victor Hugo, and Dumersan all figured. Arnoux had known a number of famous actresses; the young men leaned forward to listen to him. But his words were drowned by the din of the music, and, as soon as the quadrille or the polka was over, everyone rushed for a table, called the waiter, laughed; bottles of beer and fizzy lemonade popped among the greenery, women cackled like hens; sometimes, two gentlemen tried to fight; a thief was arrested.'

70. 'The guests arrived early in carriages, light one-horse carts, two-wheeled charabancs, old cabs without hoods, delivery vans with leather curtains . . .' 'and the young folk from the nearest villages in traps where they stood in a row, holding the sides to keep from falling, going at a trot and very much shaken up.'

71. 'You could see beside them, not speaking a word in her white dress from the first communion, which had been lengthened for the occasion, some gangling girl of fourteen or sixteen, their cousin or elder sister, no doubt, ruddy-faced, embarrassed, her hair greasy with rose pommade, and very afraid of soiling her gloves.'

72. *Three Novels by Flaubert*, p. 132.

73. 'The procession, keeping together at first like a single coloured scarf, which undulated through the countryside along the narrow path winding between fields of green wheat, soon stretched itself out and divided into separate groups, which lingered to chat.'

74. 'The countryside was flat, they could be seen from afar; and the villagers wondered what on earth were these two extraordinary objects, bounding on the horizon.'

75. '*Madam* bought herself a hat, some gloves, a bouquet. *Monsieur* was much afraid they would miss the curtain.' 'Bovary, out of prudence, kept the tickets in his hand, in his trouser pocket, which he pressed against his body.' 'Why had she not, like Lucy, resisted, entreated?' 'With him, through all the kingdoms of Europe, she would have travelled from capital to capital, sharing his hardships and his pride, gathering the flowers that were thrown to him . . .'

76. 'A fine voice, an unshakeable assurance, more temperament than intelligence and more pomposity than lyricism completed and heightened this splendid specimen of the charlatan, part hairdresser and part toreador.'

77. 'All the drawn out pocket handkerchiefs mopped red foreheads.' 'From the very first scene he enthralled. He pressed Lucy in his arms, left her, returned, seemed in despair; he produced flashes of anger, then elegiac rumblings of infinite sweetness.'

78. 'the citizens stared, their eyes full of astonishment at this thing, so extraordinary in the provinces . . .' 'the gardens of the almshouse, where old men in black jackets stroll in the sun, along a terrace, green with ivy.'

79. 'Toward six o'clock, the carriage drew up in a lane of the Beauvoisine quarter, and a woman alighted from it, who walked with her veil lowered, without turning her head.'

80. *L'Idiot de la famille*, II, 1278.

81. *Ibid.*, p. 1285.

82. *Selected Literary Criticism*, p. 263.

83. Henry James, *The Art of the Novel*, pp. 329 and 142.

84. 'A tender sob shook her. Her arms opened and standing up they embraced one another in a long kiss. The floor creaked. A woman was beside them. Rosanette.'

85. 'Mme Arnoux had recognized her and was gazing at her with wide staring eyes, full of surprise and indignation. At last Rosanette said, "I've come to see M. Arnoux on business." "He's not here, as you see." "So he isn't," the Maréchale replied, "Your maid was right. Please excuse me." And, turning to Frédéric: "So you're here are you, my dear." This familiarity in her presence, like a slap in the face, made Madame Arnoux turn scarlet.'

86. 'Frédéric felt something soft beneath his foot; it was the hand of a sergeant in a grey coat lying face-down in the gutter. New groups of workers were coming up, pushing those who were fighting towards the guardhouse. The firing became heavier. Wine shops were open and people went in from time to time to smoke a pipe or drink a glass of beer and then came back to fight. A lost dog was howling. That raised a laugh.'

87. Henry James, *The Wings of the Dove* (Penguin, Harmondsworth, 1965), p. 232.

88. Henry James, *The Golden Bowl* (Penguin, Harmondsworth, 1966), p. 504.

81. *The Wings of the Dove*, p. 56.

90. Benjamin Constant, *Adolphe* (Garnier, Paris, 1965), pp. 90 and 62.

91. 'When all was over at the cemetery Charles came back home. He found no one downstairs, went upstairs, to the bedroom, saw her dress still hanging at the foot of the alcove; then, leaning against the writing table, he remained until evening lost in sorrowful reverie. After all, she had loved him.'

92. 'What astounded them above all was that earth, as an element, does not exist.' 'The skeleton surprised them . . . they learned the parts of the human frame and were amazed by the spinal column . . . The metacarpals upset Bouvard.' 'They were surprised that fish should have fins, birds wings, and seeds shells.' 'In the galleries of the museum they viewed the stuffed quadrupeds with astonishment, the butterflies with pleasure, and the metals with indifference.'

93. 'Two men appeared. One was coming from the Bastille, the other from the Botanical Gardens. The taller, dressed in linen, walked with his hat pushed back, his waistcoat unbuttoned, and his cravat in his hand. The smaller, whose body was engulfed in a brown frock-coat, bent his head under a cap with a pointed brim. When they were half-way along the boulevard,

they sat down, at the same moment, on the same bench.

To wipe their foreheads they took off their hats, which each set down beside him; and the small man noticed in his neighbour's hat: Bouvard; while the latter could easily make out in the hat of the frock-coat's inhabitant the word: Pécuchet.'

94. 'Bouvard's friendly air quickly charmed Pécuchet. Pécuchet's serious look struck Bouvard.'

95. 'Pécuchet adopted without hesitation a hiker's stick, six feet long with a tapered steel point. Bouvard preferred an umbrella-stick or collapsible umbrella.'

96. 'they ascended to speculations on the origins of the world. Bouvard opted for the Neptunian theory; Pécuchet, on the contrary, was a Plutonian.' 'Pécuchet admired these ideas. To Bouvard they were pitiful — he had first read Augustin Thierry.' 'Bouvard, who was liberal-minded and tenderhearted, was a constitutionalist, Girondist and Thermidorian. Pécuchet, of worrying and authoritarian tendencies, declared himself Sans-Culotte and even Robespierrist.'

97. 'Pécuchet takes a black view of the future of humanity. Modern man has declined and become a machine.' 'Bouvard takes a happier view of humanity's future. Modern man is advancing.'

98. Marie-Jeanne Durry, *Flaubert et ses projets inédits*, p. 111.

99. Nathalie Sarraute, 'Flaubert le précurseur', *Preuves* (Feb, 1965), p. 11. Cf. Alan Robbe-Grillet, *Pour un nouveau roman* (Minuit, Paris, 1963), p. 139.

100. *The Novels of Flaubert*, p. 193.

101. *Ibid.*, p. 201.

102. *Ibid.*, p. 259.

103. *The Craft of Fiction* (Cape, London, 1921), p. 92.

104. *Ibid.*, pp. 60, 80, 73.

105. Georg Lukács, *Die Theorie des Romans*, 3rd ed. (Luchterhand, Neuwied & Berlin, 1965), p. 69.

106. J. P. Stern, *On Realism* (Routledge, London, 1973), pp. 5 and 28, Chapters 6 and 7.

107. 'There was Charles. His cap was pulled down to his brow and his two thick lips were quivering, which gave his face a stupid air. Even his back, his placid back, was irritating to look at, and she found displayed there on his coat all the banality of the man.'

108. 'But it was especially at meal times that she could bear it no longer . . . all the bitterness of life seemed served up on her plate, and, with the steam from the boiled meat, there rose from the depths of her soul something like clouds of disgust. Charles was a slow eater; she nibbled a few nuts, or else, leaning on her elbow, would amuse herself by making, with the point of her knife, scratches on the oilcloth.'

109. 'The shadows of evening were falling; horizontal rays of sunlight, passing through the branches, dazzled her eyes. Here and there, all around her, in the leaves and on the ground, patches of light trembled, as if humming-birds in flight had scattered their feathers. Silence was everywhere; something soft seemed to emanate from the trees; she felt her heart beating again and her blood flowing through her body like a river of milk. And she heard then in the distance, beyond the wood, from the other hillsides, an indistinct but long-continued cry, a voice which trailed on, and she listened to it in silence, as it mingled like music with the last vibrations of her tingling nerves.'

110. *Balzac to Beckett*, p. 165.

111. Anthony Thorlby, *Gustave Flaubert and the Art of Realism* (Bowes and Bowes, London, 1956), p. 44.

112. *Ibid.*, p. 41.

113. 'by the fate inherent in their characters which made them always come together again and love one another.'

114. 'He had compromised himself as Prefect by his excessive zeal for the Government's interests. He had been dismissed. After that he had been director of colonization in Algeria, secretary to a Pasha, manager of a newspaper, advertising agent, to end up as employee in the litigation department of an industrial firm.'

115. 'And they looked back over their lives. They had both missed life, he who had dreamed of love, he who had dreamed of power. What was the reason? "Perhaps it was failure to steer a straight course", said Frédéric. — "That might be it in your case. My mistake, on the other hand, was being too straightforward, not taking account of a thousand minor factors which were all important. I had too much logic and you too much feeling." '

116. *Gustave Flaubert*, p. 150.

117. *Studies in European Realism* (Grosset, New York, 1964), p. 64.

118. *Ibid.*, p. 57.

119. *Ibid.*, p. 59.

120. Balzac, *Le Lys dans la vallée* (Gallimard, Paris, 1965), pp. 168–9.

121. Brombert and Cortland, *op. cit.*, are exceptional in grasping the problem and its difficulty but neither succeeds in avoiding this dichotomy.

122. 'Then she said to him: "Sometimes your words come back to me like a distant echo, like the sound of a bell borne on the wind, and it seems to me that you are there beside me when I am reading about love in a book." '

123. 'in order to hide this disappointment, he went down on his knees and, taking her hands, began to speak tender words to her.' 'becoming carried away by his own words, he came almost to believe what he was saying.' 'he said to her, almost in a swoon, "the sight of your foot upsets me." ' 'No one has ever been loved like this!'

124. 'Another fear restrained him — fear of being disgusted later. Besides, what a nuisance it would be! — and both out of prudence and to avoid tarnishing his ideal he turned on his heel and began to roll a cigarette.'

125. 'she wanted to know if he would marry. He swore he would not.
— Really? Why?
— Because of you, said Frédéric, taking her in his arms.'

126. *The Sentimental Adventure*, p. 98.

127. Georg Lukács, *Die Theorie des Romans*, p. 128.

## 3. *Values*

1. 'With stupidity the Gods themselves struggle in vain.' 'Stupidity and Poetry. There are subtle relationships between these two orders; the order of stupidity and the order of poetry.'

2. The mis-spellings are Flaubert's. 'Since there's a woman who comes to Papa's house and who always tells us stupid things I will write them.'

3. 'I am up to the neck in young girls' dreams.' 'At the moment I'm making all the gods speak on their deathbeds. The subtitle of my book could be: "The height of insanity." ' 'Nothing is so exhausting as delving into human stupidity.' 'I am overrun by the stupidity of my two chaps.'

4. *Selected Literary Criticism*, p. 187.

5. 'One can bet that any public notion, anything conventionally accepted, is a stupidity, since it has suited the greatest number.'

6. Henceforth in citing the *Dictionnaire des idées reçues* I shall simply italicize the word under which the entry is to be found.

7. *L'Idiot de la famille*, I, 635.

8. See the 'Postface' to Barthes' *Mythologies* (Seuil, Paris, 1957).

9. E. and J. de Goncourt, *Journal*, 17 December 1873.

10. Sartre, *L'Idiot de la famille*, II, 1245.

11. 'It would be bloody good fun to propose it to her. Can you imagine the bill the Garçon would make out in this situation? "For the company of a man like myself, so much. Extra charges: for having made a clever remark, for having been charming and polite, etc." '

12. 'I shout aloud, I laugh, I drink, I sing out, ha! ha! ha! ha! ha! ha!, and I give the Garçon's laugh, I beat on the table, I pull out my hair, I roll on the floor.'

13. *S/Z*, p. 212.

14. 'I want to produce such an impression of weariness and boredom that one might believe in reading the book that it had been written by an imbecile.'

15. Sartre, *L'Idiot de la famille*, II, 1505.

16. 'What a strange life a man must lead who stays there, in that little cabin, moving the two keys and pulling the wires; the unintelligent cog in a machine which is mute for him, he can die without having known any of the events he has been informed of, any of the many words he has transmitted. The point? the point? the significance? Who knows? . . . Are we not all, a bit more or less, like this worthy fellow, speaking words we have been taught and which we learn without understanding them?'

17. Claude Lévi-Strauss, *Le Totémisme aujourd'hui* (PUF, Paris, 1962), p. 130.

18. Marie-Jeanne Durry, *Flaubert et ses projets inédits*, p. 349.

19. 'Roman et objets: l'exemple de *Madame Bovary*', *Europe* 485–7, 'Flaubert', (Sept–Nov, 1969), p. 186.

20. 'People were resting their two hands on their two thighs.' *Ibid.*, p. 187.

21. 'The "stupidity" of everything makes itself felt. Stupidity, that is to say particularity as opposed to generality. "Smaller than" becomes the awful sign of mind. The demon of possible orderings.' *Oeuvres* (Pléiade, Paris, 1960), II, 64.

22. Cf. *Madame Bovary — Nouvelle version*, ed. J. Pommier and G. Leleu (Corti, Paris, 1949), p. 458; and Maxime du Camp, extract from *Souvenirs littéraires*, in Flaubert, *Oeuvres complètes*, I, 29.

23. *Gustave Flaubert*, p. 96.

24. *La Pensée sauvage* (Plon, Paris, 1962), pp. 34–6.

25. Michel Crouzet, 'Le Style épique dans *Madame Bovary*', *Europe* 485–7 'Flaubert' (Sept–Nov, 1969), p. 159.

26. Though I am much indebted to Sartre's brilliant discussion of reading (*L'Idiot de la famille*, II, 2028–42), I should like at least to dissociate myself from the reasoning by which he decides that Flaubert does not read books from beginning to end.

27. Cf. Sartre, *L'Idiot de la famille*, II, 1703–6.

28. *Ibid.*, II, 2042.

29. *L'Idiot de la famille*, I, 628, Cf. I, 626–9.

30. *The Concept of Irony*, p. 274.

31. *Ibid.*

32. Seznec, *Les Sources de l'episode des dieux dans la Tentation de Saint Antoine* (Vrin, Paris, 1940) and *Nouvelles Etudes sur la Tentation de Saint Antoine* (Warburg Institute, London, 1949). Foucault, 'La Bibliothèque fantastique' in *Flaubert*, ed. Raymonde Debray-Genette (Didier, Paris, 1970).

33. 'Marcion: The Creator is not the true God!
Saint Clement of Alexandria: Matter is eternal!
Bardesanes: It was created by the seven Planetary Spirits.
The Hernians: The angels made souls!
The Priscillianians: The Devil made the world!'

34. 'We have martyrs more martyred than yours, more difficult prayers, better outbursts of love, and trances at least as long.
Antoine: But no revelation, no proofs!
Then all wave in the air papyrus rolls, wooden tablets, scraps of leather, cloth strips.'

35. 'That one is worth all the rest of hell. Nebuchadnezzar did not dazzle me as much, nor the Queen of Sheba charm me so deeply. His way of speaking of the gods makes one want to know them.'

36. *Oeuvres*, I, 613.

37. *Selected Literary Criticism*, p. 273.

38. 'She wanted to become a saint. She bought rosaries, she wore amulets; she wanted to have in her room, at the head of her bed, a reliquary set in emeralds to kiss every evening.'

39. 'Emma compared herself to those great ladies of yesteryear, whose glory she had dreamed about over a portrait by La Vallière, and who, trailing so majestically the elaborate trains of their long dresses, retired from society to spill at Christ's feet all the tears of a spirit that life had wounded.'

40. A broad phonetic transcription makes clear the relationships between vowels:/ʒ dõna õe gra dine/. Note the presence of three nasal vowels in close proximity.

41. 'He opted for painting, since the demands of that profession would bring him closer to Mme Arnoux. He had, therefore, discovered his calling. The goal of his existence was now clear and the future assured.'
   'There was discussion of the immortality of the soul; comparisons were made between professors.'
   'He was primarily concerned about the Rhineland frontier. He claimed a knowledge of artillery and went to the tailor of the Ecole Polytechnique.'
   'longed to travel or to go back to live in her convent. She desired both to die and to live in Paris.'

42. 'It was cold and the air reeked of a heavy fog which obscured the house-fronts. Frédéric inhaled it with delight . . . Since the pavement was slippery they swayed a bit, and it seemed to him as if the wind were rocking them both in the midst of a cloud.'

43. Cf. Sherrington, *Three Novels by Flaubert*, pp. 92–6, 100–9, 117–19, 239–46, and 249–315 passim.

44. 'It was all loves and lovers, damsels in distress swooning in lonely lodges, postillions slain all along the road, horses ridden to death on every page, dark forests, heart-aches, solemn oaths, sobs, tears, and kisses, moonlight boat-rides, nightingales in the groves, gentlemen as brave as lions, as gentle as lambs, too virtuous to be true, always impeccably dressed, and who wept like fountains.'

45. 'pallid landscapes of dithyrambic regions, which often show in the same picture palm trees and pine trees, tigers to the right, a lion to your left, tartar minarets on the horizon, Roman ruins in the foreground beside kneeling camels; — the whole scene framed by a well-kept virgin forest, with a huge perpendicular sunbeam trembling on the water, on which can be seen, white scratches on a steel-grey background, here and there, swans swimming.'

46. 'Why couldn't she lean on the balcony of Swiss chalets or shut up her melancholy in a Scottish cottage, with a husband dressed in a black velvet coat with long tails and who wore soft boots, a pointed hat, and white cuffs.' Cf. Emma's vision of life in Paris, I, 594.

47. 'Silences de Flaubert', in *Figures* (Seuil, Paris, 1966), pp. 223–9. Genette's best example is Emma's reverie, I, 640–41.

48. 'She was the beloved of all the novels, the heroine of all the plays, the undefined *she* of all the volumes of poetry. On her shoulders he found the amber skin of the *Odalisque bathing*; she had the long-waisted dresses of feudal chatelaines; she also resembled the *Pale Woman of Barcelona*, but above all else she was an angel!'

49. *The Concept of Irony*, p. 73.

50. *On the Aesthetic Education of Man*, ed. and trans. Wilkinson and Willoughby (Oxford University Press, 1967), pp. 105, 192–207.

51. *Oeuvres*, I, 1467.

52. *The Stoic Comedians* (Beacon Press, Boston, 1962), p. 12.

53. Kierkegaard, *The Concept of Irony*, p. 324.

54. 'in wielding an irony fraught with uncertainty, brings about a salutary uneasiness in the writing: he refuses to halt the play of codes (or does so badly), with the result that (and this is no doubt the true test of writing as writing) one never knows whether he is responsible for what he writes (whether there is an individual subject behind his language); for the essence of writing (the goal and meaning of the activity which makes up writing) is to prevent any reply to the question, who is speaking?' *S/Z*, p. 146.

55. Proust, 'A propos du "style" de Flaubert', in *Chroniques* (Gallimard, Paris, 1927), pp. 202–3.

56. *Gustave Flaubert* (Chapter 10, pp. 221–85), pp. 261–3.

57. *Ibid.*, p. 264.

58. 'The women, dressed in brilliant colours, wore long-waisted dresses, and, seated on the tiers of the platform, they were like large clumps of flowers, speckled with black, here and there, by the dark suits of the men.'

59. *Qu'est-ce que la littérature?*, pp. 162–3.

60. 'A propos du "style" de Flaubert', pp. 203–4.

61. 'human speech is like a cracked drum on which we tap out melodies that only make bears dance when we seek to make the stars weep.'

62. 'she, who was perhaps expecting to see her nephew's very portrait, so limited was her intelligence.'

63. 'They became associated in her mind, the parrot being sanctified by the relation with the Holy Ghost, which, on its part, came alive and more intelligible to her. The Lord, to give man the Word, could not have chosen a dove, since those birds have no voice, but rather one of Loulou's ancestors. And Félicité prayed before the picture but from time to time turned ever so slightly towards the bird."

64. William Empson, *Some Versions of Pastoral* (New Directions, Norfolk, Conn., 1960), p. 55. Cf. pp. 25–9 and 43–66.

65. Anthony Thorlby, *Gustave Flaubert and the Art of Realism* (Bowes and Bowes, London, 1956), pp. 58–9.

66. For further exploration of this theme, see Veronica Forrest-Thomson, 'The Ritual of Reading Salammbô', *Modern Language Review* 67:4 (Oct, 1972), to which the following discussion is greatly indebted.

67. Jean Rousset, 'Positions, distances, perspectives dans Salammbô', *Poétique* 6 (1971), p. 154. Denis Porter, 'Aestheticism versus the Novel: The Example of *Salammbô*', *Novel* 4:2 (Winter 1971), pp. 102 and 105.

68. *The Historical Novel* (Beacon Press, Boston, 1963), pp. 187 and 190.

69. *Gustave Flaubert*, p. 145.

70. *The Novels of Flaubert*, p. 108.

71. Cf. Veronica Forrest-Thomson, 'The Ritual of Reading Salammbô', pp. 787–94.

72. 'They marvelled at her attire; but she cast over them a long horrified gaze; then, letting her head sink between her shoulders and spreading wide her arms, she cried several times: "What have you done! What have you done!"'

73. 'they tried to grasp these vague legends which played before their imagination, through the mists of theogonies, like phantoms in clouds.'

74. 'Positions, distances, perspectives dans *Salammbô*', p. 154.

75. 'and, pressing her hands to her heart, she remained for several minutes with her eyes closed, savouring the agitation of all these men.

'Mâtho the Libyan leaned towards her. Involuntarily she approached him, and, drawn by her recognition of his pride, she poured him a long stream of wine into a golden cup in order to make her peace with the army.'

76. *The Historical Novel*, p. 189.

77. *Three Novels by Flaubert*, p. 155.

78. *Ibid.*, p. 223.

79. *Ibid.*, pp. 229–30.

80. *Ibid.*, pp. 187–8.

81. *Ibid.*, p. 222.

82. *Ibid.*, p. 205 n.

83. *Ibid.*, p. 206.

84. Veronica Forrest-Thomson, 'The Ritual of Reading *Salammbô*', p. 788.

85. *Ibid.*

86. 'He drew back, elbows behind him, gaping, nearly terrified. She felt as if supported by the power of the Gods; and looking him straight in the eye she asked for the Zaïmph, she demanded it with proud and fluent words, Mâtho did not hear; he was gazing at her, and for him her garments blended with her body.'

87. 'An irresistible curiosity drew him on, and, like a child who reaches out his hand to an unknown fruit, trembling all the while, with the tip of his finger, he touched her lightly on her breast; the rather cool skin yielded with an elastic resistance.'

88. 'They had stopped speaking. Far away the thunder rolled. Sheep bleated, frightened by the storm.'

'Salammbô was overcome by a lassitude in which she lost all consciousness of herself. Something both very intimate and yet impersonal, the will of the Gods, made her abandon herself to it.'

89. 'surprised not to feel the happiness she had previously imagined. She remained melancholy in her fulfilled dream.'

90. 'Mâtho gazed about him and his eyes fell on Salammbô. With the first step he had taken she had risen; then, unconsciously, as he drew near she had moved forward, little by little, to the edge of the terrace; and soon, as all things external were blotted out, she had seen only Mâtho. A silence had descended on her soul, one of those abysses in which the whole world disappears beneath the weight of a single thought, a memory, a look. This man, who was coming towards her, drew her.'

91. Veronica Forrest-Thomson, 'The Ritual of Reading *Salammbô*', p. 792. Cf. Maurice Schroder, 'On Reading *Salammbô*', *L'Esprit créateur* 10:1 (Spring, 1970), p. 28.

92. 'an unknown amulet, found by chance in dangerous circumstances, became a god; or again it might be a name, merely a name, that was repeated with no attempt to grasp what it might mean.'

*Afterword*

1. *Selected Literary Criticism*, p. 175.

2. *Essais critiques*, p. 164.

3. D. H. Lawrence, 'Surgery for the Novel — or a Bomb?', in *A Selection from Phoenix* (Penguin, Harmondsworth, 1971), p. 193.

# Bibliography

*Texts*

Flaubert, *Oeuvres complètes*, ed. Bernard Masson (Seuil, Paris, 1964), 2 vols.
Flaubert, *Correspondance* (Conard, Paris, 1926–33), 9 vols, and *Supplément* (Conard, Paris, 1954), 4 vols. The forthcoming edition in the Bibliothèque de la Pléiade will supersede the Conard.

*Critical Works*

The best general studies of Flaubert are the longest and the shortest: Jean-Paul Sartre, *L'Idiot de la famille* (Gallimard, Paris, 1971–  ), 4 vols, and Anthony Thorlby, *Gustave Flaubert and the Art of Realism* (Bowes and Bowes, London, 1956). Two other general studies which may be consulted with profit are Albert Thibaudet, *Gustave Flaubert* (Gallimard, Paris, 1935), and Victor Brombert, *The Novels of Flaubert* (Princeton University Press, 1966). A number of excellent articles will be found in the issue of *Europe* devoted to Flaubert, 485–7 (Sept–Nov, 1969).

More specialized studies of particular interest:
Peter Cortland, *The Sentimental Adventure* (Mouton, The Hague, 1967).
Marie-Jeanne Durry, *Flaubert et ses projets inédits* (Nizet, Paris, 1950).
Alison Fairlie, 'Flaubert et la conscience du réel', *Essays in French Literature* 4 (Nov 1967).
   'Some Patterns of Suggestion in *L'Education sentimentale*', *Australian Journal of French Studies* 6: 2–3 (1969).
Veronica Forrest-Thomson, 'The Ritual of Reading *Salammbô*', *Modern Language Review* 67: 4 (1972).

Michel Foucault, 'La Bibliothèque fantastique', in *Flaubert*, ed. Raymonde Debraye-Genette (Didier, Paris, 1970).

Gérard Genette, 'Silences de Flaubert', *Figures* (Seuil, Paris, 1966).

Claudine Gothot-Mersch, 'Introduction', *Madame Bovary* (Garnier, Paris, 1971).

J. Pommier and G. Leleu, *Madame Bovary — Nouvelle Version* (Corti, Paris, 1949).

Marcel Proust, 'A propos du "style" de Flaubert', *Chroniques* (Gallimard, Paris, 1927).

Jean-Pierre Richard, 'La Création de la forme chez Flaubert', *Littérature et sensation* (Seuil, Paris, 1954).

R. J. Sherrington, *Three Novels by Flaubert* (Oxford University Press, Oxford, 1970).

Stephen Ullmann, *Style in the French Novel* (Blackwell, Oxford, 1960).


General works relevant to the approach adopted herein:

Roland Barthes, *S/Z* (Seuil, Paris, 1970).

Jonathan Culler, *Structuralist Poetics* (Routledge, London, 1974).

Veronica Forrest-Thomson, 'Levels in Poetic Convention', *Journal of European Studies* 2 (1971).

Geoffrey Hartman, *Beyond Formalism* (Yale University Press, New Haven, 1970).

Fredric Jameson, *Marxism and Form* (Princeton University Press, Princeton, 1971).

Paul de Man, 'The Rhetoric of Temporality', in *Interpretation: Theory and Practice*, ed. Charles Singleton (Johns Hopkins Press, Baltimore, 1969).

# Index

The most important discussions of a topic are indicated by page numbers in bold type. Works are indexed under their authors

Self-consciousness: of texts, 16, 18-19, 67, 91-3, 103-5, 110-12, 212-25; of authors, 30, 53, 69, 103-5; unself-consciousness as goal, 68-9; and reverie, 175; and irony, 185-6

Sentence: importance of, 17; as synthesis, 57, 76; as petrification, 58, 202-3; as surface, 59, 71; structure of, 75-6, 95, 140, 203, 206; and irony, 200-206

Seznec, Jean: 181

Sherrington, R. J.: 100, 112-13, 114-15, 116-19, 216-18, 221, 254

Shlovsky, Victor: 233

Sign: signifier denied a full signified, 65-6, 73, 108, 179; desire for motivation 66, 108-9, 160-61; arbitrariness, 105-6, 128-9, 179, 209, 225-7

Sollers, Philippe: 135

Starkie, Enid: 110-11

Starobinski, Jean: 82

Stendhal (Henri Beyle, pseud.): 81-2, 84, 128

Stern, J. P.: 249

Sterne, Laurence: 38

Stevens, Wallace: 72-3

Stupidity: **157-85**; of life, 34; attractions of, 73, 158, 173, 177; as a mode of, comprehension, 164, 169, 173-4, 184-5; of objects, 74, 170-72; of language, 160-61, 164-7; of thought, 167-71; of masterpieces,

172-5, 177; and reverie, 173-5; structure of, 178-80; of *La Tentation de St Antoine*, 180-84

Style indirect libre: 62, 113, 140

Symbol: attachment to symbolic reading, 49, 63-4, 88, 101-6, 132; resistance to symbolic reading, 63-7, 76, 96, 100; parody of symbolic reading, 91-4; uses of symbolic reading, 217-27, 224-8

Temporal structures: 28-31, 37-8, 41-2, 45, 51, 155-6

Theme: indeterminacy, 76, 107 **136-56**; importance of, 90-91, 93; in Balzac, 99-100; relation to plot, 135; novels' indifference to, 137-9; relation to reading, 18, 230

Thibaudet, Albert: 92, 137, 204, 212-13

Thorlby, Anthony: 145, 211

Thought: characterized, 43; gratuitousness and stupidity of, 132-3, 166-71, 182; question of value, 173-6; and irony, 194-5

Valéry, Paul: 170-71, 184

Vigny, Alfred de: 32

Voltaire (F. M. Arouet, pseud.): 175

Wordsworth, William: 55